DISABILI

AND PRACTICE:
APPLYING THE
SOCIAL MODEL

Edited by
Colin Barnes and Geof Mercer

The Disability Press
Leeds

First published 2004
The Disability Press
Centre for Disability Studies
School of Sociology and Social Policy
University of Leeds
Leeds LS2 9JT.

Produced by Media Services at the University of Leeds.

British Library Cataloguing in Publication Data
A catalogue record for this book is available from the British Library

Library of Congress Cataloguing in Publication Data
A catalogue record of this book has been requested

ISBN 0-9528450-9-1 (pbk)

Contents

The Disability Press

The Disability Press aims to provide an alternative outlet for work in the field of 'disability studies'. It draws inspiration from the work of all those countless disabled individuals and their allies who have, over the years, struggled to place 'disability' on to the political agenda. The establishment of The Disability Press is a testament to the growing recognition of 'disability' as an equal opportunities and human rights issue within the social sciences and more widely in society.

The Centre for Disability Studies at the University of Leeds has provided funding for this volume. We also wish to record our thanks to the School of Sociology and Social Policy at the University of Leeds for its continuing support.

Colin Barnes and Geof Mercer

Acknowledgements

This is the second volume that we have edited based on contributions to a seminar series on 'Implementing the Social Model of Disability: from Theory to Practice' organised by the Centre for Disability Studies (CDS) at the University of Leeds. The first volume, *Implementing the Social Model of Disability: Theory and Research* was published earlier this year (2004) by The Disability Press.

Our thanks to the Economic and Social Research Council for a grant to help with this series, and also to the participants and particularly those presenting papers at the third and fourth seminars on which this volume is based.

Last, but certainly not least, our special thanks to Marie Ross who has showed endless patience and editing skills in completing the Index and preparing the whole volume for publication.

Contributors

Colin Barnes is Professor of Disability Studies at the Centre for Disability Studies, School of Sociology and Social Policy, University of Leeds.

Karen Beauchamp-Pryor is a PhD student, with a visual impairment, based in Social Policy at the University of Wales, Swansea.

Paul Brown is a Director of the Scottish Higher Education Funding Council Scottish Disability Team at the University of Dundee.

Grant Carson is the Co-ordinator of the Glasgow Disabled Persons Housing Service, based at the Centre for Independent Living in Glasgow.

Dave Gibbs is Research Manager at Derbyshire Coalition for Inclusive Living, and has worked in the disabled people's movement since 1981.

Dan Goodley is Reader in Applied Disability Studies, School of Education at the University of Sheffield.

Malcolm Harrison is Reader in Housing and Social Policy in the School of Sociology and Social Policy at the University of Leeds.

Jennifer Harris is Senior Research fellow in the Social Policy Research Unit, University of York undertaking research in disability studies.

Geof Mercer is a Senior Lecturer in the School of Sociology and Social Policy and a member of the Centre for Disability Studies at the University of Leeds.

Charlotte Pearson is a Research Fellow at the Strathclyde Centre for Disability Research, University of Glasgow.

Debby Phillips is Senior Lecturer in Social Work and Researcher at the Cornwall Business School, Combined Universities of Cornwall, Camborne.

Sheila Riddell is Professor of Inclusion and Diversity, Moray House School of Education, University of Edinburgh.

Alan Roulstone is Reader in Disability Policy at the University of Sunderland. He has been much influenced by the writings of Vic Finkelstein.

Anne Simpson is Head of the Special Needs Service at the University of Strathclyde and Manager of the Teachability Project.

John Speirs is the Co-ordinator of the Glasgow Disabled Persons Housing Service Employment Project, located in the Centre for Independent Living in Glasgow.

Teresa Tinklin is Research Fellow in the Centre for Educational Sociology, University of Edinburgh.

Alastair Wilson is Senior Research Fellow, Centre for Applied Educational Research, University of Glasgow.

Gerry Zarb is the Disability Rights Commission's Head of Health and Independent Living Strategy. He has extensive experience in policy and research.

CHAPTER 1

Changing Disability Policies in Britain

Geof Mercer and Colin Barnes

Introduction

The reforms in social policy associated with the establishment of the welfare state in Britain during the 1940s contained a number of initiatives designed to improve the lives of disabled people. However, the lack of meaningful progress towards social inclusion was highlighted, particularly from the 1970s, by an increasing number of campaigns by newly organised groups of disabled people. Their grievances ranged widely: against continuing forcible institutionalisation, segregation in 'special needs' services, higher rates of poverty and unemployment, lower educational qualifications, and the greater restrictions on leisure and social relationships compared with the rest of the population.

Disabled activists also developed a radical critique of the dominant 'personal tragedy' approach to 'disability' that characterised policy and service provision, as well as public attitudes generally. This regarded the person with an impairment as a 'victim' of their functional limitations and accorded policy priority to individual, medical treatment and rehabilitation, and state social welfare benefits. This also presumed a more general dependence on informal care provided by family and friends, together with the voluntary sector and charities. In contrast, disabled activists and emerging organisations *of* (that is, controlled by) disabled people advanced a social interpretation (model) that stressed the 'disabling' and exclusionary character of contemporary society (UPIAS 1976; Finkelstein 1980; Oliver 1983; Barnes 1991). This required policy action to overcome these barriers to social inclusion and to provide support for disabled people to lead 'ordinary lives'.

In this chapter, we will trace the recent growth of disability policies, with particular attention to the last decade. Our general conclusion is that, while there have been improvements in disabled people's everyday lives, and new opportunities to challenge their social exclusion, this remains substantial and wide-ranging. Too often, reforms have lacked ambition and resources, and not been appropriately directed at exclusionary barriers. Hence, the continuing relevance of exploring a social model approach to disability theory and policy practice.

The emergence of the modern welfare state

Following the experiences of economic depression in the 1930s and the Second World War, a 'post-war settlement' between capital and labour led to wide-ranging social policy reforms. In developing a blueprint for this welfare state, Beveridge (1942) targeted the elimination of the 'five giants' – want, disease, ignorance, squalor and idleness. In return, the state would pursue a policy of full employment as well as comprehensive social and welfare reforms. These included: the development of: the National Health Service (NHS); universal and free primary and secondary education; compulsory insurance contributions for all employees and the self-employed to cover for unemployment, and old age, together with various non-contributory benefits; family and child care support; and an expansion in council house building. However, there was also continued reliance on informal 'care' and support from family and friends, and a still active voluntary and charity sector.

These reforms represented a compromise between three overlapping 'welfare settlements': political-economic; social; and organisational (Clarke and Newman 1997: 1-8). At the 'political-economic' level, Keynesian macro-economic policies were at the heart of government thinking. These centred on a commitment to full employment that proved crucial in winning agreement for, and maintaining through National Insurance contributions, the welfare reforms. This national pooling of risk underpinned the political and ideological bases of the welfare state. It became the litmus test of a civilised society: where citizenship determined support for basic social needs (Marshall 1950). In practice, it offered a compromise between 'market-driven' (that is, through labour market participation) and 'state-guaranteed citizenship' (Clarke and Newman 1997: 1).

The 'social settlement' incorporated specific notions about the family and work that presume the 'norm' of a household headed by a wage-earning male providing for the rest of the household. Similarly, those with an accredited impairment were viewed as reliant on the family and friends. This view of disabled people as in need of 'care and attention' was regarded as 'natural', and was also used to justify state regulation of their lives (Barnes, Mercer and Shakespeare 1999).

The 'organisational' settlement comprised 'a commitment to two modes of co-ordination: bureaucratic administration and professionalism' (Clarke and Newman 1997: 4-8). Public service norms and values complemented claims that the new system would be impartial in its dealings with different sections and interests in the population. Similarly, the claim to expertise and neutrality in identifying and 'treating' social problems provided the rationale for professional control of service delivery. This was most evident in the influence of the medical profession within the National Health Service (NHS), but was also apparent in the role of professionals in education and, to a lesser extent, personal social services, something that attracted increasing criticism from social scientists (Wilding 1982). In addition, disability activists highlighted the unacceptable authority exercised by the 'caring professions' in their lives and the perception of disabled people as a dependent group with 'special needs' (Barnes 1991).

Disability and social policy: separate paths?

In the immediate post-1945 years, state policy on disability largely comprised specialised, segregated institutions, such as 'special education' schools, long-stay asylums and hospitals, and diverse residential accommodation (Humphries and Gordon 1992). The increase in the number of disabled people following the 1939-1945 War, and a heightened social obligation to 'do something' for them, triggered specific policy responses to address the problems facing disabled people. These included the Disabled Persons (Employment) Act 1944, as well as provisions within the Education Act 1944, plus the National Health Service Act 1946, and the 1948 National Assistance Act.

The Disabled Persons (Employment) Act 1944 was the first piece of legislation to extend the focus from specific impairment groups to consider disabled people in general. It sought to enhance their participation in paid work, while setting up a variety of 'rehabilitation' services and vocational training courses. It introduced the notion of reserved occupations for disabled workers, an employment quota scheme compelling all employers with more than 20 employees to employ disabled people, established the employment resettlement service and set up a nation-wide network of sheltered workshops. However, its implementation was not vigorously pursued and little effort was made to penalise employers who failed to satisfy the recruitment target. Similarly, the 1944 Education Act promoted the education of disabled children alongside their non-disabled peers in primary and secondary schools, although it allowed that integration was conditional on adequate tuition and funding (Tomlinson 1982). As a result, the legislation encouraged the establishment of a system of segregated special education rooted in medical impairment categories.

Not surprisingly, the National Health Service Act 1946 reinforced the view of 'disability' as a medical (rehabilitation) issue. While long-term services and medical aids to enable disabled people to live at home were highlighted, funding resources were concentrated on acute care and services. The 1946 National Insurance (Industrial Injuries) Act continued the division of disabled people according to the source of their impairment, in providing benefits for injury, disablement or death caused by workplace accidents, but with liability transferred from the employer to the state. The 1948 National Assistance Act repealed the old Poor Law and mandated local authorities to provide residential and other services for anyone 'substantially handicapped by illness, injury or cognitive deformity', and maintain a register of those in receipt of services (but not assess wider support needs). However, little funding was allocated to expand non-residential services for disabled people. Instead, there were more significant moves to allow local authorities to delegate services to approved voluntary/charitable agencies. One outcome was the establishment of the Leonard Cheshire Homes in 1948 that subsequently became the largest single voluntary provider of residential accommodation for people with physical impairments in the UK (Drake 1999).

This legislation built the foundations for statutory provision for disabled people in the second half of the twentieth century. In practice, it sowed the seeds of a 'life apart' with separate/segregated and minimal provision, and their continued exclusion from the key institutions and processes of mainstream society (Humphries and Gordon 1992).

Seeking a 'community' solution

The emergence of protest action by groups of disabled people was initially concentrated on those incarcerated on long-stay institutions. This ran parallel to academic studies that highlighted the failure of institutional regimes to satisfy the emotional, social or physical needs of residents (Goffman 1961; Townsend 1967). The growing outrage was fuelled by a series of scandals involving the negligence and abuse of inmates which were externally confirmed in a succession of government-sponsored inquiries (Martin 1985).

The government decided to shift the policy focus to 'care in the community' having been persuaded that these offered an irresistible combination of better quality and cheaper services than institutional alternatives. Even so, as it subsequently acknowledged, the calculation of economic benefits did not take into account the contribution of unpaid informal 'carers', or the inadequate level of community provision (DHSS 1981). In 1961, it was announced that the number of beds in long-stay, segregated hospitals would be halved. Subsequent plans for community-based services included sheltered housing schemes and workshops, with the 'mentally disordered' and the 'physically handicapped' identified as key priority groups (Jones *et al.* 1983). However, there was no comparable increase in resources for non-hospital services.

The Government also introduced changes in local social service provision in The Local Authority Act 1970 and The Chronically Sick and Disabled Persons Act (CSDA) 1970. The latter was promoted as a 'Charter for the Disabled' (Topliss and Gould 1982). For example, Section 2 covered local authority services for disabled people, including practical assistance in the home, help with recreational activities, and aids and adaptations in the home. The CSDA also instructed local authorities to provide for the housing needs of disabled people (Section 3); and access to public buildings (Section 4), including 'University and school buildings' (Section 8). In practice, the main developments were in areas such as residential and day centre facilities, respite care, meals on wheels, aids and adaptations, with most emphasis placed on the role of social workers, occupational therapists and physiotherapists. However, the now familiar caveat that services should be provided only if local authorities deemed it 'both practicable and reasonable' supplied an easy justification for inaction. As a result, local authority services were widely criticised as inadequate to bring about a significant improvement in the quality of disabled people's lives.

Restructuring the welfare state

In the mid-1970s a global economic crisis heralded a 'new right' (or 'neo-liberal') critique of an interventionist welfare state and its 'excessive' expenditure on the grounds that it was more likely to create than resolve economic and social problems. In 1979, the newly elected Conservative Government, headed by Margaret Thatcher, outlined a programme designed to 'roll-back' and restructure the state, notably by introducing market competition into the delivery of welfare services in order to promote their efficiency and effectiveness. The broad political consensus around Keynesian macro-economic policies, full employment and widening social citizenship were overturned, while 'managerialism' was embraced as a strategy to increase efficiency and reduce the stultifying power of entrenched bureaucratic-professional interests (Pollit 1993; Clarke and Newman 1997). The policy shift was outlined in major reviews of social policy, and specifically health and social care, in the 1980s (Griffiths 1988). These underscored the National Health Service and Community Care Act 1990 that provided a quasi-market framework, with greater involvement of the private and voluntary sectors, and gave an important stimulus to managerialism in public sector services with its introduction of centralised targets and performance measurement.

From a very different direction, social constituencies sidelined in the birth of the welfare state, including women, minority ethnic groups and disabled people, campaigned against their exclusion from mainstream policies. These attacks represented an unravelling of the 'settlement' between capital and labour that underscored welfare state legislation in the 1940s. Through the 1970s, there was a noteworthy growth in the politicisation and organisation of disabled people, with a growing number of disabled people looking to translate the social model of disability into practical action (Davis 1990). This was reinforced by abundant evidence from government surveys that disabled people still languished at the bottom of the social hierarchy, with disabling structures and processes resistant to state attempts at improvement, and effectively remained 'second-class' citizens (Martin and White 1988; Martin, White and Meltzer 1989; Grundy et al. 1999).

Rather paradoxically, the neo-conservative critique of the welfare state, with its emphasis on market competition (and citizenship), and encouragement of individualism opened up new possibilities for disability politics. A number of new disability policy strands can be identified. The stress placed on user involvement, evident generally in the proliferation of Consumer Charters, was enacted more specifically in the Disabled Persons (Services, Consultation and Representation) Act 1986. There was also slow recognition of disabled people's campaigns for appropriate support to live 'independently' in the community. In England and Wales, the 1948 Social Security Act had made it illegal for local authorities to make cash payments in lieu of services to disabled people in order to purchase their own personal assistance. However, in the 1980s and 1990s a few authorities were persuaded by local groups of disabled people to administer payments indirectly, that is, through a third party (typically a voluntary group or independent trust) (Zarb and Nadash 1994). A separate but linked development led to the establishment of the Independent Living Fund in 1988 to provide cash payments to disabled people. This was viewed as a temporary measure but proved as extremely popular with disabled people who saw an opportunity to achieve more choices and control of their lives (Morris 1993). By the mid-1990s, the Conservative Government were finally persuaded that cash payments fitted with its agenda to promote market competition and individual choice in welfare by passing the Direct Payments Act 1996.

The period since the 1980s also witnessed concerted campaigns by disabled people's organisations (internationally and in Britain) for anti-discrimination legislation. This finally led to the passage of the Disability Discrimination Act (DDA) in 1995. While the DDA failed to satisfy disabled people's ambitions, attracting criticism for being located in a medical approach to disability, as too limited in its scope, and for allowing 'justifiable discrimination', it opened up new possibilities in disability politics. This was reinforced by the increasing adoption of a human rights perspective (Sayce 2000), with early interventions by the United Nations and more recently, from the European Union (Doyle 1999).

New Labour's strategy for disability policy

The New Labour Government elected in 1997 stressed its inclusionary goals by targeting low-income and socially disadvantaged groups in general, while also targeting measures at disabled people. New Labour gave centre stage to its 'welfare-to-work' programme, with the philosophy of, 'work for those who can and security for those who cannot' (DSS 1998a). There was also a major emphasis on modernising and reforming the welfare state, with an emphasis on applying private sector methods and providers, particularly performance outcome measures, for example, with league tables for hospitals, schools, and social services. Even so, New Labour retained many of the previous Conservative administration's economic policies including control on public spending until 2001.

In respect of disability, the Disability Rights Commission (DRC) was founded in 2000 to bolster the implementation of the DDA (although there are currently moves to merge the DRC with its equivalents for 'race' and sex discrimination into a general equality organisation). Interestingly, the DDA has been used rather more intensively than previous equal opportunities legislation, while the initial focus on employment cases has concentrated more on dismissal and unfair treatment rather than recruitment (Meager et al. 1999). The passage of the Special Educational Needs and Disability Act (SENDA) in 2001 extended the Disability Discrimination Act 1995 to cover schools, further and higher educational institutions. This means that it is now illegal to treat a disabled student less favourably (without justification) as a result of their impairment, or to fail to make 'reasonable adjustments' to include them, such as physical features, auxiliary aids and services. If education was central to social inclusion then disabled children's experience required urgent action: in the late 1990s, 45 per cent of disabled children (16-29 year olds) left without educational qualifications compared with 13 per cent of the whole age group. Segregated education has been widely criticised for this shortfall.

The remit of the DDA also covered housing, transport, and the built environment. Additional employment rights, and rights of access to businesses and organisations providing services will become law in October 2004. Whatever improvements in social inclusion can be attributed to the DDA, there was also considerable scope for bolstering policy intervention to promote social inclusion.

New Labour also became an enthusiastic advocate of direct payments in lieu of services for disabled people. It expanded the eligibility criteria to include older and younger disabled people, people with learning difficulties, and carers. Moreover, their relatively slow and uneven development across the country led to the decision in 2002 to make it mandatory for local authorities to offer the direct payments option to disabled people. Its social inclusion agenda was further illustrated by a new strategy for people with learning difficulties outlined in the Department of Health White Paper *Valuing People* (DoH 2001). It presaged a shift from a 'medical' to a 'social' model approach, with an emphasis on 'Rights, Independence, Choice and Inclusion' (DoH 2001: 23).

Apart from cash payments, including direct payments and those offered to people on low incomes through the Social Fund (since 1988), personal social services operate as a key facilitator of social inclusion. They are overseen by a system of national and local inspection and evaluation, expanded by New Labour, including the Social Services Inspectorate, the Care Standards Commission, and the General Social Care Council.

Social services are central to supporting independent living for older disabled people, from washing and dressing, meals, social activities, and supporting 'informal carers' financially and with breaks, although unpaid care remains crucial for so many older disabled people. Nevertheless, personal social services have received much lower increases in funding since New Labour came to power than the NHS (DoH 2002). Government policy has moved towards focusing resources on those in most need, and charging 'clients' for services as a way of generating more revenue. This places heightened pressure on informal 'carers' and the voluntary sector, and leads to greater social isolation and more institutionalisation of older disabled people. In a rare instance of devolution affecting social policy, the Scottish devolved Parliament decided to make all personal 'care' free at the point of use.

Welfare-to-Work

As an illustration of New Labour disability policy, its 'welfare-to-work' programme has probably become the pre-eminent example. Given disabled people's low levels of economic activity – 31 per cent compared with 77 per cent for non-disabled people (Labour Force Survey 1997) – and the much higher reliance on social security benefits, they were an obvious target for policy action. New Labour's welfare-to-work initiative sought to move people off benefits into paid employment, and improve job retention (such as when they experienced sickness), and reduce the reliance on 'sheltered' employment. It included the introduction of a New Deal for Disabled People (NDDP) in 1997: a package of schemes that often entailed partnerships between the public, private and voluntary sectors. Additionally, disabled people were one of the potential beneficiaries of the introduction of the National Minimum Wage (NMW) in April 1999, because of their over-representation in low-paid jobs. However, there were concerns that some groups, such as people with learning difficulties, would lose out because employers thought them less productive.

After its re-election in 2001, the Labour Government established a new Department for Work and Pensions, along with Jobcentre Plus by amalgamating the Employment Service and parts of the Benefits Agency (Burchardt 2003). Yet despite recognition of the wider barriers facing disabled people in the paid labour market (DWP 2002), welfare-to-work policies relied overwhelmingly on a supply-side approach to assist claimants become more 'attractive' to employers. Particular emphasis was placed on the unemployed person's motivation and capabilities and adapting to changing labour market demands. These were supplemented by: subsidies to employers recruiting unemployed people (re-training, direct wage subsidies, reduced payroll taxes); training unemployed people in new skills; giving unemployed people work experience; and providing improved job search assistance. In contrast, apart from the NMW, demand-side policies to generate jobs and economic development were far less prominent (see Chapter Two).

Yet while New Labour's 'welfare contract' called for a 'life of dignity and security' (DSS 1998: 80) it was less certain about how this applied to those who cannot expect to work. Total expenditure on benefits for 'sick and disabled people' has trebled since the late 1970s and now accounts for one-quarter of social security spending. Contributory factors include widening eligibility, increasing take-up, a growing impact of extra-cost benefits, and an increase in the prevalence of impairment, notably with an ageing population. Hence, disabled people remain disproportionately reliant on social security benefits for all or part of their incomes, with two fifths of disabled people of working age on incomes below half the national average (Burchardt 2000).

The balance of the social system inherited by New Labour was shifted to stimulate entry into the labour market, although in order to qualify for welfare benefits, the disabled person still has to stress their incapacity for work. A particular government concern was that the social security system acted as a disincentive to seeking employment, as demonstrated by the more 'generous' level of Incapacity Benefit (IB) compared to Unemployment Benefit. This commitment to 'make work pay' underscored the main provisions of the Welfare Reform and Pensions Act 1999, and the replacement of the Disability Working Allowance (DWA) by the Disabled Person's Tax Credit in the same year. In addition, moves were made to integrate employment, social security, and taxation measures, along with organisational restructuring, to simplify the provision of benefits and support services, such as the merger of Benefits Agency, Employment Service and local authorities in a 'one-stop shop'.

The consequences for disabled people have been uneven (Powell 2002). Employment rates have risen since 1997, for both men and women, faster than for the non-disabled population (Burchardt 2000). Yet there were still many disabled people who had considerable difficulty obtaining appropriate paid work. Barriers, such as inaccessible workplaces, transport to work, and discriminatory attitudes and practices by employers and discrimination from other employees, proved resistant to change. Again, social security changes had a differential impact on the disabled population, with more targeting of benefits at those deemed in most need, with greater means testing and controls on unemployed disabled people.

This overview of disability policy largely ignores the possible impact of economic globalisation on welfare regimes, as well as important international initiatives, notably from the United Nations and the World Health Organization, to 'standardise' approaches to disability. Similarly, British membership of the European Union has stimulated its own 'external' influences on social policy, as with the projected harmonization of social security. However, broad objectives have not yet been translated into specific policies. Equally, the moves toward devolution within the UK since 1999 have opened up new possibilities for contrasts in social policy between Scotland, Wales, Northern Ireland and England.

Outline of chapters

The contributions to this collection demonstrate how the disability studies literature increasingly reflects the theoretical diversity evident in the social sciences. In early British debates on the social model, there was an obvious influence of conflict and neo-Marxist approaches (UPIAS 1976; Oliver 1983; Abberley 1987). Subsequently, feminist and interpretative influences grew in significance, while most recently 'post-modernism' and 'post-structuralism' have gained prominence (Corker and Shakespeare 2002). This has obvious implications for debates about disability and implementing the social model.

In Chapter 2, Alan Roulstone reviews the range of policy initiatives designed to further enhance disabled peoples' employment opportunities since 1944, with particular emphasis on the impact of the Disability Discrimination Act and the New Labour Government's emphasis on a 'welfare to work' strategy. He concludes that the overall impact in reducing the levels of unemployment, under-employment and wider social disadvantage has been very limited. A major weakness has been the lack of engagement with disabled people in developing effective policies to confront, for example, the wide-ranging barriers to paid employment, the professionally-led nature of services, and the nature of work in an 'inclusive' society.

In Chapter 3, Grant Carson and John Spiers examine the introduction of an innovative labour market employment and training project for unemployed disabled people based at the Centre for Independent Living in Glasgow. The authors trace the experiences of the first cohort of disabled people who moved into temporary paid employment in the housing sector (where they were able to explore suitable housing options for disabled people). The project identified key issues in supporting disabled people in these placements, including training plans, clarifying organisational expectations and possible changes. Overall, the success of this cohort in moving into full-time employment or further training highlighted the potential of such initiatives.

In Chapter 4, Malcolm Harrison critically examines the influence of 'environmental determinism' in writings on housing – notably assumptions about the impact of the physical qualities of dwellings and the immediate neighbourhood on behaviour, health, and overall well-being. This approach overlaps with social model accounts that regard inaccessible buildings and spaces as a major source of 'disability', reinforced by wider financial and management constraints. Harrison argues that housing and disability researchers, just as much as policy makers and architect-designers must be careful not to over-emphasise the potential of technical solutions or consider housing and physical planning in isolation or separate from the wider social context.

Three chapters then deliver a wide-ranging review of the higher education (HE) system with detailed evidence of experiences in England, Scotland, and Wales. In Chapter 5, Paul Brown and Anne Simpson explore the relative impact of social model thinking compared with the medical or individual approach to disability on HE policy in Scotland. They argue that economic factors have a determining importance in driving institutional change, as is illustrated by their analysis of the general arrangements through which institutions are responsible to funding councils, and the larger political agendas that these arrangements represent. In their examination of HE provision for disabled students, there seems little coherent direction, although insofar as financial arrangements and rewards hold sway, they conclude that the medical approach still exercises the central influence.

In Chapter 6, Sheila Riddell, Teresa Tinklin and Alastair Wilson report on their investigation of disabled students in higher education in Scotland and England. They explore contrasting approaches to disability as a unitary category, and as a subjective, complex and multi-dimensional identity in researching access into, and the experience of, higher education. This involved quantitative data analysis of patterns of participation in higher education along with a qualitative investigation of the ways in which students negotiated their position by deploying a range of cultural identities. The authors indicate that impairment and disability are major factors in students' lives, but not always the determining aspects.

The enactment of the Special Educational Needs and Disability Act 2001 has forced higher educational institutions to re-think their policies and practices towards disabled students. In Chapter 7, Karen Beauchamp-Pryor reviews recent developments in Wales. She contends that disabled people have had relatively little influence on the design and implementation of HE policies, compared to major charities and professional bodies. The Welsh Assembly has acknowledged the barriers confronting disabled people, but has not taken effective action to promote their social inclusion. Instead, a medical model approach remains dominant, with the potential of a social model interpretation to bring about radical change as yet unrealised.

In Chapter 8, Jennifer Harris discusses a central aspect of current social care practice: the assessment of need for 'community care' services. She explores a specific attempt to shift towards an outcomes approach that incorporates key elements of the social model of disability in routine assessment and review documentation. In exploring its implementation as part of a research and development project, she highlights the problems experienced by many professionals in moving towards a framework that emphasises user-defined aspirations and was perceived as encouraging increased managerial intervention. In contrast, service users welcomed the greater accountability and personal control afforded by this outcomes approach to assessment.

In Chapter 9, Charlotte Pearson, reviews the growth in direct payments to disabled service users to organise their own personal assistance. She highlights the relatively slower progress in Scotland compared with England. This is explained in terms of the greater resistance in Scotland to the marketisation of social care among local authorities, and the lower focus of disability activism on securing direct payments. Moreover, while the numbers of direct payments users are increasing, levels of funding and other support remain uncertain. Policy makers have to be convinced that direct payments are part of a wider demand for social justice and the right to independent living.

In Chapter 10, Dave Gibbs criticises the notion of 'social model services'. Drawing on his experience of working with the Derbyshire Coalition of Inclusive Living (DCIL), he argues that it must be more than a service provider and that the people DCIL supports are not simply passive 'users'. Instead, DCIL service programmes overlap with its other functions, such as lobbying and campaigning. Moreover, while public services for disabled people have effectively acted as a means of control, DCIL provides general support for inclusive living. Hence, the political goal is to redefine public services by drawing on an applied social understanding of disability, rather than pursuing separate 'social model services'.

Debby Phillips in Chapter 11 explores the impact of professional health and social care systems in the daily lives of women labelled as having learning difficulties. She explores the power dynamics evident in the 'carer/cared-for' relationship. Many of her research participants criticised the involvement of health and welfare professionals in their lives and dismissed suggestions that these took the form of a partnership. Nevertheless, there was some evidence of alliances with female support staff, such as in non-medicalised, alternative health practices. Yet, overall, professionals failed to recognise the importance to people with learning difficulties of life style adjustments, periods of transition, and issues concerning parenting and sexuality.

In Chapter 12, Dan Goodley also illustrates aspects of the professional domination of the lives of people with the label learning difficulties. He suggests that enabling theory, practice, and politics can gain considerably by turning to narrative and discourse analysis rooted in post-structuralism. This entails turning the analytical spotlight on people's narrative accounts: particularly, how education constructs and regulates the person with 'learning difficulties'. A priority is to scrutinize social exclusion in terms of institutional practices and discourses. These value, promulgate, and divide access to knowledge in historically specific ways. Additionally, the achievement of diverse forms of resistance by people with learning difficulties must be recognised.

In Chapter 13, Gerry Zarb examines the significance of independent living to social inclusion, and its links with the social model of disability. He explores independent living as a civil and human rights issue, illustrated by interventions from the Disability Rights Commission. He expresses reservations about the efficacy of anti-discrimination legislation, and acknowledges concerns that individual rights solutions may clash with a social model approach which stresses the collective emancipation of disabled people. As the continuing significance of exclusion, institutionalisation and segregation demonstrates, much needs to be done to win the argument about the merits of independent living, and its status as a universal human right.

Review

This chapter provides a broad overview of the development of disability policy starting with the legislative foundations of the welfare state established in 1940s. This is set within more recent efforts to 'roll back' and restructure the welfare state, as well as the broader struggles by groups of disabled people for more equal opportunities for inclusive living. Criticism that the welfare state in general and disability policy in particular has 'failed disabled people' is based on wide-ranging evidence of continued social exclusion. It remains a 'fact of life' for disabled people, who are denied the same opportunities to lead 'ordinary' lives that non-disabled people take for granted.

The contributors to this collection provide detailed case studies in many different areas of social policy and social life that illustrate the disabling barriers and attitudes remain very resistant to policy reforms, although changes are taking place. They also demonstrate some of the competing interpretations of the social model approach, as well as ways in which it can be applied in order to inform radical policy action.

Bibliography

Abberley, P. 1987: The concept of oppression and the development of a social theory of disability. *Disability, Handicap and Society*, 2 (1), 5-19.

Barnes, C. 1991: *Disabled People in Britain and Discrimination*. London: Hurst and Co.

Barnes, C., Mercer, G. and Shakespeare, T. 1999: *Exploring Disability: A Sociological Introduction*. Cambridge: Polity.

Beveridge, Sir W. 1942: *Social Insurance and Allied Services*, Cmd 6406. London: HMSO.

Burchardt, T. 2000: *Enduring economic exclusion: Disabled people, income and work*. York: York Publishing Services for the Joseph Rowntree Foundation.

Burchardt, T. 2003: Disability, capability and social exclusion. In J. Millar (ed.), *Understanding Social Security*. Bristol: The Policy Press, 145-166.

Clarke, J. and Newman, J. 1997: *The managerial state: Power, politics and ideology in the re-making of social welfare*. London: Sage.

Corker, M. and Shakespeare, T. (eds) 2002: *Disability/ Postmodernity: Embodying Disability Theory*. London: Continuum.

Davis, K. 1990: *Activating the Social Model of Disability: The Emergence of the Seven Needs*. Derby: Derbyshire Coalition of Disabled People.

DHSS 1981: *Care in Action*. London: HMSO.

DoH 2002: *Departmental Report 2001-2002*. London: The Stationery Office.

DoH 2001: *Valuing People: A new strategy for learning disability for the 21st century*, Cm 5086. London: The Stationery Office.

Doyle, B. 1999: From welfare to rights? Disability and legal change in the United Kingdom in the late 1990s. In M. Jones and L.A.B. Marks (eds), *Disability, Divers-ability and Legal Change*. The Hague: Kluwer Law International/ Martinus Nijhoff Publishers, 209-26.

Drake, R. 1999: *Understanding Disability Policies*. Basingstoke: Macmillan.

DSS 1998: *New ambitions for our country: A new contract for welfare*. Cm 3805. London: The Stationery Office.

DWP 2002: *Pathways to work: Helping people into employment*. Cm 5690. London: The Stationery Office.

Finkelstein, V. 1980: *Attitudes and Disabled People*. New York: World Rehabilitation Fund.

Goffman, E. 1961/68: *Asylums: Essays on the Social Situation of Mental Patients and Other Inmates*. New York: Doubleday/ Harmonds-worth: Pelican.

Griffiths, R. 1988: *Community Care: Agenda for Action*. London: HMSO.

Grundy, E., Ahlburg, D., Ali, M., Breeze, E. and Slogett, A. 1999: *Disability in Great Britain: Results from the 1996/97 disability follow-up to the Family Resources Survey*. DSS Research Report No 94. Leeds: Corporate Document Services.

Humphries, S. and Gordon, P. 1992: *Out of Sight: The Experience of Disability 1900-1950*. London: Northern House Publishers Ltd.

Jones, K., Brown, J. and Bradshaw, J. (eds.) 1983: *Issues in Social Policy*. London: Routledge and Kegan Paul.

Marshall, T. H. 1950: *Citizenship and Social Class*. Cambridge: Cambridge University Press.

Martin, J.P. 1985: *Hospitals in Trouble*. Oxford: Blackwell.

Martin, J. and White, A. 1988: *OPCS Surveys of Disability in Great Britain: Report 2 – The financial circumstances of disabled adults living in private households*. London: HMSO.

Martin, J., White, A. and Meltzer, H. 1989: *OPCS Surveys of Disability in Great Britain: Report 4 – Disabled adults: services, transport and employment*. London: HMSO.

Meager, N., Doyle, B., Evans, C., Kersley, B., Williams, M., O'Reagan, S. and Tackey, N. 1999: *Monitoring the Disability Discrimination Act (DDA) 1995*. DfEE Research Report No 119. London: DfEE.

Morris, J. 1993: *Independent Lives? Community Care and Disabled People*. Basingstoke: Macmillan.

Oliver, M. 1983: *Social Work with Disabled People*. London: Macmillan.

Pollitt, C. 1993: *Managerialism and the Public Services*. Oxford: Blackwell.

Powell, M. (ed.) 2002: *Evaluating New Labour's welfare reforms*. Bristol: The Policy Press.

Sayce, L. 2000: *From Psychiatric Patient to Citizen: Overcoming Discrimination and Social Exclusion*. Basingstoke: Macmillan.

Tomlinson, S. 1982: *The Sociology of Special Education*. London: Routledge and Kegan Paul.

Topliss, E. and Gould, B. 1982: *Provision for the Disabled*. Oxford: Blackwell with Martin Robertson.

Townsend, P. 1967: *The Last Refuge*. London: Routledge and Kegan Paul.

UPIAS 1976: *Fundamental Principles of Disability*. London: Union of the Physically Impaired Against Segregation.

Wilding, P. 1982: *Professional Power and Social Welfare*. London: Routledge and Kegan Paul.

Zarb, G. and Nadash, P. 1994: *Cashing in on Independence*. Derby: BCODP.

CHAPTER 2

Disability, Employment and the Social Model

Alan Roulstone

The rise of the social model of disability has provided a significant challenge to the way academics, practitioners, researchers and policy makers conceptualise the 'problem' of disability (Oliver 1990; Swain et al. 1993; Barnes et al. 1999). The social model of disability offers a new framework and language of identifying, understanding and responding to disability. Here, the focus has rightly shifted to the social and institutional barriers that impact on people with impairments. Former shibboleths of the medical model have been questioned: professionally-led services, assessment regimes based on non-disabled constructions of disability, warehousing of disabled people in day centres and inflexible and often depersonalising service provision.

The language of choices and rights rather than assessments and needs has now been asserted across the UK at least as aspirations. The advent of the Disability Discrimination Act 1995 and the establishment of a Disability Rights Commission, despite their shortcomings, add to the feeling that disabled people should be a strong voice in any decisions that affect their lives.

One key area in which the social model of disability has still to permeate is that of paid employment. Despite recent changes in official language (Department for Education and Employment 1999) and small-scale adoption of social model ideas, UK disability employment research, policy and provision continue to be rooted firmly in the medical model of disability. At best, government research and policy operate with a mix of medical and social models of disability. The overall picture of UK disability employment policy points to a continued adherence to a deficit approach to understanding disabled peoples' inferior employment position.

The employment position makes clear the need for a re-evaluation of the deficit model if we are to begin to make a difference to disabled peoples' employment options. Disabled people are substantially more likely to be unemployed or economically inactive. In Spring 2002 the economic activity rate (in or looking for paid work) was about 50 per cent for people judged to have a long-term disability (sic), and 79 per cent for the whole UK population. The unemployment rate was 9 per cent for disabled people and 5 per cent for non-disabled people (Labour Force Survey 2002). This amounts to a substantial number of disabled people not in paid employment. Economic activity is particularly low for people with visual impairments with recent research suggesting that 75 per cent of working age people with 'sight problems' were not in paid employment (Bruce et al. 2000; RNIB 2002).

Disabled people are more likely to be under-employed in terms of the quantity of paid work they do and to be earning less per hour even for the same work (Burchardt 2000). There is substantial evidence that disabled people face significant attitude barriers in employment contexts (French 1988; Graham et al. 1990; Morrell 1990; Thomas 1992; Roulstone 1998; Goldstone and Darwent 2000)

The stark nature of disabled people's employment position and the apparent failure of much employment policy and provision in altering this situation, necessitates an urgent review of the influence of the medical model to date and the need to bring in social model understandings. We can begin this process by reflecting on the transformatory power of the social model of disability. As Oliver and Barnes argue, we have to be:

> shifting the focus squarely away from the functional limitations of impaired individuals and on to contemporary social organisations with a plethora of disabling barriers (1993: 271).

This provides the basic framework for a new way of viewing disability, so what can be said about the application of this social model to service provision in an enabling society?

> Services of the future then, must ensure that users and their organisations play a central and decisive role in any assessment and goal setting process. The role of the service provider should be just that – to provide services (Finkelstein and Stuart 1996:173).

There are a number of key ways in which the social model of disability needs to be applied to questions of disability and employment:

- As a revised and fundamental overhaul of the way the disability

problem is framed, for example in research, the benefits system and
in policy making.

- A critical application of key social model and independent living
themes to the question of disability and employment: for example,
choices and rights, enabling language, confronting professional
power.
- As a new vocabulary for enhancing employment opportunities and
experiences.

Disabling research

As mainstream policy and practice are directly informed by research, it is
vital that the nature and models underpinning disability employment
research are understood. Key government-led research, such as the Labour
Force Survey (LFS), General Household Survey (GHS) and Social Trends
all adopt ICIDH type 'disability' schemas and all seek to explain disability
and employment difficulties in terms of bodily deficits. The LFS asks
disabled respondents whether '...the health problem or disability affects
the kind of paid work they can do' (cited in Blackaby et al. 1999: 2).
Additionally, the LFS subdivides 'main disability' into 'problem'
categories, so that all 'long-term disabled' are classified as 'problems with
arms and hands', 'problems with back and neck' and so on (Labour Force
Survey 1999).

The General Household Survey adopts a more general focus in asking
'whether their disability/illness limits their activities in any way' (Blackaby
et al. 1999: 3). Here the causal direction of the research 'problem' is
assumed to be from the deficits of the disabled person in shaping
employment opportunities and experiences. It is difficult to see how
subsidiary questions can break free of these epistemological constraints.
Indeed even when we look at research designed expressly to map and
explore the employment experiences of disabled people, we see the
medical model remaining at the core of these studies.

The OPCS report *Disabled Adults: Services, Transport and Employment*
(Martin et al. 1989), the SCPR study *Employment and Handicap* (Prescott-
Clarke 1990) and more recent studies drawing on established datasets
(Blackaby et al. 1999; Sly et al. 1999; Goldstone and Darwent 2000) all
adopt medical schemas as tools of variable analysis or as guides to disabled
people's 'functional ability'. For example, the OPCS survey that had a
major impact on neo-liberal reforms of disability and employment policy,
identified 13 'types of disability' and calculated a 10 point 'severity' scale

(Martin et al. 1989: 2). However, the perceived relationships between types of disability led to the aggregation of disabilities into 5 groups: physical, mental, seeing, hearing and 'other'. The research adds an additional layer of complexity by devising a 'Classification of Complaints'. Here 16 classes of complaints are identified. These complaints, for example those of eye complaints and of the digestive system, are deemed to be the 'complaints causing disability' (Martin et al. 1989).

Of significance, disability and the functional problems caused by a bodily or 'mental complaint' are seen explicitly as key factors in limiting disabled workers and job seekers. For example, in trying to understand the reasons why disabled respondents were not working the researchers devised the following categories:

- Your health problem makes it impossible for you to do any kind of paid work
- You have not found a suitable paid job
- You do not want or need a paid job (Martin et al. 1989: 75).

It is worth reflecting that the major government-led research which includes disability, most notably the LFS, GHS and OPCS, have at no point consulted about the shape, language, focus or execution of these studies. We are only now beginning to connect what the key tenets of a social model would be in the field of employment. It could be argued that disability research is simply a sub-set of wider positivist research assumptions, however even official qualitative follow-up research bears all the hallmarks of a medical model of disability. We can take it that the medical model has many guises and has a logic which straddles all forms of disability research. Andrew Thomas's qualitative study *Working with a Disability* asserts:

> Employers were not part of the research design; this report considers employment from an employee's perspective and is based on their accounts of the facilitators and barriers they experienced in working with a disability (Thomas 1992:1).

This sounds promising in focusing on barriers and facilitators, factors external to the individual disabled employee. However a reading of the wider report makes clear the centrality of the medical model in the research:

> The occupational experiences of employees in this study were often inter-linked with the onset or deterioration of their disability ... almost all of the study sample had experienced a change in their working life as a result of their disability (Thomas 1992:71).

However, the adoption of the medical model ICIDH schema is only made clear by Thomas (1992: 9) in a footnote in the research report, and is justified as being 'consistent with other research'. Although much effort is invested in conveying the experiences of disabled workers, there is a strong sense of the incommensurability of medical and social model epistemologies. Research agendas, study design and the relationships of research production are firmly established here as with most medical model research.

The social model and employment

In setting the agenda for research on disability and employment in a medical model, it is not surprising that much UK policy and practice has been geared to rehabilitating individuals or for assessing employability, partial capacity, work readiness and being deemed 'unemployable'.

The period 1944 to 1995 has largely been characterised by the dominance and overshadowing presence of the Tomlinson Report (1943) and the 1944 Act. There is now a well-established literature identifying the limitations of disability and employment policy and a full reprise of these is unnecessary. However it is worth connecting these early influences with longer run employment policy and practice. Key influences of the medical model of disability are:

- provider-led services;
- limited impact on employment barriers; and
- professional power.

Provider-led services

The UK Employment Service (now part of the newly formed Jobcentre Plus) has developed a key role over the last 50 years in identifying disabled workers and job-seekers needs. One such responsibility has been to administer the 'Access to Work Scheme' (AtW). Although clearly of value to disabled people in its role of providing workplace aids and adjustments (Thornton and Lunt 1995) there is much evidence that the nature of provision is often disempowering (Glickman 1996; Roulstone 1998; RNIB, 2002; Roulstone et al. 2003). In comparison, official governmental research presents a favourable picture of the working of the AtW scheme (Beinart 1996; Thornton et al. 2001). Examples of disempowerment relate to the narrowness of eligibility requirements, the bias towards providing for those already in work, the time taken to deliver, the lack of disabled people's own perspectives on needs, budget-led assessments and the fragmented nature of provision.

These all mirror the criticisms of deficits in community support for disabled people (Morris 1993; Barnes 1997). Accountability to disabled people is entirely absent at a local and regional level. Whilst ACDET, the successor to the National Advisory Council on Employment of Disabled People despite their criticism of the AtW provide a rather anodyne forum, one appointed by the DFES and performing an advisory rather than outcomes and monitoring function. The newly established Disability Employment Advisory Committee (DEAC) has also been established as a purely advisory body, whilst unlike ACDET the minutes of DEACs meetings are not made public. Here, advice is deemed to be 'in confidence' in marked contrast to the workings of ACDET (Department for Work and Pensions 2002). It is also noteworthy that AtW and Jobcentre Plus are staffed predominantly by non-disabled people.

Limited impact on employment barriers

Despite a plethora of policy developments designed to further enhance disabled peoples' employment opportunities since 1944, the overall impact in reducing the levels of unemployment, under-employment and wider social disadvantage (Burchardt 2000) has been very limited. Those developments promising most in terms of reducing workplace barriers have regrettably delivered the least and have been actively allowed to fall into disuse. The UK quota system, a scheme emanating from the 1944 Disabled Persons Act has been the most dramatic example.

In contrast to the more individualised approach to barriers embodied in ADL and more radical in principle than the voluntarist approach of persuasion recently exampled in the 'see the person' campaign, the quota system was based on more corporatist ideas. Here, the need to plan and audit disabled people's access to employment is backed up with legal and financial sanctions. There are different schools of thought on the quota system's failure (Barnes 1991; Doyle 1994; Thornton and Lunt 1995). However it could be argued that the quota scheme's demise was not because it was unworkable but that it came nearest to breaking out of a deficit model of disability and represents the most ambitious feature of the 1944 Act. The repeal of the quota system with the advent of the DDA 1995 has led some to argue that these two approaches are largely incompatible. However, there needs to be more debate about a social model approach to common barrier reduction, one which transcends individual and voluntarist ideas. The promise of the Disability Discrimination Act 1995 however is clearly limited by its medical model underpinnings. Invested with much promise (Cooper 2002:17), the Act offers redress for 'treatment less favourable' and where the reason relates to disability and where the 'treatment' was not 'justified'. Additionally a failure to make a 'reasonable adjustment' also comes within the remit of the Act. Despite the involvement of a small number of disabled people, and in spite of the Act being a compromise with the more radical aims of the UK Disabled People's Movement, the Act adopts established medical model tenets (Gooding 1996; Roulstone 2003).

Disability as restriction is taken to result from impairment, as Gooding notes:

> The DDA creates a new legal definition of a 'disabled person'. It does not however replace the previous definitions of 'disability' and 'handicap' contained in other legislation ... and focuses solely on the inability to perform certain physical and mental functions caused directly by the 'impairments' of the individual (Gooding 1996: 9).

A reading of the body of case law to date, much of which focuses upon section 2 the Employment Provisions of the Act (Income Data Services 2000) suggests that much attention focuses upon a claimant's ability to meet key tests of disability for the purposes of the Act. Research suggests that over 80 per cent of cases submitted to a tribunal are unsuccessful in establishing treatment less favourable due to the failure to meet key legal test. Here a claimant's 'disability', its adverse affects, have to be 'long-term', 'substantial' and have an adverse affect on 'normal day-to-day activities' (Gooding 1996: 11). These terms are informed by established statutes, most notably the Chronically Sick and Disabled Persons Act 1970, and reflect established medical model assumptions that to qualify for the benefits of disability legislation a person must establish they are disabled enough to qualify for these benefits. This has implications for people with unseen impairments (Roulstone 2003) and fluctuating conditions (Gooding 1996).

As with most disability legislation the Disability Discrimination Act (DDA) 1995 is abstracted from the organisational realities of the social world. Of note, very few cases have been submitted under section 2 around recruitment given the difficulty in establishing 'treatment less favourable'. Most cases have focused on dismissal and alleged failure to make reasonable adjustments (Meager et al. 1999; Income Data Services 2000). As with all anti-discrimination legislation the reactive nature of legal redress suggests the DDA is likely to have only a supportive role for more active and planned programmes of barrier reduction. This support has been made more likely given the recent announcement by the Disability Rights Commission (DRC) of a limit of 75 funded cases per year from 2000-2004 (DRC 2002a). The failure to go beyond individualised notions of justice towards more general barrier reduction are evident in the fact that no formal investigations of major organisations have been undertaken to date, whilst the following suggests the DRC are themselves unsure about their commitment to rooting our systemic discrimination:

> The experience of the other commissions (CRE, EOC) has not been uniformly encouraging ... The EOC for example has not conducted a formal investigation for several years, as a result of previous difficulties (DRC 2002b).

Professional power

There is now much evidence that as with health and social care professions, Employment Service staff remain the most powerful stakeholder in the disability relationship (O'Bryan et al. 2000; Roulstone et al. 2003). There is also evidence that service providers do attempt to maintain professional and financial control by carefully managing information when discussing possible provision (Glickman 1996; Roulstone 1998). These approaches reflect the more substantial literature on information control and professional rigidities in health and social care (French 1988; Morris 1993; Stevenson and Parsloe 1993). An attendant assumption has often been that disabled people do not know what is best for them and that this is best left to experts (McKnight 1983; Barnes 1997).

In the field of disability and employment support it is noteworthy that no inspectorates, independent reviews and publicly available service standards attach to this work. The professional standards, ethos and accomplishments of employment professionals is largely a 'closed book' with few insights being available. However, New Labour's adoption of cross-departmental working and the merging of agencies as with the newly formed Jobcentre Plus may hold some promise in encouraging more joined-up working and transparent professional work with disabled people.

Joint Investment Plans hold similar promise for better joint working to the advantage of disabled workers and job seekers. However at the time of writing there is evidence that Jobcentre Plus faces many challenges in reducing established professional boundaries, the initiative being launched well before the pilot scheme was completed (House of Commons Work and Pensions Select Committee 2002).

One key example of the failure to engender an holistic approach to disability employment support is given in the recent case of Kenny versus Hampshire Constabulary. Kenny, a disabled job seeker was interviewed for a civilian post with Hampshire Constabulary. It was clear that Kenny would need support in aspects of his work which were not available from his colleagues. An offer of employment was made subject to the personal assistance being provided. Kenny was asked if a relative could assist but he felt this to be inappropriate. The Employment Services were asked if they would fund a Personal Assistant. Due to the length of time in providing support Hampshire Constabulary withdrew the job offer. Kenny took the employer to an Employment Tribunal but it decided that he had not been treated less favourably (Roulstone 2003). This demonstrated a noteworthy failure to join two key planks of support: the Access to Work scheme and the powers of the DDA.

Applying the social model of disability to employment

As stated earlier, the social model of disability has led to significant changes in the way disability is viewed. Challenges to the language of disability are paralleled by fundamental revisions of the perceived roots of disability. Here the language of choices, rights, and active involvement urgently need to be translated into the realm of employment and job seeking. In policy and practice terms such choices and involvement can begin to draw on broader street-level applications of the social model. Borrowing from wider uses of the social model we need to begin to look at:

- user-led research;
- living and working in the mainstream;
- flexible policies;
- direct payments; and
- disabled people's input into key legislation and reform.

User-led research

Despite a growing body of research increasingly reflecting the social model of disability in the field of employment (Roulstone 1998; French 2000; Roulstone et al. 2003), the continued dominance of official research in informing policy and programme development has to be challenged. This is not to impugn the value of large-scale studies but a fundamental questioning of the value of the medical model assumptions on which they rest.

There is then an urgent need to openly challenge the government's continued adherence to medical model research and the value of the results of these studies. This could be tackled at many levels from lobbying the Minister for Disabled People on the issue of reappraising the model to active attempts to offer up alternative research designs and premises and the use of social model research findings to date in support of the value of the model. It is perhaps unlikely that disabling research alone will lead to the direct action that has been motivated by immediate concerns over benefit reform (Hyde 2000; Roulstone 2000), the limited moves toward civil rights legislation (Oliver and Campbell 1996), and inaccessible transport (Barnes, Mercer and Shakespeare 1999). However, if we view official research and its findings as a key constitutive of policy and programme design and development we can begin to see its importance as a locus of change.

Living and working in the mainstream

Developments are already afoot within the Disabled People's Movement towards open employment. As with debates around institutional segregation (Ryan and Thomas 1980) and 'special schools' (Armstrong and Barton 1999) there seems to be a growing awareness that segregated employment is not in tune with wider constructions of citizenship. This has been spurred on by New Labour's emphasis on active citizenship and rights-responsibilities discourse at the heart of the Welfare Reform Green Paper (Department for Social Security 1999). The notion of welfare-through-work however has to be seen as both important but also as constrained by a liberal epistemology based largely on access. This mirrors Len Barton's (1996) discussion on educational mainstreaming where he rightly challenges the assumption that access and integration equals inclusion. We need to avoid any *a priori* assumption of access equalling enabling and inclusive experiences.

Clearly the historically low pay received in section 2 (sheltered and supported) employment (Barnes 1991; Hyde 1996) suggests that this should not be accepted as equating to citizenship, however there are likely to be long-run debates about the value of intermediate labour markets, with some staunchly opposed (O'Bryan et al. 2000) whilst others are strongly in favour of their retention (RNIB 2002). The dilemma of choices and rights here is clear, however in going beyond a liberal epistemology we can both reflect on the nature of employment and ask why it is that sheltering is required in the twenty first century. What is it being sheltered from and why?

The recent development of Workstep highlights the Government's commitment to emphasising mainstream open employment as the ultimate goal (Department for Work and Pensions 2002). We do however need to reflect on the complex motivations that might attach to this programme development. It is clear that many New Labour policy and programme developments have been Treasury-driven (Roulstone 2000) and that encouraging open employment at all costs is not necessarily the equivalent of choices and rights where getting employment is a higher consideration than the experience of employment.

Flexible policies

Key improvements in reducing the rigidities of work and welfare systems can already be identified: the Disabled Persons Tax Credit (DPTC) does in principle make work more accessible for those able to work 16 plus hours. The tax credit is seen as a less stigmatising way of boosting disabled workers income. The extension of the Incapacity Benefit 'linking rule' from 8 weeks to one year (Jacobs and Winyard 2002) allows greater ease of movement between work and benefits, whilst increased earnings disregards for Independent Living Fund claimants may also encourage greater labour market participation.

Sadly counteracting policies have also been rolled out which have created a generally punitive feel to disability employment policy in the 1990s (Hyde 2000; Roulstone 2000). Attempts to differentiate 'real' and contrived claims to the 'disability category' (Stone 1985) have led to invidious distinctions being made, based largely on the medical model but of note not based on independent medical opinion; each quite distinct points. Inflexibilities continue to inhere in the '16 hours rule' that is still applied to the DPTC that make it very difficult to build-up hours over a period of time without financial penalty. Whilst the benefits trap continues to work against those with more substantial supported living packages wishing to enter supported employment (O'Bryan et al. 2000).

The importing of a social model into a systematic scrutiny of disability policy and the disability benefits system would likely produce more responsive policies and programmes. Moreover, this development should help break down invidious distinctions based on medical model notions of percentage loss (Social Security General Benefit Regulations 1982), abstract notions of 'incapacity' (O'Bryan et al. 2000) and 'capability' tests (Social Security Incapacity for Work General Regulations 1995). A need to review the discrepancies between the more inclusive (if imperfect) definitions of disability in the DDA and the highly restrictive definitions and constructions of disability contained in benefit regulations is clear and imperative. It would help if staff involved with disabled people in getting and keeping work had experience of impairment.

Direct payments

The question of the value of direct payments for disabled people living in the community is now well established by the Disabled People's Movement here in the UK (Kestembaum 1993; Lakey 1994). There have also been some small-scale discussions about blurring the boundaries of where this support and assistance should take place, with early connections with employment-based support being mooted (O'Bryan et al. 2000). However these have not permeated debates about the role and form of the key programme measure in Access to Work (AtW). This important scheme as noted above, remains inflexible, provider-driven, budget-focused, is sometimes adversarial in its dealings with employers and employees and does not dovetail with the Employment Code of Practice emanating from section 2 of the Disability Discrimination Act 1995. Alongside a more joined up approach to supporting reasonable adjustments, AtW has to be opened up for routine and disabled-led scrutiny.

It is noteworthy that a programme as important as the AtW scheme should not allow any unfettered input of disabled people in aiding the review, redesign of the scheme. Unlike health and social care, employment support remains something of a closed book. The official evaluations of AtW are surprisingly favourable and very different to those which adopt a social model of disability as part of their research design. In social model terms, choices and rights to an equitable, open, responsive scheme requires independent scrutiny which itself is shaped by disabled people. In concrete terms this should involve the enhanced numerical and qualitative involvement of disabled people in the running of AtW and should attempt to map wider developments such as direct payments on to possible future reforms of the scheme. Indeed, ACDET, disbanded but reformed as the DEAC, suggested that direct payments should be considered by the Government (Hansard 10 July 2000). The ACDET also made the related points that disabled people's knowledge and experience were simply 'not taken seriously enough', that AtW unduly focused on disability rather than need, and that Disability Employment Advisors require Disability Equality Training and awareness of complex impairment issues to provide a more tailored service.

Disabled people's input into key legislation

There is an urgent need both to review substantially legislation that impacts on disabled people, but also to ensure that disabled people are allowed to enter the realm of law making more fully and that law is increasingly scrutinised for its enabling potential. Legislation drafted with the express intention of helping disabled people make out in a disabling society is not living up to its promise and potential. In the field of employment, the most urgent needs are for a review of the further potential and impact assessment of the Disability Discrimination Act 1995 part 2 and its accompanying Code of Practice.

Laws, regulations and statutory instruments underpinning Direct Payments, employment related benefits and 'advisory' mechanisms around disability, employment and training all need to be scrutinised and where possible radicalised by the involvement of disabled people. The disbanding of ACDET coincided with some of their most far-reaching recommendations. There is an urgent need to develop a more influential disability-led forum which is permanent, outcomes-focused and which requires greater accountability on the part of the Minister for Disabled People. It is not inconceivable that in time a disabled person may gravitate to the role of minister, it too beginning the process of breaking down barriers to disabled people's claims to informed choice in employment options.

Conclusion

This chapter has explored the development of a social model informed approach to understanding and reviewing employment policy, programmes and practice. Although employment should not be seen as the only viable route to citizenship in the twenty first century, access to supportive and sustainable employment environments should be the shared goal of disabled people and stakeholders who are paid to enhance such opportunities. A key message here is that disabled people should be more involved at every level from reforming the way we look at the disability and employment 'problem', through the challenging of professionally-led nature of services to a questioning of the nature of employment in an enabling society.

Bibliography

Armstrong, F. and Barton, L. 1999: **Disability, Human Rights and Education**. Buckingham: Open University Press.

Barnes, C. 1991: **Disabled People in Britain and Discrimination, A Case for Anti-Discrimination Legislation**. London: Hurst and Co.

Barnes, C., Mercer, G. and Shakespeare, T. 1999: *Exploring Disability, A Sociological Introduction*. Cambridge: Polity.

Barnes, M. 1997: *Care, Communities and Citizens*. London: Longman.

Barton, L. 1996: Sociology and Disability: Some emerging issues. In L. Barton (ed.), *Disability and Society: Emerging Issues and Insights*. London: Longman.

Beinaret, S., Smith, P. and Sproston, K. 1996: *The Access to Work Programme. A Survey of Recipients, Employers, Employment Service Managers and Staff*. London: SCPR.

Blackaby, D., Clark, K., Drinkwater, S., Leslie, D., Murphy, P. and O'Leary, N. 1999: *Earnings and Employment Opportunities of Disabled People*. DfEE Research Brief 133.

Brechin, A., Liddiard, P. and Swain, J. 1983: *Handicap in a Social World*. Sevenoaks: Hodder and Stoughton.

Bruce, I., McKennell, A. and Walker, E. 2000: *Blind and Partially Sighted in Britain: The RNIB Survey*. London: HMSO.

Burchardt, T. 2000: *Enduring Economic Exclusion: Disabled People. Income and Work*. York: Joseph Rowntree Foundation.

Cooper, V. (ed.) 2002: *Law, Rights and Disability*. London: Jessica Kingsley.

Department for Education and Employment 1999: *From Exclusion to Inclusion: A Report of the Disability Rights Task Force on Civil Rights for Disabled People*. London: DfEE.

Department for Social Security 1999: *New Ambitions for Our Country: A New Contract for Welfare*. Green Paper, Cmd 3805. London: DSS.

Department for Work and Pensions 2002: *Workstep: A Handbook for Providers*. London: Employment Service.

Disability Rights Commission 2002a: *Legal Strategy 2001-2003*. London: DRC.

Disability Rights Commission 2002b: *DRC Future Objectives: A Personal Communication from Nick O'Brien, Director of Legal Services*. London: DRC.

Doyle, B. 1994: *New Directions Towards Disabled Workers' Rights*. London: Institute for Employment Rights.

Finkelstein, V. and Stuart, O. 1996: Developing New Services. In G. Hales (ed.), *Beyond Disability: Towards and Enabling Society*. London: Sage.

French, S. 1988: The Experiences of Disabled Health Professionals. *Sociology and Health and Illness*, 10 (2), 70-88.

French, S. 2001: *Disabled People and Employment*. Aldershot: Ashgate.

Glickman, M. 1996: Disability and the Cost Minimising Imperative. *Rehab Network*, Autumn.

Gooding, C. 1996: *Disabling Laws, Enabling Acts, Disability Rights in Britain and America*. London: Pluto Press.

Goldstone, C. and Darwent, T. 2000: *Disabled Jobseekers: A Follow-Up Study of the Baseline Survey*. DfEE Research Brief No 195. London: DfEE.

Graham, P., Jordan, D. and Lamb, B. 1990: *An Equal Chance or No Chance?* London: The Spastics Society.

House of Commons Work and Pensions Select Committee on Education and Employment. *'One' Pilots-Lessons for Jobcentre Plus*. 1st Report, March. House of Commons Reports, London.

Hyde, M. 1996: Fifty Years of Failure: Employment Services for Disabled People in the UK. *Work, Employment and Society*, 10 (4), 683–700.

Hyde, M. 2000: From Welfare to Work? Social policy for disabled people of working age in the United Kingdom in the 1990s. *Disability and Society*, 15 (2), 327–41.

Income Data Services 2000: *Monitoring the Disability Discrimination Act 1995*. London: IDS.

Jacobs, L. and Winyard, S. 2002: *Social Security, Visually Impaired People and the Labour Government. Briefing paper*. London: RNIB.

Kestembaum, A. 1993: *Making Community Care a Reality*. Nottingham: Independent Living Fund.

Labour Force Survey 1999: London: Office for National Statistics.

Labour Force Survey. 2002: London: Office for National Statistics.

Lakey, J. 1994: *Caring About Independence: Disabled People and the Independent Living Fund*. London: Policy Studies Institute.

McKnight, J. 1983: Professionalised Service and Disabling Help. In Brechin, A., Liddiard, P. and Swain, J. (eds) *Handicap in a Social World*. Sevenoaks: Hodder and Staughton, in association with The Open University Press.

Martin, J., White, A. and Meltzer, H. 1989: *Disabled Adults: Services, Transport and Employment*. London: HMSO.

Meager, N., Doyle, B., Evans, C., Kersley, B., Williams, M., O'Regan, S. and Tackey, N. 1999: *Monitoring the Disability Discrimination Act (DDA) 1995*. London: DfEE.

Morrell, J. 1990: *The Employment of People with Disabilities: Research into the Policies and Practices of Employers*. Sheffield: Employment Services.

Morris, J. 1993: *Independent Lives: Community Care and Disabled People*. Basingstoke: Macmillan.

O'Bryan, A., Simons, K., Beyer, S. and Grove, B. 2000: *A Framework for Supported Employment*. York: Joseph Rowntree Foundation.

Oliver, M. 1990: *The Politics of Disablement*. Basingstoke: Macmillan.

Oliver, M. and Barnes, C. 1993: Discrimination, disability and welfare: from needs to rights. In J. Swain et al. (eds), *Disabling Barriers, Enabling Environments*. Milton Keynes: Open University Press and Sage.

Oliver, M. and Campbell, J. 1996: *Disability Politics: Understanding Our Past, Changing Our Future*. London: Routledge.

Prescott-Clarke, P. 1990: *Employment and Handicap*. Social and London: Community Planning Research.

Roulstone, A. 1998: *Enabling Technology, Disabled People, Work and New Technology*. Buckingham: Open University Press.

Roulstone, A. 2000: Disability, Dependency and the New Deal for Disabled People. *Disability and Society*, 15 (3), 427-443.

Roulstone, A. 2003: The Legal Road to Rights? Disabling Premises, Obiter Dicta and the Disability Discrimination Act 1995. *Disability and Society*, 18 (2), 117-131.

Roulstone, A., Price, J., Gradwell, L. and Child, L. 2003: *Thriving and Surviving at Work: Disabled People's Employment Strategies*. Report for the Joseph Rowntree Foundation. Bristol: Policy Press.

Royal National Institute for the Blind 2002: *Work Matters: Enabling Blind and Partially Sighted People to Gain Employment*. London: RNIB.

Ryan, J. and Thomas, F. 1980: *The Politics of Mental Handicap*. London: Free Association Books.

Sly, F., Thair, T. and Risdon, A. 1999: *Disability in the Labour Market: Results of the Spring 1998 Labour Force Survey*. March. London: HMSO.

Social Security General Benefit Regulations 1982: London: HMSO.

Social Security Incapacity for Work General Regulations 1995: London: HMSO.

Stone, D. 1985: *The Disabled State*. Basingstoke: Macmillan.

Swain, J., Finkelstein, V., French, S. and Oliver, M. 1993: *Disabling Barriers, Enabling Environments*. Milton Keynes: Open University Press and Sage.

Thomas, A. 1992: *Working with a Disability: Barriers and Facilitators.* London: Social and Community Planning Research.

Thornton, P. and Lunt, N. 1995: *Employment for Disabled People: Social Obligation or Individual Responsibility?* York: Social Policy Research Unit.

Thornton, P., Hirst, M., Arksey, H., Tremlett, N. 2001: *Users' Views of Access to Work.* Sheffield: Employment Service.

Tomlinson Report 1943: *Report of the Inter-Departmental Committee on the Rehabilitation and Resettlement of Disabled Persons.* Cmd 6415. London: HMSO.

CHAPTER 3

Developing a User-Led Project: creating employment opportunities for disabled people within the housing sector

Grant Carson and John Speirs

Introduction

> One of the most significant factors undermining the rights of disabled adults to participate fully and equally in society is their systematic exclusion and marginalisation from the labour market (Smith 1992: 1).

This chapter examines the development of a unique and innovative intermediate labour market scheme that was the first of its kind in the United Kingdom. This Employment Project was designed to enable a small group of people with significant impairments to move from long-term unemployment into temporary paid work, specifically in the housing sector, with a view to securing a permanent job afterwards. It was sponsored by The Centre for Independent Living in Glasgow (CILiG) which had already established the Glasgow Disabled Person's Housing Service (GDPHS) in September 1999 to supply information and advocacy on housing and associated independent living options for disabled people.

The GDPHS Employment Project was planned so that the disabled participants were located in temporary positions in housing associations where, as part of their work experience, they gathered information on accessible housing in Glasgow. In so doing, they would also enhance the general aim of the GDPHS to support disabled people's housing needs.

We will begin by outlining the approach taken by the CILiG in developing user-led services and more particularly the GDPHS, before describing and assessing the implementation of the Employment Project.

This will include an extended case study of the work placement experiences of one of the disabled participants. Finally, we will review the main outcomes and overall progress of the Project.

Supporting independent living: a social model approach

The CILiG was launched in 1995 to offer a full range of independent living support, advice, training and advocacy services to disabled people who wanted to manage their own personal assistance packages. From the outset, the CILiG rejected the traditional view of an individualised or medical model of disability, with its focus on a person's functional limitations, and the conflation of 'disability' and 'impairment' that still characterises government policy, as is clearly illustrated by the approach taken in the Disability Discrimination Act (DDA) 1995. Instead, the CILiG actively promoted the social model of disability which defines disability as a societal construct emerging from the social and environmental barriers and discrimination experienced by people with impairments (Oliver 1990).

Combating institutional discrimination

The social interpretation of disability demonstrates obvious parallels with analyses of other forms of discrimination based on 'race' and gender. Moreover, despite the availability of legal redress in the last quarter of the twentieth century, and the growing acceptance of the level and extent of social exclusion, progress in overcoming such discrimination has been limited.

As was argued in the report sponsored by the British Council of Organisations of Disabled People *Disabled People in Britain and Discrimination* (Barnes 1991), institutional discrimination against disabled people is embedded in the institutions and organizations of contemporary society. It arises where the needs of disabled people are systematically ignored or met inadequately, and if 'agencies are regularly interfering in the lives of disabled people as a means of social control' (Barnes 1991: 3), in ways not experienced by non-disabled people. From this perspective, institutional discrimination:

> incorporates the extreme forms of prejudice and intolerance usually associated with individual or direct discrimination, as well as the more covert and unconscious attitudes which contribute to and maintain indirect and/or passive discriminatory practices within contemporary organizations. Examples

of institutional discrimination on social policy include the way the education system is organized, and the operation of the labour market (Barnes 1991: 3).

Traditional notions of disability based on an individual or medical model have frequently been reproduced uncritically, and 'confirmed' in the approach to disability as a 'personal tragedy', so that people with impairments are demeaned as in need of 'care' and dependent on others (Oliver 1990). The effect has been to disregard or deny the relevance or merit of equal opportunity policies and practices to advance the social inclusion of disabled people.

Building a housing service for disabled people

The CILiG is a democratically accountable user-led organisation with 85 per cent of Directors and 70 per cent of staff identifying themselves as disabled people. Its philosophy and practice is firmly located in the social model approach of seeking ways to challenge disabling barriers and promote social inclusion (UPIAS 1976). This has been widely adopted by disabled activists and their organisations in Britain over the last quarter of the twentieth century. Another important early influence was Derbyshire Coalition of Disabled People's (DCDP) formulation of the 'seven needs' of disabled people (Davis 1990; Davis and Mullender 1993). These arose from detailed discussions among disabled people about an alternative social interpretation of disability and how this might be translated into 'practical action'.

There was considerable agreement on the significance of 'housing of good basic design, appropriate technical aids, and a flexible system of personal assistance' (Davis 1990:6). Similarly, it was argued that crucial life choices facing disabled people, such as moving out of an institution or away from their family home, depended on accurate information about, for example, national and local policies, benefit systems, housing providers, aids and equipment. However, such information had to be interpreted and used effectively, hence the importance of advice and peer counselling. In addition, achieving social integration depended on accessible built environment and transport opportunities. For DCDP, these areas comprised the seven 'primary' needs: information, counselling, housing, technical aids, personal assistance, transport, and access and housing. Taken together they 'put flesh on the social model of disability' (Davis 1990: 7). Needless to say, once these are met, a further level of 'secondary' needs materialises, notably education, employment and leisure.

Looking specifically at accessible housing, Glasgow has a complex and extremely fragmented housing sector with a high proportion of flatted accommodation, particularly in older tenements. In 2002, over 800 disabled people in Glasgow were classified as a 'top medical priority' and more than 200 of this group had been waiting for more than two years for suitable housing. Moreover, Glasgow City Council (2001) reported that the average waiting time for a priority one adaptation was 329 days, and further that there was a shortfall of over 13,000 houses for disabled people of all ages and impairment groups. This large unmet demand was mirrored in the *Scottish House Condition Survey 1996* (Scottish Office 1997). It indicated that there were only around 24,000 dwellings (approx 1 per cent of total) in Scotland that could be classified as suitable for use by the 'ambulant disabled' although there were 124,000 'ambulant disabled' households. This clear failure to meet disabled people's needs was exacerbated because, for example, only 2,000 of the 5,000 wheelchair accessible houses were actually occupied by 'full-time' wheelchair users. More recently, the *Scottish House Condition Survey 2002* (Communities Scotland 2003) reported that the number of dwellings meeting the lowest level of the barrier free standard for disabled people had risen to 89,000 but this still only represented 4 per cent of the total housing stock.

An early issue for the GDPHS was that social landlords, such as the more than eighty Housing Associations in Glasgow controlling over 48,000 properties, were unable to supply a detailed breakdown of their housing stock, and the level and location of accessible and adapted units that they were managing. The most frequent reason given was that they did not have, or could not spare the necessary staff resources to gather and collate this information. Coincidentally, at this time, Government strategists were emphasising the important role that housing had to play in creating a fairer and more equal society:

> Good housing has a vital part to play in promoting social inclusion, and although it cannot, on its own, provide a panacea for all the ills of social exclusion, a decent secure and affordable home for all is fundamental to the development of the sort of inclusive and participative society the Government wants in Scotland (Scottish Office 1999: para. 2.4).

Against this background, the CILiG prepared an application for European Union Objective 3 funding to develop a specialist housing information, advice and advocacy service for disabled people in housing need. It was the first democratically accountable, user-led organisation to obtain this type of European funding in Scotland. As a result, the Glasgow Disabled Person's Housing Service (GDPHS) was set up in September 1999, and became operational in mid-2000. It initiated an information and advocacy service for disabled people by gathering and collating information on the accessible housing stock in Glasgow as well as producing a centralised register of disabled people in housing need. Once these two registers had been fully developed, the GDPHS was able to deliver a matching service to assist disabled people to find 'the right house for the right person at the right time'. Equally, it permitted housing providers to register vacant accommodation suitable for disabled people. By the end of 2003, the GDPHS held information from some 80 different housing associations/social landlords covering over 48,000 properties.

The GDPHS Employment Project

The Intermediate Labour Market model for moving people from long-term unemployment into permanent work concentrated on ways of improving their general employability. The focus was on a temporary (up to one year) contract with a comprehensive 're-engagement package' ranging from the direct work experience through to basic skills and vocational training, personal development and confidence building (Marshall and Macfarlane 2000). In order to avoid displacing those already in work, schemes have stressed activities not currently undertaken by the employing organisation. There has also been considerable emphasis on placements that will produce wider community benefits.

Typically, employment projects and programmes have drawn on a diverse range of local, national (e.g. New Deal) and European funding sources. The CILiG's application specifically targeted the European Social Fund and this resulted in an award of more than £97,000 in September 2000. Prior to making its bid, the CILiG commissioned a feasibility study and consultation exercise. These suggested that many social landlords were keen to develop and improve their services for disabled people, and to increase their opportunities for working in housing organisations. The CILiG developed the programme, secured the funding and employed the core co-ordinating staff.

The GDPHS Employment Project adopted a two-prong strategy:

1) It made available additional resources to social landlords to enable them to develop their policies and services for disabled people. This included the development of a city-wide database of adapted properties, plus improved referral and information networks to

match those seeking accessible accommodation with relevant housing providers. It also encouraged housing management and development policies that were more appropriate and responsive to the needs of disabled people.

2) It offered employment and training opportunities to selected disabled people in order to assist them to develop skills, experience and qualifications in all aspects of social housing. No distinctions were drawn against people with different types of impairment. Thus, the GDPHS participants demonstrated a broad range of impairments such as 'mental distress', head injury, hearing impairments (including a sign language user), visual impairments and physical impairments (such as Muscular Dystrophy, and Spina Bifida).

The GDPHS successfully negotiated twelve full-time placements based within housing associations in and around Glasgow. Each placement provider agreed to contribute £4,000 towards the cost of the project. Furthermore, in order to overcome the lack of incentive to leave relatively higher levels of welfare benefits, wage levels for those disabled people recruited to the Project were set at £212 per week. This amounted to an average annual salary of £11,000, which meant that all of the disabled recruits were better off financially in work than on benefits, by between £28 and £134 per week net. The Intermediate Labour Market model also stressed the significance of offering not only a temporary job but making available appropriate training and support to enable the disabled participants to move on to a 'regular' paid job at the end of their contract.

Furthermore, in order to satisfy the demand for wider community advantage, the Project expected disabled participants, as part of their placement, to gather and collate information on the numbers, types and locations of adapted and accessible houses. In this way, the project produced a unique synergy by creating employment for disabled people who in turn helped other members of the disabled population to find suitable housing accommodation.

Overall, during the course of their placement, participants:

- carried out a number of tasks/assignments aimed at improving the data on accessible housing throughout Glasgow;
- assisted the housing associations in which they were placed to develop more effective systems to match supply and provision of adapted housing; and
- were involved in a formal training programme in one of the following areas: housing management, urban regeneration,

administration, information and communications technology (ICT), and finance.

The first participants began their work placement in early 2001.

Recruitment

A number of criteria were identified to select the first cohort of twelve unemployed disabled people for their one-year, temporary placement with a housing association. These comprised a combination of assessment of the candidate's suitability for the project (based on motivation, enthusiasm, previous experience and qualifications) and measuring the level of disadvantage they had previously faced in accessing and retaining employment (based on length of employment, access issues, and the type of benefits received). Those individuals who received the Disability Living Allowance at the medium or higher level (that is, on the basis of assessed degree of impairment) were specifically targeted because official statistics indicate that this category incorporated the most disadvantaged and under-represented in the labour market (Martin, White and Meltzer 1989). To date, around two thirds of the project participants fitted this classification. While it was recognised that disability is not directly related to degree of impairment as measured by welfare benefits assessments, it was felt to be a reasonable 'proxy' indicator of social disadvantage in the present context.

All applicants were subjected to further rigorous checks in order to match the skills of the candidate to the specific requirements of the placement organisation, while also acknowledging the relevance of previous work experience, educational and training qualifications. The recruitment process spanned four main stages: the application and interview; a pre-selection or induction course; an interview with a placement provider; before making a final decision whether to enlist the individual on to the Project.

Personal Development

Once selected, each participant was offered financial support in order to pursue wider personal development and training. Examples of the type of course or activity chosen by the first cohort on the pilot project ranged from training in British Sign Language Level II, purchase of two personal computers for use at home by project workers, yoga classes, through to taking the European Computer Driving Licence. Indeed, all of those who stayed with the project for a complete year achieved a Standard Vocational Qualification at Level 2 or higher.

Aside from the added value of these activities, other benefits were unforeseen. For example, one recruit had been on a National Health Service (NHS) waiting list for a lightweight wheelchair for around 2 years which she could lift in and out of her car. Without it, her level of independence was greatly reduced. Yet within three weeks of starting on the GDPHS scheme, she was supplied with a suitable lightweight chair through the Department of Employment's *Access to Work* programme (see Thornton et al. 2001). This is designed to identify and address disabled people's needs in terms of equipment, adaptations or arrangements that allow them to gain, or remain in, employment. The Project ensured that the access needs of each participant were identified and agreed in partnership with the participant, staff of the GDPHS, the placement provider and *Access to Work*, prior to commencement of the placement. To date the Project has assisted in accessing over £100,000 worth of equipment, adaptations and support for the participants.

The Employment Project also contributed mentoring support to the workers and professional advice to organisations on the management of the placement. Again, if an employer required assistance to adapt their workplaces or acquire specialist equipment for use by a worker, the GDPHS was ready to assist with obtaining public funding.

Case Study: Sasha's story

Sasha (a pseudonym) is a 27-year-old Glasgow woman from an Asian family; she is Deaf and had never been in paid employment. She had completed an access course in administration at a local college one year before joining the GDPHS Employment Project. Sasha's family had actively discouraged her from working and this affected how she interacted with other people. She lacked confidence and social skills due in no small part to the 'cotton wool treatment' she received from her family. However, she was determined to get a job and ultimately wanted to work in an organisation that supported Deaf people.

Sasha's experience illustrates how a broad range of barriers both excludes disabled people from entry into the labour market and isolates them after joining the workplace. She had two placements in housing associations but these experiences could hardly have been more different. Her first post was in Glasgow city centre where she became a member of the housing services administration team. After discussions between Sasha, the GDPHS Employment Project staff, the placement provider, and staff administering the Department of Employment *Access to Work* scheme, all of her communication and access needs required for working in the housing association were addressed. These comprised:

- a textphone and phoneflash;
- a pager (hooked up to the fire alarm system);
- sign language interpreters;
- a work-related signing course delivered to all of the staff that worked directly with Sasha (this was specifically designed, with Sasha's involvement, to teach basic sign language techniques); and
- a Deaf Awareness course delivered by RNID.

There was a settling-in period for the first couple of months but at this point everything appeared to be going well. Sasha was enjoying the experience of working in a 'real' salaried post, while the housing association staff had completed their work-related signing course, and seemed positive about working with a Deaf person and familiarising themselves with the diverse barriers that confronted Sasha in the workplace.

However, after about three months, Sasha began to express dissatisfaction with her relationship with the line manager. She also felt that there was a breakdown in communication with other staff members and that she was getting less and less to do. When questioned about this, her line manager said 'Sasha was not doing the job properly, so she was not given that work to do again'. Nevertheless, there had been no discussions about possible support or training issues that might allow her to overcome any difficulties or misunderstandings. For her part, Sasha reported that she was not aware of making any mistakes. How was she supposed to know that she was not doing the job properly if nobody let her know that there was a problem?

Thereafter, the work relationship deteriorated quickly. Sasha felt isolated, frustrated and excluded, and the early confidence that she had gained soon disappeared. She believed that she was being treated differently from other members of staff and that her support needs were not being met. At the same time, her line manager and other staff expressed growing dis-satisfaction with the placement and it was terminated.

Sasha was then re-located in a housing association on the south side of Glasgow. Again, joint discussions between the main stakeholders resulted in a training and support plan that covered:

- Disability Equality Training for all staff;
- a work-related signing course for all staff;
- training to make the most effective use of the time that Sign

Language Interpreters spent at the placement;

- addressing access issues, installing all the equipment and completing other necessary adaptations and arrangements; and
- supplying Sasha with a yearly planner that detailed all aspects of her work experience, such as a work plan, team meetings, training days and locations.

In contrast to her first placement, this second experience remained positive throughout her stay. Sasha began as a member of the finance team, where she was attached to a more experienced member of staff. When that person was absent from work for a considerable period, Sasha took on her role. When this individual returned to work, she was moved to a different department, and Sasha was offered the post on a full-time basis. As a measure of the rise in Sasha's confidence, when informed that she was to be recommended for this higher-grade position, she immediately approached the director and asked for (and received) a significant pay rise! At the time of writing (mid-2003), over a year has passed and Sasha continues to occupy this post.

How can two housing associations of similar size, deliver such different work experiences? First, on both placements a plan was drawn up that identified issues in three key areas: access, support mechanisms and staff training. Nonetheless, several important differences emerged. With respect to access, while there were concerns about equipment, adaptations and related matters in both placements, there was less awareness of the barriers confronting Deaf people in the first placement or commitment to overcoming them.

Second, it was largely left to Sasha to sort out everyday issues. There was little encouragement for staff to discuss how the placement was going, let alone exploring collaborative action to maximise the support for Sasha. In contrast, in the second placement, a joint action plan was drawn up between staff and Sasha to make the most effective use of the time when a sign language interpreter was available, for example, in covering meetings, information, support and training issues. It was also evident that the staff and management in placement two showed more recognition of, and willingness to respond positively to, Sasha's obvious lack of work experience and wider isolation from 'mainstream' society. The many possibilities for a breakdown in communication between herself and other staff were therefore dealt with quickly rather than ignored. The regular review meetings set up between Sasha, the GDPHS Employment Project staff and the placement line manager permitted an earlier identification and closer monitoring of any concerns and allowed more scope for prompt intervention to address these difficulties. It is perhaps worth adding that the second placement housing association had a very good reputation for delivering an inclusive service to tenants as well as encouraging good employee-management relations.

A third area of difference between the placements emerged in staff training and development. In the second workplace, staff were expected (and embraced the opportunity) to participate in Disability Equality Training. While staff in both locations took part in a work-related sign language course, those in the second placement showed a greater appreciation of the importance of practicing and improving their new language skills by signing with Sasha on a regular basis. This difference in the level of commitment was further confirmed by the decision of ten staff to undertake and complete a British Sign Language Level 1 course.

The overall impression derived from Sasha's experience in the first placement was that there was an expectation that she should 'fit in' with established work routines. The pattern of institutional discrimination was both overt and covert and revolved around the ways in which Sasha was treated differently and unfairly because of her impairment. When staff began to question Sasha's performance, the management's claim to promote inclusion was overtaken by arguments that having a Deaf worker created 'problems' for the organisation. Instead of exploring the nature of these difficulties, management decided that the 'solution' was to ask Sasha to do more menial tasks (because these required the least amount of supervision) or to ignore her presence in the workplace. No feedback was given that she was not doing the job in the way or to the standard expected. This progressive exclusion from regular work tasks and communication reached the point where Sasha felt demoralised and extremely pessimistic about her prospects for finding any other paid employment.

Conversely, placement two was a far more positive experience from the outset. In the early meetings with senior staff members it was obvious that they were more sensitive to the issues and barriers facing a Deaf person in the workplace. They viewed the Employment Project as a development opportunity for existing members of staff and the organisation as a whole, as well as providing a positive work experience for Sasha. The management and staff were committed to involving Sasha in all aspects of the work experience and were very open to learning about and implementing new forms and techniques of communication, while also stressing her responsibilities and role as an employee. They treated Sasha as a regular member of staff with different access needs and embraced the opportunity to develop as an organisation, with her co-workers happy to talk to Sasha on everyday and work-related matters. Sasha quickly felt that she was being welcomed and treated as a fellow worker. She was carrying out a demanding role within the housing association, but received appropriate levels of support until she was competent enough to carry out the job as required. When issues arose or mistakes were made, there were appropriate communication channels and advice to address these promptly and efficiently. After all, the Employment Project was set up to promote the inclusion of disabled people in the workplace, by building their confidence and self-belief.

Sasha's experience also demonstrates the importance of co-operation between the Project Team and the placement associations. Continuing communication and exchange of experiences proved difficult in placement one: indeed, management staff members were reluctant to involve the Project Team in monitoring the experience and performance of the disabled trainees, until it was too late. Instead, the placement was viewed as an additional burden, and efforts were made to minimise potential access, support or training issues that might arise. Such instances raised basic questions about the commitment and attitude of staff individually and collectively in the provider organisation to the Project's aims. Yet, for the most part, the majority of the discriminatory practices entailed indirect rather than overt hostility. Conversely, a major reason for the much more positive outcomes achieved in Sasha's second placement was the very different attitudes of the staff and their preparation for the placement and working with a disabled colleague. This included a comprehensive training plan, together with a framework for monitoring its implementation.

The GDPHS: an evaluation

Recent independent evaluations of Intermediate Labour Market projects suggest that some have achieved positive outcomes of over 60 per cent of the participants progressing into permanent employment, with an overall average of 53 per cent in 1999/2000 – a figure slightly in excess of New Deal adult training programmes (Marshall and Macfarlane 2000). Significantly, over 90 per cent of those who obtained a job were still in work six months later, a much higher figure than that achieved by comparable 'return-to-work' programmes.

In the first two years of the GDPHS Employment Project, twenty-six disabled people, with a range of impairments and an average length of unemployment of eight years, were recruited. Of this group, fifteen successfully completed their European Computer Driving Licence and fourteen undertook a training qualification in Housing Administration. Fifteen participants moved into full-time employment (representing 58 per cent of the intake) and four into full-time higher education (15 per cent). Moreover, seven individuals from the first intake who moved into full-time employment were still in work one year later.

These positive outcomes have been reinforced by preliminary economic calculations of the costs and benefits of the Project. These suggest major financial returns over its two-year life span, at both the local and national government levels. These are as a result of the reduced costs of welfare benefits, lower wastage in housing adaptations, higher levels of income from rents and Council Tax, and additional income tax and national insurance contributions.

A further key feature of the GDPHS Employment Project was that it was overtly framed as an alternative to existing mainstream provision that drew on social model thinking. But how far, and in what ways, has it differed from a mainstream housing service? The central elements of the GDPHS comprised:

- an analysis of disabling social and environmental barriers to the social exclusion of people with impairments, and ways to tackle and overcome them (such as the 'benefits trap', access, communication, attitudes of employers, access to training);
- respect for the variety of individual support needs (not 'one size fits all');
- recognition of the dignity and expertise of disabled participants – including their own assessment of their support needs;
- an emphasis on quality rather than quantity in terms of 'outputs'; and
- addressing the basic shortcoming caused by the lack of involvement by disabled people in housing provision that leads to inappropriate and inadequate services and attempting to bring about organizational change in structures, process and culture through the participation of disabled people.

Together these elements outline an ambitious policy or service for the target (disabled) group. However, while the Employment Project has been delivered within a theoretical framework firmly based on the social model, its practical implementation has highlighted a number of contentious issues.

One concern has been the tension between a collective, structural approach and one located at the individual level. In order to prepare disabled people for work, action must be directed to individual needs as well as directing attention to more structural concerns such as improving the accessibility of workplaces to include disabled people. We need to do both. Also, within a social model analysis we must recognize that it is individuals with impairments who experience structural/ institutional barriers. The impact of these external barriers on individual self-esteem and confidence can be destructive and generate further internal barriers (oppression) so that even individual disabled people begin to believe the criticism from others that they are 'not up to the job', or 'just can't cut it' (Mason 1990). In these circumstances, support from a peer group (or user-led organization) is crucial in helping to diagnose the problem, and explore alternative remedies.

A second area worthy of note is the importance of flexibility in seeking organisational change. There are limits on how far and how quickly dominant cultural norms and values around work can be challenged, ranging, for example, from work patterns, task definition and allocation, through to modes of dress and communication. A specific example would be the information and advice as well as the communication support required to enable people with learning difficulties to participate meaningfully in decision making process at the workplace.

In addition, funders demand clarity in the identification of the target group as well as confidence that the recipient organisation can demonstrate that it will give 'value for money' in how the funding has been used. In the case of the GDPHS, this required evidence of the assessment or screening of disabled people so that they fitted the target criteria in terms of the degree of their impairment. Notwithstanding such concerns, employers should not need the 'sweetener' of cheap (project placement) labour to employ disabled people: they should ensure that disabled people have equal opportunities to find paid employment and flourish in the labour market.

Conclusion

Disability, within a social model approach, is a socio-political issue that concerns society as a whole. It should not be considered an issue only for disabled people, but something that potentially will affect anyone with an impairment. Disability is created by the failures of people, organisations and social systems to anticipate and/or respond appropriately to the everyday support needs of people who have an impairment. As the GDHPS Employment Project in general and the case study of Sasha's experience illustrate, institutional discrimination against disabled people is deep-seated and wide-ranging, but positive moves towards inclusion are possible with adequate support and training, aids and equipment, information, advice and peer counselling. The contrasting experiences of disabled participants in their work placements reveal ways in which the attitudes, everyday practices and routines of non-disabled people/employees constrain equal opportunities for disabled people. This picture reinforces the significance attached by organisations of disabled people to promoting the concept of user involvement in the design and delivery of services. This is based partly on the right to self-determination and partly on the belief that it leads to more effective, higher quality, services.

For its part, the GDPHS has now become an established part of the local housing service landscape. It has developed databases of disabled people's housing needs and preferences of the profile of available and planned accessible and barrier-free housing in Glasgow. These greatly help disabled people in their search for appropriate accommodation, while also facilitating the task of social landlords with accessible housing in finding suitable disabled clients. Additionally, the GDPHS has branched out to provide training and consultancy for housing providers, notably Disability Equality Training, and briefing courses on the DDA and its implications. In summary, the GDPHS now comprises a successful one-stop shop for disabled people in housing need, located in an accessible environment, and which is supported and managed by disabled people working for the CILiG – a user-led organisation of disabled people.

Bibliography

Barnes, C. 1991: *Disabled People in Britain and Discrimination.* London: Hurst and Co., in association with the British Council of Organisations of Disabled People.

Communities Scotland 2003: *Scottish Housing Condition Survey 2002.* Edinburgh: Scottish Office.

Davis, K. 1990: *Activating the Social Model of Disability: The Emergence of the Seven Needs.* Derby: Derbyshire Coalition of Disabled People.

Davis, K. and Mullender, A. 1993: *Ten Turbulent Years: A Review of* Centre for Social Action, University of Nottingham.

Glasgow City Council 2001: *Internal report*. Glasgow: Glasgow City Council Housing Department.

Oliver, M. 1990: *The Politics of Disablement*. Basingstoke: Macmillan.

Marshall, B. and Macfarlane, R. 2000: *The intermediate labour market: A tool for tackling long-term unemployment*. York: York Publishing Services for The Joseph Rowntree Foundation.

Martin, J., White, A. and Meltzer, H. 1989: *OPCS Surveys of Disability in Great Britain: Report 4 – Disabled adults: services, transport and employment*. London: HMSO.

Mason, M. 1990: Internalised Oppression. In R. Rieser and M. Mason (eds), *Disability quality in the Classroom: A Human Rights Issue*. London: Inner London Education Authority.

Scottish Office 1997: *Scottish Housing Condition Survey 1996*. Edinburgh: The Scottish Office.

Scottish Office 1999: *Investing in modernisation – an agenda for Scotland's housing*. Cm 4272. Edinburgh: The Stationery Office.

Smith, S. 1992: Disabled in the Labour Market. *Economic Report*, 7 (1), 1-3. London: Employment Policy Institute.

Thornton, P., Hirst, M., Arksey, H. and Tremlett, N. 2001: *Users' Views of Access to Work*. Sheffield: Employment Service.

UPIAS 1976: *Fundamental Principles of Disability*. London: Union of the Physically Impaired Against Segregation.

CHAPTER 4

From Gans to Coleman to the Social Model of Disability: physical environmental determinism revisited

Malcolm Harrison

Background

The aim of this chapter is to discuss ideas about housing environments and their impact on people's lives, and to consider relationships with the social model. The writer does not claim any particular knowledge about impairment or disability, but approaches the topic from the perspective of someone studying and teaching housing. There is, however, a personal element behind this chapter. It reflects stages in the development of my thinking about the environments in which people live; from the time when I was a student of town planning (thirty-five years ago), to the present, when I work in a social policy framework, just a few doors away from members of the Centre for Disability Studies at the University of Leeds. There is therefore a slow (and at present unfinished) learning process or intellectual journey underpinning my discussion, so I hope readers will forgive the personal tone the chapter sometimes has.

So much has been written about the social model that it seems unlikely that especially unexpected insights are 'waiting around the corner' from people in fields like housing and planning. This is not to deny the value of deepening or extending our understanding of how things work, or of clarifying connections and qualifying our interpretations. It is just to acknowledge that academics are good at 're-inventing the wheel', and to alert readers that the novelty of the present chapter lies more in its focus than in any claim to a new contribution to social model debates. In earlier work I attempted an overview of the UK housing and disability field (alongside ethnicity and gender), placed within quite a complex theoretical account of 'difference within difference', 'structure' and 'agency' (Harrison with Davis 2001). That analysis, however, did not get very far into questions about 'residence environments' as such, and accepted the significance of physical barriers without much amplification or qualification. This chapter is a tentative effort to engage more directly with the question of environments and causation.

An approach resting on *environmental determinism* implies that features of the environment tend to have a determining influence on outcomes of various kinds. For most of the present chapter this thinking is being defined fairly narrowly, and refers to what is in effect physical (or perhaps 'architectural' or 'design') determinism, as applied to environments where people live. It may be assumed by physical environmental determinists that there is a substantial impact on people arising from the physical qualities of their dwellings and immediate neighbourhood surroundings; these qualities may be assumed to influence behaviour, health, satisfaction or well-being. The connection with disability issues is evident, given the significance of barriers in terms of physical problems of access and use. Thus it might be felt that there is good fit between physical environmental determinism and the social model of disability, insofar as the house, its steps and stairs, its doorways, and the lack of space seem to 'create disability' (Oldman and Beresford 2000: 430). Despite the force of this argument, we need to consider how far physical features actually do have determining effects, or are independently crucial in causation. It is important that housing researchers, policy makers and design practitioners do not over-emphasise technical solutions developed by looking at housing and physical planning in isolation. It is worth remembering that 'housing' may be a potential component in disabling or enabling environments not only through its physical characteristics, but also through its administration, services and finance (see Harrison with Davis 2001: chapter 5).

Gans and Coleman: from enlightenment to pseudo-science?

Physical environmental determinism has had a long history as a strand within the thinking of town and country planners, housing providers and politicians. For concerned professionals or politicians it has often seemed self-evident that if dwellings and surrounding neighbourhoods were changed, this would alter people's lives substantially, on dimensions ranging from health to interactions with neighbours. What were perceived in any particular period as higher physical standards, superior designs and improved environments could be presented as major contributions to social advancement, while concepts of housing and environmental needs could be thought of primarily in physical terms. Desirable though improved physical housing standards can be, there have been potential problems with this approach.

One difficulty is that evidence for direct positive effects from physical changes has sometimes been difficult to come by, contested, or potentially complicated by the presence of other causative factors, such as changes in income (Harrison *forthcoming*). Histories suggest that certain programmes to improve matters via physical strategies actually had more significant negative than positive results, especially once the worst housing structures and health problems had been dealt with. Examples may be found in the later periods of large-scale slum clearance (Dennis 1970; McKie 1971), and the high-rise council housing era in Britain (for a general introduction to multi-storey housing and its prospects, see Towers 2000). It is sometimes assumed that these instances proved the failure of centrally-inspired interventionist programmes from the 1940s onwards, but the 'prefabs' experience suggests that failure was not inherent in intervention and central planning (Vale 1995; Stevenson 2003). Rather, what proved crucial was probably the gap between assumptions and realities as far as the social and economic effects of some of the physical changes were concerned.

A second problem persists as a general issue when physical standards for quality and design are being planned or deployed in the cause of meeting needs. The development and implementation of physical arrangements tends to involve formulation of standards, interpretation or implementation by experts, professionals, bureaucrats or other influential decision-makers. Environmentally deterministic ideas can be embedded in the under-standings that the experts have of their own roles, and serve as implicit foundations for assumptions that might not stand up well if tested against real households. Standards for physical environments have been a province for experts acting as 'guardians' of quality, preservation or improvement, and a belief in the primacy of the physical sometimes generated arguments which look archaic today. Some past claims went far beyond a practical knowledge of materials, design and safety, or the boundaries of regulating public health. Assertions about aesthetic judgements, for instance, might appear in defence of new proposals, existing treasured buildings, or precious rural environments. Here is an example from a town and country planning professionals' gathering of 1959. The speaker is addressing the planning and protection of physical environments, and demonstrates paternalism and moral righteousness:

> To be rational was to recognize that a general and popular concept might be full of sin and that it should be disregarded ...The obvious guide in all things was knowledge of accepted, beautiful artifacts. In that the dictum of the expert must be accepted, and the advice of acknowledged experts should guide us in forming our surroundings (cited in Harrison 1975: 262).

Standpoints of this kind reflected faith in expertise or authority citing concepts of the public interest. Action could be cast in terms of a battle against irrational lay opinions, unacceptable behavioural practices, or commercialism and the market.

In any event, designs, plans and standards for housing and neighbourhoods might be focussed in professional practice on physical targets, without necessarily always paying substantial regard to specific occupiers or factors shaping individual notions of 'home' and housing needs. This did not make the specific physical design goals of professionals necessarily 'wrong' in any general sense, and in any case the ideas frequently shared an agenda with other ways of looking at progress and needs (such as concerns about housing costs and affordability). Nonetheless, claims about environmental effects and benefits deserved to be scrutinised, tested, modified and qualified, with more space being made for considering the 'human agent'.

Herbert Gans

The 1960s and 1970s saw extensive debates about planning, its problems and its failings. The claims and activities of professionals were scrutinised and challenged (see, for instance, Dennis 1970: 182-345, on slum clearance practices), while the issue of participation was raised not only by critics in Britain and the USA but also by UK government itself (Arnstein 1969; Ministry of Housing and Local Government, Scottish Development Department and Welsh Office 1969; Department of the Environment and Welsh Office 1973). A particularly important contributor whose work was available in the debates of the late 1960s was the sociologist Herbert Gans. He had an impressive record of detailed empirical investigations in the USA (see Gans 1962, 1967), as well as direct commentary on planning (for instance, Gans 1969). One essay included in his book *People and Plans* was especially useful, for in it he sketched the difference between a 'potential' and an 'effective' environment (Gans 1968: 4-11). If writing a piece of similar purposes today we would give more attention to gender, age and disability than was given then, but the essay (apparently prepared initially in 1958) nonetheless retains much value even after several decades. His basic conception was that the physical environment was relevant to behaviour insofar as it affected the social system and culture of the people involved or as it was taken up into their social system. Between the physical environment and empirically observable human behaviour there existed a 'social system and a set of cultural norms' which defined and evaluated 'portions of the physical environment relevant to the lives of people involved' (Gans 1968: 5), and structured the way people would use and react to this environment in their daily lives. Referring to an example of planning for a park, Gans says that planners might believe that creating a park would provide pleasure, aesthetic satisfaction and better health, through the exposure to fresh air, sunlight and grass. It is not the park alone, however, but 'the functions and meanings which the park has for the people who are exposed to it' that affect the achievement or non-achievement of the planners' aims (1968: 6).

The passing of time has actually made this park example more instructive than in 1968. In the UK today we might be more wary than once we were about creating easily-accessible public open space. Sadly, questions could be asked about who would maintain it, and whether it would become a dumping ground for rubbish, or a depository for needles or burned-out vehicles. Some might see such spaces as areas of danger, depending upon the persons frequenting them. Gans wrote that the park proposed by the planners was only a potential environment. The social system and culture of those who use it determine to what extent the park becomes an effective environment. We can extend this argument readily to housing design, estate planning and internal dwelling features, with implications for how we think about adaptations and improvements. With respect to the influence of physical factors on behaviour, what Gans then referred to as a 'man-made artifact' is a potential environment, and the conception of that artifact in the culture is the effective environment. The effective environment, he says, may thus be defined as 'that version of the potential environment that is manifestly or latently adopted by users' (1968: 6).

This piece by Gans became a reference point for my thinking about causation and environments, and proved a valued aid when teaching students over many years. Of course many subsequent writers made contributions touching on similar or adjacent intellectual territory.

Alice Coleman

It is probable that crude forms of physical environmental determinism had been modified or even discredited in some spheres of professional debate in Britain by the end of the 1970s, although it would require documentary research to test this. It seemed to me at the time that at the very least the intellectual debate had altered, with a measure of enlightened recognition that causation is a complex matter, and with less faith in professionals. A physical environmental determinist perspective clearly had something to contribute for specific issues such as the impact of dangerous materials in housing, but grandiose claims seemed unlikely to make much headway.

In 1985, however, Alice Coleman's *Utopia on Trial* appeared. She reported a heavily funded research project aimed at studying design and layout in mass housing schemes, and mapping and testing these to see which aspects were associated with 'various lapses in civilised behaviour'. These lapses were a somewhat selective combination; litter-dropping, graffiti-scrawling, vandalism, pollution by excrement, and 'family breakdown leading to children being placed in care' (1985: 2). Designs were treated as having a 'disadvantaging effect', and a 'design disadvantagement score' was obtained for each block of flats (1985: 3, 5, 123, 126). Coleman claimed to be placing what she referred to as the planned 'Utopia', the 'ideal environment', on trial (1985: 3), and she pointed to design features being responsible for 'many aspects of social decline' (1985: 173). Her ways forward revolved around design modification, which was held relevant to everything from levels of litter to reduction in crime (1985: 5). The project was large, involving a team of up to six people over five years (five being credited as supporting contributors on the title page), and had the 'generous financial support' of the Joseph Rowntree Memorial Trust (1985: vii).

Although there was a stress on the 'scientific' nature of this enterprise, it was well received neither by some scholarly reviewers, nor apparently by departmental civil servants (see for instance, Hillier 1986; Spicker 1987; also Coleman 1985: 181). Leaving aside doubts about the statistical analyses, problems of moving from association to causation, and the issue of how difficult it is to assemble any uncontested set of measures or indicators of 'social malaise', the project was in any case open to challenge at the conceptual level for its limited coverage of potential key causative variables. A critic could argue that Coleman undervalued many social and economic variables which might create or contribute to social problems, behavioural patterns or tensions on estates, highlighting instead housing and estate design. We find little from her about youth cultures, family structures and histories, levels and sources of income, debts and living costs, ethnic relations, or policing practices. When social factors are referred to, it is primarily in relation to her selective framework of indicators (noted above), and the discussion is narrow. Thus, while poverty is mentioned, a short analysis diminishes its role as a causative issue in estate life or in what she refers to as 'social breakdown' (see Coleman 1985: 83, 85, 86, 172; cf Spicker 1987). An unusual argument is developed to intimate that perhaps design may be an important factor in causing unemployment, rather than unemployment itself being a potential major cause of problems on estates (Coleman 1985: 86-87). Although Coleman avoids commitment to being an environmental determinist (see 1985: 5, 19-20, 25, etc.), there is plenty to indicate her belief that planning, layout, design and physical features are likely to have direct and very important effects on behaviour.

The paperback version of *Utopia on Trial* featured ringing endorsements from the *Daily Mail, Mirror, Sunday Times, New Society*, and *London Standard*. The well known architectural commentator Patrick Nuttgens was reported saying that she had 'done a public service', since 'It won't do ever again for academic sociologists to say that architecture does not affect people's behaviour' (Coleman 1985: front inner page). The book went to a second edition in 1990, and a new preface noted that a large sum had now been provided by central government to support systematic trials of Coleman's physical solutions to housing design faults in selected estates (Coleman 1990: ix). Apparently, Coleman's ideas had found much favour with Thatcher's government, and − it is said − with the prime minister herself. Having criticised the mass housing enterprises of post-war reformers (where there were indeed things to learn from the over-optimistic assumptions and false hopes for social advance), Coleman highlighted a similar path by elevating design as a means of social benefit. She seems to have been engaging, like those post-war designers but on a much smaller scale, in social engineering built upon physical foundations. This is not to say that she lacked concepts about the social features of estate life. Pejorative and pathologising remarks indicate moral perspectives and firm feelings about social order and control. This is the only time when I have noticed the word 'sluts' used judgementally by someone setting out their stall as a scholar:

> ... at the other end there are a few who will always be sluts or criminals, even in ideal conditions (Coleman 1985: 20) ...

Living in a high-rise block does not force all its inhabitants to become criminals ... it puts temptation in their way and makes it probable that some of the weaker brethren will succumb (p. 22).

To the present writer, Coleman's work was a step backwards. Though formulated nearly thirty years earlier, the ideas of Gans seemed infinitely more appreciative of the contingent nature of physical environmental effects on behaviour and on satisfactions.

Partly in response to the Coleman debate, I began reformulating my own thoughts in terms of intervening variables, building on Gans. It seemed reasonable to conceive of effects from physical environments being significant under some economic conditions, in the context of some health conditions, given certain social networks and interactions, and so forth. I envisaged an array of intervening or 'confounding' factors operating along-side or 'between' the physical environment and any specific effects it might have, and activating, modifying, nullifying or amplifying those effects. Thus nothing much could be 'taken as given' about the impact of most physical features of a local environment without knowing quite a lot about the people living there, and the impact of other factors upon them. There would be exceptions, but generally these would be for relatively limited or extreme kinds of cases (such as dangerous building materials or services).

Environmental determinism and the social model of disability

My thinking began to shift as I encountered social model ideas through Leeds colleagues in the late 1990s. The argument that disablement is brought about through physical environmental as well as socio-economic barriers is persuasive. I therefore wondered whether I had been wrong about how to evaluate physical factors. My initial response involved ideas about the potentially determining but varying significance of physical barriers, with their impact perhaps conditioned by some continuum of 'vulnerability', reflecting differences relating to age, gender, illness and impairment. This formulation, however, seemed to take me in the direction of a rather more deterministic model than before, perhaps open to challenge on the grounds that it did not build in individuals' diversity or capacities for action.

Agency and structure

To avoid an over-deterministic account I needed to include human agency, but felt that this in turn would gain from a consideration of relationships with 'structural' factors. This is because even though we cannot fully assess the impact of barriers until we know about people's resources and actions, individuals do not think and act in a vacuum. One way forward seemed to be to start with the character of 'environment' in its broadest sense, and the contributions agency makes to it, rather than with intervening variables or barriers as such.

In general terms 'structure' can be treated as being about the resources and environments (socio-economic, political, and to some extent physical) that come to us from the past, and help condition our choices and opportunities in the present. This does not mean that what we can think of as structural factors determine events, but that they set the stage and scenery, provide a range of possible texts and performance traditions, and lay out suits and props for the actors, opening up opportunities as well as posing constraints. Physical environments are part of the heritage that we all encounter, and part of the stage on which we move, but these environmental features take on their full meanings and significance to some extent in combination with other kinds of resources and other elements of the broader environment. At the same time actors are not necessarily inert receivers of environment in any of its manifestations, social, economic or physical. Not only can 'agency' imply resistance, subversion, collaboration, challenge, construction, and a myriad of other effects, but structural factors themselves may be influenced by interaction with agency and are manifested through it. People clearly have important effects now and for those who come after them. Social, economic and physical environments are shaped and re-shaped over time, as are the sets of ideas that we absorb or invoke when we discuss, evaluate or write about them.

How does this approach to environment relate to the social model? Two benefits of the social model are its clear recognition of the 'big picture' of constraints and practices, and its capacity to inform broader accounts highlighting structure. At the same time agency can be catered for particularly via focussing on mobilisation and resistance, as well as in terms of identifiable human contributions in processes that are oppressive. We need to add to this, however, that structural factors may facilitate and resource people as well as hinder them, and that agency is extensively involved beyond its manifestations in resistance, struggle or domination (for several manifestations of agency in housing see Harrison with Davis 2001: 41-42). Amongst other things, agency may encompass contributions to receiving, interpreting and shaping the environments into which we are cast, building on opportunities as well as facing obstacles, and (for present purposes) constructing and developing the meanings of home and locality.

As the flaws in physical environmental determinism suggest, when we consider barriers, constraints and opportunities in specific policy fields, people's perspectives and active roles need to be kept in mind. This may apply for many kinds of 'environmental' factors (including socio-economic ones and those in the realm of ideas). This is despite the fact that certain practices and forces potentially contribute so strongly to regulating everyone's lives that the scope for substantially subverting or avoiding them may be limited in the short-run.

The inter-meshing of physical, social and economic environmental factors
Another strength of the social model (and of disability studies) is a potential for integrated approaches to the various aspects of environment and disablement that people face. There is a good fit here with seeing 'the home' as much more than a physical object, with what has already been said above about the limitations of physically-focussed assumptions about causation, and with concepts of 'environments' implicit in notions of structural factors. A holistic approach to neighbourhood and residential environments perhaps might better reflect what disabled people have already understood about the social model, and the simultaneous and interlocking effects for any household of physical, social and economic barriers and resources in specific localities.

This implies being cautious in two ways. Although it is useful to highlight particular physical environmental barriers and possibilities for improvement, this should not lead into disaggregating aspects of environ-ment in a formulaic way that suits the divisions of professional expertise, or follows the demarcations of academic preoccupations and 'disciplines'. The physical component of the barriers envisaged through the social model is not necessarily an uncontested or separable matter for debate, even if at first glance we might have considered the impact of the built environment a relatively non-controversial element within a social model approach. In addition, at a practical level it would be unfortunate if design, housing and planning practitioners and researchers were to focus on classifications, categorisations, measurement, design methods and techno-logical advances without a full regard for the ways in which physical features are actually 'received' by housing consumers. People's various resources and their specific capacities to develop, cope and adapt may affect the relative importance they place upon the detailed design of some physical features. (For further insights, in respect of visually impaired children, see: Allen, Milner and Price 2002: note p. 12; and JRF 2002: 1).

An unfinished journey

When reviewing the impact of physical factors, we need reasonably informed perspectives on the nature, forging and development of the broader environment of home and residence, and the wider meanings of housing 'quality'. Ideas about both agency and structure can be kept in mind when we analyse these things. For instance, we might try to distinguish between potential effects derived initially from 'external' forces (longstanding low levels of investment in services, low incomes in older age, racialisation processes, persistent barriers in labour markets, etc.), and those arising from current activities and preferences of local people. Although a little mechanical, this might facilitate an agency/ structure type of discussion of environmental effects, interactions and contingencies, at the level of locality and dwellings, and the placing of physical design features in relation to this.

As a start towards a better account, I have recently begun trying to use selected secondary sources (books, studies, etc.) to help me to summarise the key types of social, economic or behavioural factors that constitute important features helping shape residence experiences (or what the environment of the home and neighbourhood might mean to residents), and to locate physical environment features in relation to this array. Socio-economic factors in the environment may be highly significant in influencing the 'realisation' of the home. Leaving aside the physical qualities of the dwelling, an analysis of factors which might influence residents' perceptions of housing and locality would be likely to include (amongst others): general socio-economic and demographic conditions and trends affecting neighbourhoods; the capacity of households to exert control over their housing (and meet its costs); institutional practices; crime and neighbour nuisance; the histories of people's individual and collective activities, strategies, or investments, and the kinds and levels of social organisation and inter-personal interactions that have developed related to the neighbourhood and homes; the composition and features of households in terms of numbers, age, gender, ethnicity, impairment, chronic illness, or sexual orientation; the availability of and interactions with particular support personnel, assistants, advocates, kin, or peer group members; the relative significance of the dwelling in terms of daily time spent there; effects of hostilities locally to those who are perceived as 'different'; access to (and quality of) facilities such as public transport, schools, and shops; and intrusive or hazardous activities such as heavy or unpredictable traffic movements (for a more extensive discussion see Harrison *forthcoming*).

Policy issues

Whether a practitioner is designing for more comfortable living, for better access, or for 'smart home' technology, it may be unwelcome to be reminded that favourite professional ideas do not necessarily readily translate into an improved life for residents. The best way forward for housing, however, may not necessarily be to focus on a physical design solution or quality standard, and investing in the physical attributes of the home need not always be the most helpful way to spend money. In an ideal world, improving housing environments to 'facilitate everyday living' (Peace and Holland 2001: 14) would involve tackling numerous dimensions of 'environment', including not only physical features and equipment, but also funds, costs, or the attitudes of professionals that might be affecting the management and use of the dwellings.

This raises questions about the campaigns and policies to raise physical environmental quality standards for housing which have been so important from the nineteenth century onwards, and which have been significant recently for disabled people's access. Furthermore, where does it leave reformers' ideas about lifetime, inter-generational or flexibly-planned homes?

An initial answer might be to say that the benefits of higher standards are likely to outweigh any potential costs (such as higher building and development costs), and that those benefits are readily demonstrable for large numbers of people. There will also be future gains from preventative strategies such as creating more adaptable homes. Thus real benefits can be obtained from better physical standards and designs. Tests, reassurance or confirmation of this might be sought by more frequent research on the outcomes of improvements, fuller monitoring of costs and benefits, feedback from 'users' after the event, and more solid consultations beforehand. From a planner's point of view, facilities should be made as far as possible satisfactory in terms of the frames of reference of both the planner and the users (cf Gans 1968: 8), while modest approaches to how people's lives can be improved might cast the designer or planner more often as negotiator, investigator, advocate and facilitator.

Another way forward would be to develop more holistic strategies, placing physical improvements within a broader package, or making trade-offs between one kind of expenditure and another, even if retaining protective base-line physical standards to safeguard public health. Unfortunately, we do not live in a world where all the desirable policy options are readily available as this would require. For instance, although a particular older person might prefer a substantially increased state pension or a reduction in robberies and burglaries to the improvement of the neighbourhood physical environment, no such choice is ever likely to be on offer. Large inequalities in resources and power are at the heart of many unsatisfactory home circumstances, but politicians do not seem likely to take these on.

I will conclude, therefore, with a possible paradox about policy choices: physical policies may be desirable even though they are not necessarily the best route forward in terms of principles or spending. It is plausible to argue that physical solutions have a lot to offer reformers politically, despite doubts about environmental determinism and uncertainties about gains made for individual households. In today's Britain it may be easier to secure ongoing and extensive support for improved mandatory physical housing standards than it is to get agreement and continuity for financial support for other ways of improving people's lives. A better physical environment to some extent can be argued for independently of debates about redistribution and taxation, as well as opening the possibility of rights claims around concepts of fairness and equality of access. Perhaps focussing on improved universalistic physical standards may have political advantages (by contrast with other levers) for people who are actively pressing for more equality. Indeed, more lasting gains might be secured by obtaining environmental rights in the physical environment than by seeking to enlarge those selectivist services and financial supports which can continue to be cast, by opponents of 'social rights', as 'gifts' acquired through the taxation of the 'deserving', and which may invite the participation of professionals in shaping the meanings of home and daily lives.

Bibliography

Allen, C., Milner, J. and Price, D. 2002: *Home is where the start is: the housing and urban experiences of visually impaired children*. Bristol: The Policy Press.

Arnstein, S. 1969: A ladder of citizen participation. *Journal of the American Institute of Planners*, XXXV (4), 216-224.

Coleman, A. 1985 (1990): *Utopia on trial: vision and reality in planned housing*. (2nd edn.) London: Hilary Shipman.

Dennis, N. 1970: *People and planning; the sociology of housing in Sunderland*. London: Faber and Faber.

Department of the Environment and Welsh Office 1973: *Public Participation in General Improvement Areas,* Area Improvement Note 8. London: HMSO.

Gans, H. 1962: *The urban villagers: group and class in the life of Italian-Americans*. New York: The Free Press.

Gans, H. J. 1967: *The Levittowners: ways of life and politics in a new suburban community*. London: Allen Lane/ Penguin Press.

Gans, H. 1968: *People and plans: essays on urban problems and solutions*. New York: Basic Books.

Gans, H. 1969: Planning for people, not buildings. *Environment and Planning*, [A], 1 (1), 33-46.

Harrison, M. 1975: British town planning ideology and the welfare state. *Journal of Social Policy*, 4 (3), 259-274.

Harrison, M. *forthcoming*: Defining housing quality: disability, standards, and social factors. Revised version of paper from ESRC Workshop on Housing Quality, Disability and Design, University of London, June 3rd, 2003.

Harrison, M. with Davis, C. 2001: *Housing, social policy and difference: disability, ethnicity, gender and housing*. Bristol: The Policy Press.

Hillier, B. 1986: City of Alice's dreams. *Architects Journal*, 9th July.JRF (Joseph Rowntree Foundation) 2002: Housing and urban experiences of visually impaired children. *Findings*. November, York: JRF.

McKie, R. 1971: *Housing and the Whitehall bulldozer*. Hobart paper 52. London: The Institute of Economic Affairs.

Ministry of Housing and Local Government, Scottish Development Department and Welsh Office 1969: *People and planning*. Report of the Committee on Public Participation in Planning (Skeffington Report). London: HMSO.

Oldman, C. and Beresford, B. 2000: Home sick home: using the housing experiences of disabled children to suggest a new theoretical framework. *Housing Studies*, 15 (3), 429-442.

Peace, S. and Holland, C. 2001: Housing an ageing society. In S. Peace and C. Holland (eds.), *Inclusive housing in an ageing society: innovative approaches*. Bristol: The Policy Press, 1-25.

Spicker, P. 1987: Poverty and depressed estates: a critique of *Utopia on Trial*. *Housing Studies*, 2 (4), 283-292.

Stevenson, G. 2003: *Palaces for the people: prefabs in post-war Britain*. London: Batsford.

Towers, G. 2000: *Shelter is not enough: transforming multi-storey housing*. Bristol: The Policy Press.

Vale, B. 1995: *Prefabs: a history of the UK temporary housing programme*. London: E & FN Spon.

CHAPTER 5

The Social Model of Disability in Higher Education: attention to tensions

Paul Brown and Anne Simpson

Introduction

It is our intention in this chapter to do three things:

1. to identify and briefly describe various features of the Scottish, and sometimes the UK, Higher Education (HE) and disability landscape;
2. to look at the question of whether these features find their natural home within one theoretical model of disability rather than another;
3. to think about whether the identified features of the landscape pull in importantly different directions, in some tension with each other. Behind this is the question of whether, in the process, we can identify the dominance of one rather than another model within the HE setting, and, of course, of which model this would be.

An underlying concern is what an HE sector in which the social model prevails would look like. This in turn raises the question of whether some of the mechanisms for getting there might not, *prima facie*, seem to embody or exemplify medical or individual models. We introduce these issues at various points in the discussion, and consider the question of whether the social model end might not incorporate some medical model means.

The Scottish Higher Education and disability landscape

In looking at the salient features of the higher education and disability landscape, we will firstly think about the broad features and thereafter focus on some of the detail.

The movement to promote improved levels of participation from groups under-represented in Higher Education which occurred between 1980 and 1990 neglected disabled people. The position has been addressed by the national Higher Education Funding Councils since 1992 and progress has been made (Hurst 1999: 65).

British higher education has changed from an elite system in the mid-1980s to a mass system in the 1990s through to the present with major changes in the composition of the student population (Riddell 1998; Watson and Bowden 1999). This greater diversity is evident in the increase in higher education of mature, part-time students and those from minority ethnic communities and socially disadvantaged groups. Disabled students have also benefited from this expansion, although they continue to be under-represented in the HE system, making up just under 4 per cent of students (Tinklin et al. 2002). In December 2002 the Higher Education Funding Council for England (HEFCE) published performance indicators for the first time detailing the level of participation of disabled people in higher education institutions (HEFCE 2002).

Currently, about 4% of students in UK higher education institutions have disclosed a disability, whereas 15% of the working age population have a long-term disability substantially affecting their day-to-day activities, the DDA definition of disability (Riddell and Banks 2001). However, a much lower proportion of younger people are disabled and some disabled people, including those with significant learning difficulties, would be unlikely to qualify for higher education. It should also be borne in mind that the majority of disabled students have dyslexia or unseen disabilities such as diabetes, asthma and ME, and less than 10% have significant physical or sensory impairments. It is likely that many people with significant impairments are currently unable to access higher education due to a range of financial, physical and cultural barriers, but the extent of under-representation is difficult to quantify (Riddell et al. 2002:2).

Whilst patterns of participation in relation to social class, gender, ethnicity and geographical location have been widely documented and analysed (Paterson 1997, 1998; Osborne 1999; Riddell and Salisbury 1999), disability has been frequently omitted from analyses, partly because, until relatively recently, statistical data from the Higher Education Statistical Agency (HESA) were not available (Riddell 1998).

However, a few localised studies (Baron et al. 1996; Hurst 1996, 1999; Hall and Tinklin 1998; Riddell 1998; Riddell et al. 2004) have suggested that whilst there is an increase in support for individual disabled students, there still remain systemic barriers to be challenged; that the history and culture of an individual institution has a major bearing on policy and provision for disabled students; and that Funding Council short-term initiatives, whilst successful in instigating change, have not been linked to longer-term strategic developments either within HEIs or at a national HE policy level (Brown et al. 1997; Hall and Tinklin 1998; Riddell 1998; Tinklin and Hall 1999; Riddell et al. 2004).

To turn now from the general to the detail of the scene, we would identify the following:

1. Pedagogical concepts and theory
In addition to the general picture above, we should note the accent on the concepts of the autonomous independent learner, (a fundamentally liberal notion) (Ryan 1999: 83-84) of transferable skills and the skills of 'graduateness' as core to the goals and business of higher education, and perhaps as what gives higher education its unique flavour.

2. The advent in higher education of anti-discrimination legislation
This imports from the 1995 Disability Discrimination Act (DDA) a definition of disability substantially around functional limitation and deficit (DfEE 1995). But it also, and perhaps paradoxically, defines discrimination, in part, as the failure of those who create the environment of higher education to make reasonable adjustments to that environment (DRC 2002). Further, the Act promotes the duty to anticipate the foreseeable needs of disabled people, and to that extent, it is hostile to the *ad hoc*, reactive and individual approach to provision for disabled students. It is a further feature of the DDA Part IV that the failure to make reasonable adjustments may be justified by reference to academic standards, but only where these are central or core to a course.

3. Dedicated HE Disability Services
Since the early to mid 1990s, these services have become larger, and more embedded and developed. By 1996 all Scottish Higher Education Institutions (HEIs) had a disability Advisor/Co-ordinator (Adams and Brown 2000, *forthcoming*). Since this time disability services in some institutions have grown dramatically in terms of both numbers of permanent Co-ordinators/Advisors and a diversity of staff roles and responsibilities – e.g. many institutions now employ specialist IT support

staff and dyslexia tutors. While the remit of some services is the twofold one of being advisory to and supportive of the institution's teaching and other practitioners, and also being advisory to and providers (of equipment and other forms of assistance) for individual disabled students, the weight of work in individual services is undoubtedly skewed towards the latter rather than the former. This may be seen to define such services in individual or welfare terms, and indeed, some such services are explicitly situated within what are called 'Student Welfare Services' (Adams and Brown 2000, *forthcoming*). Such services may therefore serve as a distraction from the objectives we might expect if we were to imagine an institution driven by the ideals implicit in the social model. These we would take to be the promotion and development of whole institution accessibility. To put this differently, this would involve the dismantling of disabling barriers to the participation of disabled students rather than the 'fix', usually retro, for difficulties and problems as they arise in the course of the negotiation by a disabled student of an unfriendly and inaccessible environment.

It is worth noting here that the availability of Disabled Students Allowance (DSA) is doubtless part of the driver for the substantially individual approach of disability services. The allowance is there to be applied for, and it would seem perverse of disability advisors not to support disabled students in their applications for whatever financial support is available. It remains to be seen whether the same level of provision will be made available to students who are ineligible for DSA, such as international and some part-time students, when institutions themselves have to take on this provider role, as a result of their responsibilities under the DDA Part IV. It may be that more cost-effective provision – loaned rather than owned equipment, general study skills support rather than individual dyslexia support, for example – will be sought.

4. Academic departmental services for disabled students

Institutional structures supporting provision for disabled students often involve the establishment of the role of departmental, module, school or faculty disability coordinators or advisors. We can ask the same question of the microcosmic departmental role of the departmental disability coordinator as we did of the macrocosmic role of an institution's disability service – is the focus of work the meeting of individual disabled students' needs, or is it the development of the inclusive departmental teaching environment? Purely anecdotal evidence would suggest the former.

5. Funding formulae

Scottish Higher Education Funding Council (SHEFC) Disability Premium Funding rewards institutions financially according to the numbers of students in receipt of Disabled Students Allowance (SHEFC 2001).

6. The theoretical assumptions of Funding Council-funded disability projects

Projects such as the Scottish Higher Education Funding Council funded *Teachability: Creating an Accessible Curriculum for Students with Disabilities*, and some like-minded Higher Education Funding Council for England (HEFCE) funded projects, aim to support academic staff to identify and develop accessible provision of courses and programmes of study. The focus of this work is accessible curricula. While the concept of the accessible curriculum acquires its meaning through an understanding of the needs of those to whom curricula ought to be accessible, a major task of the work has been to convey the focus on curricula and their barriers, rather than categories of impairment (University of Strathclyde 2000). The perceptions of academic staff from some 70 plus academic departments as to the sites of barriers to access to curricula are documented in *Disability Needs Analysis, Access to the Curriculum* (SHEFC 2002). Over generalising somewhat, we would say that the perceptions lean towards the view that the problems reside with individual students and their deficits, rather than with any deficit in the teaching and learning environment of HE.

7. University and Colleges Admissions Service (UCAS) use of a system of medical classification to categorise disabled students during the application process

This process introduced in the early 1990s was intended to enable students to disclose their impairment(s) to HEIs which, as a result of accessing such information, would endeavour to put in place the necessary services and support to meet disclosed needs.

Social or individual model: which one has the upper hand?

The second overarching goal that we set ourselves for this chapter was to look at the question of whether these features find their natural home within one theoretical model of disability rather than another.

Space prohibits us from attending to all of the items listed above, and we have therefore attempted to do no more than hint above at the sorts of ways in which these may be developed towards a fuller discussion of their significance in terms of the theoretical oppositions of the social and individual/medical models. We have chosen to focus at greater length on four: pedagogical concepts and theory, the DDA Part IV, Premium Funding, and the UCAS classification of impairment. Of these, it is perhaps the UCAS classification of impairment that is most likely to elicit the claim that this is a medical model at its most extreme.

UCAS classification of impairment

Disabled people are asked to self-classify under impairment headings right at the point of application to higher education. Hurst (1996) argues that:

> there is a danger that using the categories based on disability (impairment), the focus is shifted away from a social model of disability towards an individual/medical one (p. 129).

Ostensibly, the purpose of the invited disclosure is to assist institutions of Higher Education to ensure that support is in place to enable the student who makes the disclosure to participate effectively in what higher education offers. If this really is the purpose, then are we to expect that the lists of impairment categories will convey much needed information to the planners and providers of Higher Education, such that its environment is more ready for the diverse needs of all learners, some of whom may be disabled? If so, then it might be difficult to claim, with confidence, that the impairment listing, by itself, finds its natural home within the medical or individual model. In raising this possibility, we are suggesting the need to delve behind the features and details of the landscape we have depicted in order to identify their purposes, aims and objectives. If the purpose of a medical classification is ultimately to enhance the environment of higher education for disabled learners, then it might be difficult to claim that the classification in itself belonged with the medical rather than the social model. This would, instead, be an example of exploiting medical categorisation for the purpose of progressing the social model goal of creating an enabling higher education environment through the dismantling of disabling barriers.

One would have to add that, even if the UCAS classification can really be said to embody a medical/individual model of disability, it is not a very effective embodiment, because it is not a usable instrument for the practical purposes of the institution. However, the theoretical orientation of the classification aside, two points might suggest that the classification fosters only the illusion of meaning. The first is that within any impairment heading, the range of responses that individuals might require from higher education is vast. 'Blind/partially sighted' may mean that a student within this 'category' needs Braille, space to exercise a guide dog, a sighted guide, access technology, or nothing whatsoever. Without a detailed knowledge of the individual's requirements, we are no nearer to meeting the individual's needs. But secondly, we also have to know in much more detail what the academic, social and physical settings are which will dictate what the individual might want. Students who have impairments do not have requirements in a vacuum, but only in relation to what it is that they are trying to access, and knowledge of that is at least as important as knowledge about the circumstances of any particular impairment.

These points suggest the need for a considered negotiation of the individual's impairment and associated needs with the environment of the course he/she undertakes, with particular emphasis on anything in that course which is thought to be core or non negotiable, and this in turn would appear to be taking us in the direction of highly individualised 'fixes'. But what 'fixes' precisely? How is the disclosed information used? In many institutions, it would be available for the Disability Service advisors who would usually make contact with the applicant or new student. And then what happens? Two things might happen: first, the student might be assisted to make a claim for DSA, and then individual support or equipment would flow from that. Second, the Disability Service might contact institutional staff to ask them to put in place some particular provision for the student – copies of overheads, for example, or advanced note of reading lists.

What emerges, then, is that the UCAS disclosure might result in either adaptation to the teaching environment, or in provision of personal equipment or assistance. Does the nature of the proposed solution lend support to the view that we are seeing in action one model rather than another? In either case, the categorisation under impairment headings has not been used in any meaningful way. The question, 'Would you like the Disability Service to contact you?' would have done as well as the current trigger for the subsequent interaction. The fact that it has featured as a pathway to either a solution based in adjusting the environment or providing the student with the individual solution would perhaps suggest that in itself the impairment classification is meaningless rather than theoretically laden. Furthermore, these categories of impairment in HE have not been subject to the same degree of critical scrutiny as has been the case with school level education, and as a result medical definitions continue to play a vital role in both resource allocation and information management systems (Hurst 1996; Riddell 1998). The former is most clearly manifested in the mechanism used by SHEFC to award the disability premium funding to HEIs (SHEFC 2001), to which we now turn our attention.

SHEFC's Disability Premium

In 2001, SHEFC announced its intention to introduce various premia for under-represented students (SHEFC 2001). Among those under-represented groups identified for such funding were disabled students. The disabled student premium is awarded to HEIs annually as part of the main teaching and research grant. The funding is calculated on the number of full-time equivalent (FTE) students in receipt of DSA at an institution as reported to HESA. The number of students in receipt of DSA is intended to be a 'proxy' of the number of disabled students at an institution. Such funds are intended to meet the unspecified costs institutions incur as a result of teaching and supporting disabled students (SHEFC 2001). So, such funding might appear to be in line with social model thinking on disability: it is intended for whole institutional support and change; it is awarded as part of an institution's mainstream funding allocation (signalling that such activity is mainstream to HE generally and individual HE institutions).

However, there are some fundamental aspects of the method for both collecting and calculating this premium that would suggest opposition to the social model as it might apply to Higher Education. Firstly, the DSA figures reported to HESA cannot be entirely accurate. They depend on students reporting to their institution that they are in receipt of DSA and they also depend on institutions being able to accurately record and report such figures. But probably of more importance here is the fact that funding is only awarded to institutions where some external agency 'verifies' that a student is disabled – in this case being awarded DSA is seen to be 'proof' of impairment. Further, DSA is not available to all students. Those pursuing access courses, many part-time students and those from overseas are ineligible to receive DSA. Thus it might be argued that using DSA as the basis to calculate the funds available to each higher education institution is both divisive and exclusive, in that it rewards institutions for supporting certain disabled students and not others. Indeed, if the aim were to enhance inclusive, ready-for-all provision for disabled students, then it would seem counterproductive to reward institutions for reactive, ad hoc, individual and externally (i.e. DSA) funded provision.

Furthermore, premium funding is not ring-fenced, and institutions are not questioned on its use. If such monitoring were to operate so as to promote social model ideals, then we might expect to see funding council scrutiny of institutions' plans and preparation to meet the future needs of disabled students, not, or not only, through 'support' focused on individual students, but through the dismantling of identified barriers in the core academic activity and provision. But as we suggested above in our brief discussion of current work in the area of accessible curricula, it would seem that the necessary conceptual wherewithal, as well as the political will, to support such shifts, remain to be developed. And anecdotal evidence suggests that some HEIs are moving in the opposed direction by withdrawing services previously routinely provided free to students in favour of assisting those students to claim for such services through DSA.

The DDA Part IV
The Disability Discrimination Act, Part IV Code of Practice incorporates a number of strands which might suggest the absence of any thorough-going or consistent application of any one model of disability (DRC 2002). With the exception of severe disfigurement, we have a definition of disability that is around individuals' inability to do various things, i.e. based on functional limitation and deficit. But the Code is also explicitly critical of the *ad hoc* reactive approach to making provision for disabled students, and the recommendation that reasonable adjustments be made in anticipation, on the assumption that disabled people will be present in higher education in ever increasing numbers. It is a further feature of the DDA Part IV that the failure to make reasonable adjustments may be justified by reference to academic standards, but only where these are central or core to a course. Arguably, this and other comments ought to have the effect of encouraging academic staff to look inward at their course provision, and in asking whether this or that aspect of the course is 'core' they are not asking a question that is necessarily related to students' impairments, or about disability. If many of the exhortations in the Code of Practice were to find their way into common practice, with reasonable adjustments being routinely made, and teaching staff crystal clear about what is and is not absolutely essential for students to do, then arguably the environment of higher education would be less disabling for all learners.

Such exhortations would appear to stop short of enforcement. Cases will be brought not on the basis of an institution allowing disabling environments but on the basis of individual students not having adjustments made, or being treated less favourably. However, the Disability Rights Commission Act (1999) gives the Commission the same duties, powers and responsibilities as the Commission for Racial Equality and the Equal Opportunities Commission (DfEE 1999). This theoretically might include the power to inspect and initiate action against an institution for its failure to promote and develop an inclusive climate of readiness for diverse learner needs, as opposed to supporting an individual student to bring an action. If it believes that discrimination is taking place or has taken place then the Disability Rights Commission can carry out an investigation. Yet if no individual disabled student or applicant has been substantially disadvantaged by the failure to make reasonable adjustments, can discrimination be deemed to have occurred? The anticipatory nature of the duty to make reasonable adjustments might suggest that it may have. The Code at 2.17 gives the second meaning of discrimination:

> When a responsible body fails to make a *reasonable adjustment* when a disabled student is placed, or likely to be placed, at a *substantial disadvantage* in comparison with a person who is not disabled [s 28S(2), Sch 4C paras 2 or 6] (DRC 2002: 14).

Thus if the environment is such that disabled students have not yet been placed at substantial disadvantage, but it is likely that they will be, then discrimination will actually have occurred, and the DRC investigative powers could kick in. Enforcement thus does not exclusively attach to individuals' treatment and consequent complaint.

It remains to be seen whether the DRC has the staff or the will to act in this way. But if the real enemy, in the light of the social model, is the disabling environment, then the DDA Part IV at least theoretically leaves open the possibility of its attack by the DRC.

Pedagogical concepts and theory

The notions of the autonomous or independent learner, of transferable skills, and of a special bundle of skills which go under the name of 'graduateness' are ideas often taken to be the distinctive aspirations of modern higher education. They receive corresponding attention in many of the Quality Assurance Agency for Higher Education's (QAA) *Benchmarking Standards* (QAA 2003). Nevertheless, we also observe that almost completely absent from the benchmarking standards and from discussions of the overarching goals of higher education is any implicit or explicit understanding either that the standards may be achievable in alternative ways or that in some cases, alternative standards may be both acceptable and appropriate. Such an absence may serve to exclude or disable some students unless acknowledgement is made of the ways in which adjustments, where necessary, can be incorporated.

The idea of the autonomous learner bears several different interpretations. Mowthorpe (1999) glossed the expression as meaning a learner who is organized, attends lectures, and meets deadlines. Obviously Socrates, who notoriously liked to spend time in idle chatter with his friends, would have made heavy weather of a modern degree! Fazey and Linford (1996) offer a more hopeful diagnosis: an autonomous learner is one who is 'actively involved in the learning process' (p. 186). Boud (1988) describes student autonomy in learning as 'not a characteristic of a student which resides in a student, but a relational quality of student and task' (p. 34) It is this kind of thinking, we suggest, that allows us to construct a meaningful idea of higher education as accessible to disabled people. If you cannot be an autonomous learner unless you make it to the nine o'clock class, then many people, some of whom are disabled, will never qualify as autonomous learners. But the nine o'clock class rule is too restrictive. It represents misplaced concreteness; a mere example of good student behaviour is elevated into a principle which all must satisfy.

What about the idea that higher education fosters above all certain transferable skills of information management? It may be that such a view is not intrinsically unfavourable to disabled people, whose skills may involve, for example, the organisation of complex living arrangements, planning, including financial planning, or recording and storing information, and of interpreting ambiguous and corrupt information streams.

The category of transferable skills as especially important goals of higher education leads naturally to the next category, that of 'graduateness'. On its face, each of these categories consists of a group of skills which it is the goal of higher education to produce or to certify. Does a student have the capacity to process information effectively, to summarise, to identify the main points of an argument? Then he or she has transferable skills, or perhaps 'graduate' skills. It becomes a question of fact whether a particular disabled person can achieve these skills. The skills are given, as it were; the point is, can this individual learn them?

The relational interpretation of autonomous independent learning (Boud 1988) was less welcoming of the idea that there is on the one hand a target state, and on the other a set of individuals who may or may not achieve the target. Instead it prompts us to ask: given an important subject matter - history, say, or mathematics - what barriers exist to stop people developing such a relationship to this subject that they become autonomous learners? And are there any barriers which stand particularly in the way of some disabled people?

Graduateness has this in common with the category of autonomous engagement with a subject matter, that at face value it seems to identify a common characteristic of the graduate which transcends subject specialisms. A graduate in engineering or hotel management should have a great deal in common with a graduate in art history. It is however unlikely that this will literally be found to consist in a core of common skills (as supporters of the transferable skills idea propose). Graduateness in fact is probably best conceptualised as a set of skills and attributes which are believed to characterize a graduate, as long as we remember that the content of this set shifts with time and social milieu. Having duelling scars is no longer an attribute of graduateness, nor is being able to quote Horace from memory. But the value of graduateness as a set of skills which can be invoked as a criterion that everyone must meet is that no one is precisely sure what now does make up graduateness. Thus, to some people it is obvious that a graduate must be able to get up on her feet and speak in public on a business related matter. Or she must be able to spell correctly. Or she must have the self-confidence to take responsibility. Or she must at least not be subject to disabling mental illness ... the list goes on.

If our suggestions about the shifting nature of the meaning of transferable skills and the skills of graduateness are accepted, then we are perhaps encouraged towards the view that what higher education properly consists in is socially constructed. And perhaps most specifications of the aims of education are incurably ideological. The idea of the autonomous learner stands in the liberal tradition, i.e. the view that the educated person is likely to have character qualities (an inquiring mind) which make the good citizen. The proponents of the transferable skills view are technocrats of a sort. Higher education is about the skills that hard-headed people can see are important to make society work. The idea of graduateness is the natural expression of social conservatism. As society changes, so we can expect suitably time-lagged changes in the content of graduateness.

In both of the cases where the attempt is made to characterise the aims of higher education by specifying a content - teach transferable skills, teach 'graduate' skills - the models of disability, social and individual/medical, come head to head when you try to operationalise the content. This is especially true for the graduateness idea. Because the idea of graduateness is palpably socially constructed and contested, it is obvious that a particular conception of graduateness can function - one might almost say, be intentionally deployed - to exclude people who are different in any way, including people who are disabled. Yet a person who refuses to allow a student to progress because he is timid, or stammers, or cannot spell, will typically try to interpret the position in terms of the individual model. It is a deficiency in the student which stops him achieving the given goal.

But it is also true, though less obviously, for the idea of transferable skills. The question here is rather how the important skills are to be defined. Is taking notes the important thing, or digesting information? Is visualising the important thing, or interpretation? It is here that the social model gets its purchase.

In the case of the autonomous learning model, we have seen that there are those who would interpret autonomy in a relatively concrete way as the sort of self-control and discipline which gets somebody out of bed a seven o'clock. We have suggested that this interpretation does scant justice to the ideals of Western education, as well as being inherently hostile to many disabled students.

Conclusion

The third intention for this chapter was to think about whether the identified features of the landscape pull in importantly different directions, in some tension with each other. Behind this is the question of whether, in the process, we can identify the dominance of one rather than another model within the HE setting, and, of course, of which model this would be.

We have tried to look behind the HE and disability scene in order to identify the presence or otherwise of one or another theoretical model of disability. This has involved a consideration of purpose as well as practice: we have considered the possibility that social model ends could conceivably be served by what are at least *prima facie* medical or individual model means.

If one takes the view that economic factors are likely to have determining importance in driving institutional change, one will expect such things as DSA arrangements to have greater importance in practice than theoretical consistency in the way people conceptualise disability. It is indeed likely that the general arrangements through which institutions are responsible to funding councils, and the larger political agendas that these arrangements represent, are likely to be determinative of future developments. So our concluding comment is a modest one. In the case of HE provision for disabled students, we would argue that there is evidence of a lack of coherent direction, with single initiatives and arrangements often evidencing a lack of theoretical clarity, thorough-goingness or commitment. But in so far as financial arrangements and rewards hold sway, the medical or individual models would appear to have the upper hand.

Bibliography

Adams, M. and Brown, P. 2000: The times they are a changing: Developing Disability Provision in UK Higher Education. *Conference Paper for the Pathways 5 National Conference.* Canberra: Conference Solutions.

Adams, M. and Brown, P. (*forthcoming*): Disability Provision: Coming in from the Edge. In A. Hurst (ed.) *The Accessible Millennium.* Aldershot: Ashgate Publishing.

Baron, S., Phillips, R. and Stalker, K. 1996: Barriers to Training for Disabled Social Work students. *Disability and Society,* 11 (3), 361-377.

Boud, D. 1988: *Developing Student Autonomy in Learning.* London: Kogan Page.

Brown, S., Duffy, J., Sutherland, L., Phillips, R., Riddell, S. and Amery, P. 1997: *Scottish Higher Education Funding Council initiatives in support of students with disabilities in higher education.* Stirling: Stirling University Press.

DfEE 1995: *The Disability Discrimination Act.* London: HMSO.

DfEE 1999: *The Disability Rights Commission Act.* London: HMSO.

Disability Rights Commission (DRC) 2002: *Code of Practice for providers of Post 16 education and related services.* London: Disability Rights Commission.

Fazey, D.M.A. and Linford, J.G. 1996: Tutoring for Autonomous Learning. *Innovations in Education and Training International,* 33 (3), 185-196.

Hall, J. and Tinklin, T. 1998: *Students First: The Experiences of Disabled Students in Higher Education.* Edinburgh: SCRE.

HEFCE 2002: *Performance Indicators in Higher Education in the UK, 1998-99, 1999-2000.* Bristol: HEFCE.

Hurst, A. 1996: Equal Opportunities and Access: Developments in Policy and Provision for Disabled Students 1990 – 1995. In S. Wolfendale and J. Corbett (eds), *Opening Doors: Learning Support in Higher Education*. London: Cassell.

Hurst, A. 1999: The Dearing Report and Students with Disabilities and Learning Difficulties. *Disability and Society*, 14 (1), 65-83.

Mowthorpe, D.J. 1999: *The Development of Autonomous Learners: The Learning and Teaching Institute*. Sheffield: Sheffield Hallam University.

Osborne, R. D. 1999: Wider Access in Scotland? *Scottish Affairs*, 26, 36-46.

Paterson, L. 1997: Trends in Higher Education Participation in Scotland. *Higher Education Quarterly*, 51, 29-48.

Paterson, L. 1998: Higher Education, Social Capital and the Scottish Parliament. *Scottish Affairs*, 22, 99-111.

Quality Assurance Agency for Higher Education 2003: *Benchmarking Standards*. Gloucester: QAA. http://www.qaa.ac.uk/crntwork/benchmark/ index

Riddell, S. 1998: Chipping away at the mountain: disabled students' experience of higher education. *International Studies in Sociology of Education*, 8 (2), 203-222.

Riddell, S. and Banks, P. 2001: *Disability in Scotland: A Baseline Study*. Edinburgh: Disability Rights Commission.

Riddell, S. and Salisbury, J. (eds) 1999: *Gender Equality and Educational Change*. London: Routledge.

Riddell, S., Tinklin, T. and Wilson, A. 2002: *Disabled students in higher education: the impact of anti-discrimination legislation on teaching, learning and assessment*. http://www.escalate.ac.uk/diary/reports/22Nova.rtf

Riddell, S., Tinklin T. and Wilson A. 2004: *Disabled Students and Multiple Policy Innovations in Higher Education Final Report to the ESRC*. Edinburgh: University of Edinburgh.

Ryan, A. 1999: *Liberal Anxieties and Liberal Education*. London: Profile Books.

SHEFC 2001: Circular Letter no. HE/09/01 *Main Grant in Support of Teaching and Research for Academic Year 2001-2002*, Edinburgh: SHEFC.

SHEFC 2002: *Disability Needs Analysis, Access to the Curriculum*. Edinburgh: SHEFC.

Tinklin, T. and Hall, J. 1999: Getting round obstacles: disabled students'
experiences in Higher Education in Scotland. *Studies in Higher
Education*, 24 (2), 183-94.

Tinklin, T., Riddell, S. and Wilson, A. 2002: Wider Access for Disabled
Students? *Disabled Students and Multiple Policy Initiatives in Higher
Education: Working Paper 1*, Glasgow: University of Glasgow.
http://www.ed.ac.uk/ces/pdffiles/tt_0_2_0_7.pdf

University of Strathclyde 2000: *Teachability: Creating an Accessible
Curriculum for Students with Disabilities*. Glasgow: University of
Strathclyde.

Watson, D. and Bowden, R. 1999: Why did they do it? The
Conservatives and mass higher education, 1979 – 97. *Journal of
Education Policy,* 14 (3), 243-256

CHAPTER 6

Disabled Students in Higher Education: a reflection on research strategies and findings

Sheila Riddell, Teresa Tinklin and Alastair Wilson

Introduction

This chapter has two central concerns. First, findings are presented from an ESRC-funded project investigating the impact of widening access policies for disabled students in higher education. Secondly, it seeks to develop a critique of the strategies employed in the research, drawing on recent theoretical developments in the field of disability studies. Whereas disability studies, like early feminist research, operated with a relatively simple concept of disability as a unitary category, recent theorising has conceptualised identity as subjective, complex and multi-dimensional. We explore some of the implications of these ideas for our own research, and consider whether the use of categories, such as social class and disability, may be justified on the grounds that they may be used to audit social divisions.

Theorising disability: recent developments

A key goal of early social model theory was to clarify understandings of disability and impairment with a view to facilitating the political development of the disability movement. At the heart of the Union of the Physically Impaired Against Segregation (UPIAS) definition, was the idea of disability as a social relational construct:

> The disadvantage or social restriction of activity caused by a contemporary social organisation which takes little or no account of people who have [impairment] and thus excludes them from the mainstream of social activities (Oliver 1996: 22).

Reviewing the development of a body of work associated with the social model of disability, Thomas (2004) suggested that considerable progress has been made in amassing evidence on barriers to social inclusion in the public spheres of education, employment, housing, health and welfare services, recreation, media and cultural representation, legislation and so forth (Barnes 1991; Riddell and Banks 2001). Slower progress, however, has been made in documenting barriers in less public aspects of life such as familial and sexual attachments, reproduction, parenting and childcare (exceptions are Shakespeare et al. 1996; Thomas 1998, 1999). In addition, theoretical work on disability as a social relational phenomenon is also relatively under-developed, although Finkelstein (1980) and Oliver (1990) have explored the rise of capitalism and the exclusion of disabled people, whilst Thomas (1999), Morris (1996) and Crow (1996) have commented on the intersections of gender and disability.

Recently, new challenges have been mounted by post-modern and post-structuralist writers, who critiqued the taken-for-granted distinction between disabled and non-disabled people (Corker and Shakespeare 2002; Corker 2003). We shall consider our own work in the light of these criticisms, questioning whether it is possible to research social justice issues without adopting categorical and unitary notions of concepts such as disability. In the following sections, we consider research strategies which have been used to investigate participation in higher education and the way in which our work articulates with such approaches.

Strategies for researching access to higher education

Educational research in the post-war period was informed by the political arithmetic tradition. The establishment of the welfare state prompted researchers to focus their efforts on investigating the extent to which it was succeeding in its goal of creating a more equal society. To undertake this research, ways had to be found of measuring social class, and father's occupation was used as a proxy indicator. Whilst such measures could only be regarded as rough approximations, their use in a range of studies led to their reification. For example, Glass (1954) reported that from 1928 to 1947, 8.9 per cent of all boys from non-manual backgrounds entered university compared to 1.4 per cent of all boys from manual backgrounds. The provision of full fees in 1960 along with the post-Robbins expansion of higher education led to a rise of 50 per cent in university entrance between 1963 and 1968, and by 1989 the number of university entrants had risen by 150 per cent. However, researchers continued to document the persistence of social class inequality in rates of participation by students from particular social groups (Blackburn and Jarman 1993; Egerton and Halsey 1993; Tinklin and Raffe 1999).

Research on rates of participation fed into policy developments on access to higher education by 'under-represented groups'. The Robbins Committee (DES 1963) was followed thirty years later by the Dearing and Garrick Reports (NCIHE 1997a, 1997b). Government documents on lifelong learning (DfEE 1998, 1999; Scottish Executive 1999) called for wider access for students from socially disadvantaged groups, supported by funding council initiatives (HEFCE 1998; SHEFC 1998). Social class remained the main focus of analysis, with gender, ethnicity and gender attracting rather less attention. HEFCE began publishing performance indicators on the participation of under-represented groups in 1998, focusing on participation of students from different social backgrounds and ages, 'efficiency' measured by the proportion of students completing a course and research output. From 2002, performance indicators in relation to disabled students and employment outcomes were published. The performance indicators do not cover gender and they only address ethnicity in relation to employment outcomes (HEFCE 2002). Primacy continues to be attached to measures of inclusion related to social class; information is published on pupils from state schools or colleges, low-participation neighbourhoods and social classes IIIM, IV and V. The disability indicator is based on the number of students receiving the Disabled Students Allowance. The Funding Councils make additional premium payments to institutions based on social class and disability indicators. The benchmarks published in relation to each indicator are based on the performance of other comparable institutions in the sector and are intended to signal to institutions whether they are performing better or worse than expected.

Critiques of the categorical approach

It is evident that research and policy on access to higher education have been informed by the categorical or neo-realist approach criticised so extensively by post-modern writers, although some researchers have adopted a much more reflexive and critical approach. For example, Archer (2003), whilst working with traditional conceptualisations of social class, provided an excellent critique of the way in which such measures are developed and deployed. She questioned the accuracy and validity of the measures of social class employed by the University and Colleges

Admissions Service (UCAS), which underpin the performance indicators developed by the Higher Education Statistics Agency (HESA). For example, she noted that all those who are economically inactive are classified as 'other', and in certain parts of the UK the number thus classified may be as high as per cent of the population. The categories were defined with men rather than women in mind, and do not accommodate easily families where mother and father have different occupations. In addition, as the service sector expands, more jobs are likely to be classified as IIINM, but in terms of substance, pay and degree of autonomy, these may differ little from jobs in the old manufacturing sectors. Furthermore, the categories are based on the assumption that the young person retains the social class of their family until they have an independent job. However, with the collapse of the youth labour market in the late 1970s, there has increasingly been a delay in the young person having an independent occupational location. The category assigned to them on the basis of their father's occupation may therefore have little subjective validity.

Similar criticisms of accuracy and meaningfulness have been made in relation to the measurement of ethnicity (Modood and Acland 1998) and disability (Riddell and Banks 2001). Indeed, categories used to measure disability may fly in the face of social model thinking. For example, in order to assess participation in higher education by disabled students, UCAS forms invite students to allocate themselves to one of the following categories: dyslexia, unseen disability, blind/partially sighted, deaf/hard of hearing, wheelchair user/mobility impaired, personal care support, mental health difficulties, multiple disabilities, other disability. Whilst these categories attempt to characterise an individual in relation to their impairment, recent writing in disability studies (Priestley 2001; Riddell and Watson 2003) underlines the wide range of identity positions held by disabled people, which are influenced but not determined by their impairment, generational and cultural locations.

Opponents of categorisation, drawing on the work of theorists such as Williams (1961, 1977) and Bourdieu (1990), maintain that social class, disability, gender and ethnicity should be seen as negotiated and fluid identities. In addition, categorical data, employed as a tool of managerialist culture, are criticised by those opposed to the growth of the 'audit society' (Power 1997). However, categorical data may also be used in pursuit of social justice goals (Scottish Executive 2000), and monitoring of institutional performance against equality indicators is promoted by the Equality Commissions and Government Social Inclusion Units. A number of innovative studies of access to higher education have adopted multiple strategies, using fixed categories to analyse statistical patterns of participation, whilst also exploring the way in which particular groups of students negotiate their identities within particular institutional contexts (Archer 2003). Our research on access to higher education by disabled students attempted to adopt this eclectic approach, and in the following sections we present and critique our strategies and findings.

The research project

The data reported in this chapter are drawn from the ESRC funded project *Disabled Students and Multiple Policy Innovations in Higher Education* (R000239069), conducted by researchers at the Universities of Glasgow and Edinburgh between 2001 and 2003. The research consists of three main elements: (i) analysis of statistical information from the Higher Education Statistics Agency; (ii) a questionnaire survey administered to all universities and HEIs in England and Scotland; (iii) case studies of 56 students in eight universities and HEIs, four in England and four in Scotland. The institutions selected reflected sectoral diversity, and included pre-92 universities (ancient, red-brick and plate-glass), post-92 universities and HEIs. Within each institution, we invited disabled students to participate in the research and the group of students we worked with reflected diversity in terms of gender, nature of impairment, social location and age. The student case studies were conducted by means of interviews with the student, lecturers, the disabled student's adviser and a senior manager. In addition, researchers met each student in a range of settings on three separate occasions over a period of a week.

Participation by disabled students over time and by type of impairment

A key question was whether the proportion of disabled students in higher education was increasing or decreasing over time. Table 1 suggests that a modest increase has taken place since 1995/6. On the other hand, the change might simply reflect an increased willingness to disclose an impairment. Table 2 reveals some interesting changes in relation to the impairment category in which students place themselves. Dyslexic students in 1999-2000 had become the biggest group, making up a third of the total. There has also been an increase in students disclosing a mental health problem, and a decrease in hidden impairment category. Those with personal care support needs continue to be the smallest group, accounting for only 0.3 per cent of the total.

Table 1:
Percentage of disabled students in HE, 1995-6 and 1999-2000

%	1995/6	1996/7	1997/8	1998/9	1999/00
First degree	3.7	4.4	4.7	4.9	4.8
Other undergraduate	3	2.9	3.3	3.4	3.5
Postgraduate	1.7	2	2.4	2.6	2.9

Table 2:
**First years known to have a disability by type of impairment,
1995-6, 1999-2000**

%	1995/6	1999/00
Dyslexia	17.9	32.7
Unseen disability	48.6	29.7
Blind/partially sighted	3.9	3.5
Deaf/hard of hearing	7.1	5.8
Wheelchair user/mobility impaired	4.9	4.4
Personal care support	0.2	0.3
Mental health difficulties	1.8	3.3
Multiple disabilities	3.6	7.3
Other disability	11.9	13.0
Total first years	448199	525140
Total known to have a disability	15754	22290

In each impairment category, there were significant associations between gender and impairment, and these differences are apparent in each impairment category. In relation to some impairments, the gender gap is particularly marked. For example, two thirds of dyslexic students in post-92 universities are male. Whilst Tables 1 and 2 suggest clear trends, these may reflect 'real' changes in the nature of the disabled student population in HEIs, or in the social acceptability of disclosing particular types of impairment and adopting particular disability identities.

Participation of disabled students in higher education by social class and ethnicity
We also wished to explore the relationship between various aspects of the social identity of individuals in particular institutions. Information is requested on the UCAS form about the occupation of the applicant's

parent/guardian or, where entrants are aged 21 or over, the occupation of the person contributing the highest income to the household. This information is then coded by HESA into a social class grouping using the OPCS 1990 standard occupational classification, with the student classified on the basis of their parent's occupation. In practice, this information was missing for 66.3 per cent of students and analysis should therefore be treated with caution.

Despite the potential problems posed by student's reluctance to reveal their parents' occupational status, some interesting patterns emerged. In old universities, there were no marked differences in participation of disabled and non-disabled students by social class. In new universities, disabled students were slightly more likely to have come from the more advantaged end of the spectrum than non-disabled students (Figure 1). Overall, the data pointed to the high level of social stratification which characterises British higher education. In England, social classes I, II and IIINM account for about two thirds of the population but 80 per cent of students in pre-92 and 67 per cent of students in post-92 universities. In Scotland, which prides itself on its more egalitarian tradition (Paterson 1997), 78 per cent of students in pre-92 universities and 67 per cent of students in post-92 universities were from I, II and IIINM. The social class background of disabled students (81.5 per cent in English pre-92 universities and 79 per cent in Scottish pre-92 universities) was virtually identical. It has been suggested that widening participation in HE by disabled students will have a general democratising effect on the sector. However, these figures indicate that the composition of the population of disabled students was, if anything, slightly more socially advantaged than non-disabled students in particular sectors.

Information on ethnicity was available for over 92 per cent of the undergraduates in the dataset. It was not possible to break students down into all the ethnic groupings in Scotland, because the numbers were too small for analysis (Figure 2). However, a broad comparison of white and non-white students revealed that disabled students were significantly (p<.001) less likely to come from minority ethnic groups than students with no known disability. This was true in all sectors except for HEIs in Scotland. Overall, there were more non-white students (both disabled and non-disabled) in English institutions than in Scottish ones, with the percentage of non-white students ranging from 5.8 per cent to 19.3 per cent in England, compared with 1.7 per cent to 4.1 per cent in Scotland. These figures again suggest that there are no grounds for believing that including more disabled students in higher education necessarily challenges wider social inequalities. Preece (1999) reported that forty per cent of minority ethnic students were located in London, predominantly in new universities. In both England and Scotland, a significantly (p<.001) higher proportion of disabled students in pre-92 universities were white. Thus, whilst social class stratification among disabled students mirrored that of the wider population, stratification along lines of 'race' among disabled students was even more marked than among the wider population.

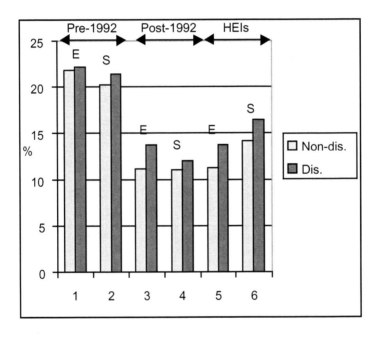

Figure 1:
Percentage of undergraduates from social class I
by sector and country

To summarise, taking these categories at face value, the inclusion of disabled students in higher education tends to reinforce rather than challenge existing patterns of social stratification. The social class profile of disabled students mirrors that of non-disabled students in different types of institution in England and Scotland, with a disproportionate number of middle class disabled students in the more prestigious pre-92 universities. In terms of other social factors, disabled students are more likely than other students to be white males aged between 19-24 years. This is related to the fact that the largest group of disabled students are dyslexic and these are likely to be male, white and middle class. This suggests that there may be many disabled students from less socially advantaged backgrounds who are currently not being included in higher education. Given that relatively socially advantaged disabled students are admitted to higher education, there still appear to be some inequalities in terms of the level of degree classification they obtain, which in England is lower than their non-disabled counterparts and in Scotland is more spread.

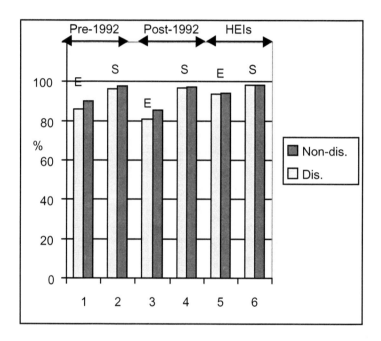

Figure 2:
Percentage of undergraduates who are white by
sector and country

There are three key points to be made about these data. First, data which appear to be relatively 'hard' become far more problematic when the provisional and relative nature of categories is recognised. This is particularly the case in relation to social class, where information is only available for a minority of students. Secondly, it is impossible to understand the extent to which disabled students are included without taking into account a number of aspects of their social location. Institutions with a particular social class and ethnicity profile appear to recruit disabled students who reflect the predominant characteristics of that institution. Considering disability in isolation from other social characteristics of students may give the impression that a higher degree of social inclusion is being achieved than is actually the case. Thirdly, given the association between social class, ethnicity and disability, it is evident that the category of disability may be too simplistic to capture the experience of disabled students. Disabled students may not be defined by others or define themselves in relation to their impairment. They may also be categorised by social class, ethnicity, gender and the nature of their impairment. Indeed, the analysis presented above raises the possibility that disability may not be the over-riding category. In order to understand the negotiated identities of disabled students, we discussed their experiences and observed them in a range of situations. Brief cameos of four students are presented below.

Morag

Morag, was a second year student studying Classics and Scottish History at an elite pre-92 Scottish University. She had attended a Scottish independent girls' school where her dyslexia was identified by the Dyslexia Institute and a psychological assessment at a university. She had chosen the University because the Wider Access Co-ordinator had responded positively to a phone call and invited her in for discussion. Also, her father had been a student at the University. She had been made a slightly lower offer than usual because of her dyslexia. She received the equipment element of DSA which was used to buy a PC and specialist software. Mostly she did not need any special adjustments, although she did get extra time in exams. Although exams were marked anonymously, once the code had been broken, special allowances might be made for poor spelling. However, Morag felt that lecturers did not understand the full extent of her difficulties, for instance, she was restricted in her use of vocabulary because of a fear of misspelling words. Her life at University was fairly quiet. She lived in a women's hall of residence and socialised mainly with the other students there. However, a quiet town-based social life was normal for many students and Morag therefore did not feel different. She felt that Christianity rather than disability was an important part of her identity.

Lewis

Lewis was in his first year at a Scottish University studying History. He had left his local comprehensive school to work as an apprentice fitter and turner. After six years undertaking 'heavy work', including a spell in a restaurant which left him 'hacked off', he decided to go to University and enrolled for an Access course at the local FE college. One University was 'on the doorstep so it seemed straightforward to come here.' However, just before he was due to start, Lewis was involved in a serious accident that left him with major head injuries. The University Disability Service provided a very high level of support, ensuring that assessments were conducted quickly, a DSA claim was made and note-takers engaged. Lewis was provided with a small laptop computer and note-takers for each lecture. Overall, he felt that the University had given him excellent support. He described himself as 'generally quite dull' and his life at university as 'quite boring'.

Fellow students were described thus:

these people are all very clever people, you know what I mean. Which makes them seem a lot older than 18. Especially since they are all the same, you know.

They were contrasted with people from the small town where he grew up and still returned to:

It's fine when I go home. I still see some people I knew ten years ago, they know what happened to me...they make allowances for it anyway.

Despite receiving excellent support, Lewis felt alienated from the University. In addition to his head injury, which he recognised had caused him major physical and psychological problems, other factors such as age and social class may have had an effect. However, despite his difficulties with balance and walking, Lewis did not see himself as disabled.

Peter

Peter was in the second year of an undergraduate degree at a post-92, inner city Scottish University studying for a professional qualification in social work. He had a visual impairment from birth and required text to be magnified. He also used voice-to-text software. Peter had received little support in his mainstream school and left with no qualifications and feeling 'disenchanted'. Subsequently, he attended his local FE college but decided to stay at home to look after his new-born daughter. He later undertook an Access Course and obtained a place at a local university which would allow him to continue to undertake childcare. Peter found the academic and administrative support provided was inadequate. The Students Awards Agency for Scotland took a long time to process his claim and the

University would not fund support before the cheque had arrived. Lecture and seminar notes were required in advance but these were rarely forthcoming and were often of poor quality. Peter described himself as a highly politicised disabled person who was willing to argue for his rights:

> I probably do think of myself as a disabled person, but disabled in the sense that I'm disabled by society, not by my physical disability. So it's more a kind of political definition I would give. I don't tend to see myself disabled in the negative sense. But I think a lot of it has come from my education.

At this point in his life, however, Peter did not have much time to engage actively in university politics, focusing his energies on completing his course and being a good parent to his daughter.

Terry

Terry was a 27 year old student studying for an MSc in Deaf Studies at an elite pre-92 English University. His father was a physician and he described the family as 'middle class' and 'not rich but privileged'. At the time of the research, Terry was an active member of the deaf community both within and outwith the university. He was diagnosed as having hearing difficulties at a relatively yearly age, but was not allowed to learn sign language or connect with the deaf community:

> when I was growing up I was kind of kept separate from the deaf community. I remember growing up and asking if I could learn sign language and kind of being refused time and time again. I remember at the age of 12 and 14 and 16 kind of being insistent about learning sign language and again, as I said, being refused.

On leaving school, Terry went to a University in London, where he learned sign language. After a brief period in another university, he moved to his current institution. He was extremely active in university politics, representing disabled students in the students' union and also for the NUS. He had also founded a new union for deaf students.

Some of Terry's lecturers could use BSL, but others required sign language interpreters and these were not always available. As a result, Terry had taken advice from two solicitors and was planning to bring a case against the university under DDA Part 4, on the grounds that it had failed to make reasonable adjustments. Despite this very high level of involvement, Terry still felt isolated:

> I feel cut off from university life as though I can't really participate socially within groups. I can't go along to open

lectures…here at the Centre for Deaf Studies it's easy because there are other deaf students and within the corridors there are academics I can talk to but other students in other departments won't necessarily be able to do that.

Cathy

Cathy, a mature student, was in the fourth year of a degree in Sociology and Politics degree at a pre-92 Scottish University where 85% of students are from state schools or colleges. Cathy had a physical impairment, acquired as an adult, which meant that she had difficulty walking and sometimes used a wheelchair. Cathy was from a working class background and left school with no qualifications. After travelling, she spent two years at college before entering university. Cathy's perception was that her status as a single parent with money problems was more salient than having an impairment. She complained, for example, that a course in women's studies was held from 3-5pm which made it inaccessible to those with childcare responsibilities:

> I can't get back to get my little girl after school. Now I pay excessively for the childcare service. Classes that are late I can't do….I've had to see lecturers more about asking for extensions and they are never very forthcoming and it's got nothing to do with disability. I've got a child, I get her to bed, I sleep with her from 8-10 and I set an alarm and get up and work till two at night…I don't believe in the assessment system. I know it's meant to be fair assessment and everyone's got the same chance, but that's rubbish. Some of my friends are out working every hour God will send. Others, their parents pay for everything.

Cathy perceived there to be a difference in identity and awareness between those born with an impairment and people like her who acquired it later in life:

> From what I've seen of my friends who are born disabled, they are very comfortable with it and call me a guest sometimes. 'Oh, here's the guest'. And my uncomfortableness is wrong. Well, not wrong …it's the whole thing of becoming disabled once you have developed as a person or been born disabled…If there was a group, I'm sure that you would find that most people had been born disabled in it.

She particularly objected to being grouped into a special area at venues such as theatres with other disabled people:

> Sometimes when you get out somewhere because it's accessible,
> you almost feel like it's "Freakers' Ball". It's horrible.

These necessarily brief and selective extracts indicate the range of identities and experiences of higher education among the 'case study' participants. The nature of a person's impairment appeared to have a significant impact on their identity and experience, and it was possible to distinguish between impairment and disability effects. For example, a deaf PhD student was uncertain about whether to pursue an academic career because of difficulties she encountered participating in and facilitating seminars. She preferred to lip read, but found it difficult having to teach a large number of students who changed every year. The disabling effects of society were evident, and arrangements might well have been made to allow her to teach fewer students in more consistent groups. However, she was doubtful that, even with such adjustments, teaching was what she wanted to do.

Students with dyslexia also did not identify closely with students with other impairments, but were prepared to use the term 'disabled student' strategically to obtain IT equipment and examination allowances. A number of students with significant impairments, on the other hand, expended much energy in trying to 'pass' as 'normal', underlining the strong normalising pressures in school and higher education. The permanency, visibility, and age at which an impairment is acquired also seemed to have a major impact on individuals' identity. Overall, students who had a view of disability as a political and social relational category were in the minority. It was also evident that students were aware of a range of identities informing their experience and sense of self, and prioritised different aspects of their identity at different times in their life and for a range of strategic purposes.

Conclusion

We began this chapter by discussing calls from within disability studies to move away from binary conceptions of disability in order to develop more subtle understandings of its social relational aspects. Subsequently we discussed post-war approaches to researching access to education, which traditionally employed categorical data. However, there has been a rejection of binary understandings of social class, gender, and ethnicity, with a new emphasis on exploring the subjective meaning of these divisions within everyday contexts (Reay 1998; Ball 2003). Whilst social theorists have increasingly drawn attention to the inadequacy of binary social divisions, equality policies and legislation emphasise the need for institutions to monitor their performance by employing fixed categories to evaluate participation rates of under-represented groups. Even when researchers employ qualitative methods to investigate cultural experiences of particular groups, categorical conceptualisations of disability, social class, gender or ethnicity generally underpin their analyses. The research discussed here attempted to combine an analysis of patterns of participation in higher education with an investigation of the way in which individuals negotiated their position in higher education by deploying a range of cultural identities. We believe that the combination of these two research strategies provided insights into the complexity of patterns of participation and negotiated identities.

The quantitative data reveal the problematic data of the labels employed, not just in relation to disability but also in relation to social class, 'race' and gender. They also indicate that the term disability cannot be seen as a master category. Wider patterns of social stratification in HE were reflected in the social composition of disabled students in particular universities. Middle class white students occupied a disproportionate share of places in pre-92 universities, and this pattern prevailed in relation to the distribution of disabled students in different institutions. Despite the fact that disabled students are a highly selected (and self-selected) group, they still have poorer degree classifications than other students, although their completion rates are better. This suggests that disability works in complex ways with a range of other variables to structure the experiences of those identified as disabled. These inter-relationships between variables have important implications for policy and practice, and could not have been accessed without the use of categorical data.

The qualitative data presented here illuminate the way in which students negotiate identity within the constraints of their individual biographies and social locations. Like the quantitative data, the case studies suggest that impairment and disability are major factors in students' lives, but are not necessarily always the defining aspect. Unsurprisingly, the social context of particular institutions plays a major part in determining the experience of impairment and disability. In the 1980s, feminists expended a great deal of energy in trying to decide whether patriarchy or capitalism had primacy in structuring women's lives. The question remained unanswered, possibly because it was not the right one to ask in the first place. The arguments made by Anne Phillips (1999) in *Which Equalities Matter?* are probably more helpful in emphasising that individuals accentuate and privilege particular aspects of identity in order to attain political and strategic goals. This may be useful in thinking through the relationship between disability and other 'equality' categories.

Finally, despite the fragility of the categories employed in the modernist project of tracking inequalities over time, we believe that this is a worthwhile endeavour, so long as it is backed up by careful attempts to place these findings in the context of lived experience.

Bibliography

Abberley, P. 1992: Counting Us Out: A Discussion of the OPCS Disability Surveys. *Disability, Handicap and Society*, 7 (2), 139-55.

Archer, L. 2003: Social class and higher education. In L. Archer, M. Hutchings and A. Ross (eds), *Higher Education and Social Class: Issues of Inclusion and Exclusion*. London: Routledge.

Ball, S.J. 2003: *Class Strategies and the Educational Market: The Middle Classes and Social Advantage*. London: Routledge.

Barnes, C. 1991: *Disabled People in Britain: The Case for Anti-Discrimination Legislation*. London: Hurst & Co.

Blackburn, R.M. and Jarman, J. 1993: Changing inequalities in access to British universities. *Oxford Review of Education*, 19 (2), 197-215.

Bourdieu, P. 1990: *The Logic of Practice*. Cambridge: Polity Press.

Corker, M. 2003: Deafness/Disability – problematising notions of identity, culture and structure. In S. Riddell and N. Watson (eds), *Disability, Culture and Identity*. London: Pearson Education.

Corker, M. and Shakespeare, T. 2002: Mapping the terrain. In M. Corker and T. Shakespeare (eds), *Disability/Postmodernism*. London: Continuum.

Crow, L. 1996: Including all of our lives. In C. Barnes and G. Mercer (eds), *Exploring the Divide: Illness and Disability*. Leeds: The Disability Press.

DfEE 1998: *The Learning Age: A Renaissance for a New Britain*. London: HMSO.

DfEE 1999: *Learning to Succeed: Coherence and Diversity for Adult Learners*. London: HMSO.

DES 1963: *Report of the Committee on Higher Education* (Robbins Report). London: HMSO.

Egerton, M and Halsey, J.H. 1993: Trends in social class and gender in access to higher education in Britain. *Oxford Review of Education*, 19 (2), 183-196.

Finkelstein, V. 1980: *Attitudes and Disabled People: Issues for Discussion*. New York: World Rehabilitation Fund.

Glass, D.V. (ed.) 1954: *Social Mobility in Britain*. London: Routledge and Kegan Paul.

Hall, J. and Tinklin, T. 1998: *Students first: the experiences of disabled students in higher education*. Edinburgh: SCRE.

HEFCE 2002: *Performance Indicators in Higher Education in the UK, 1999-2000, 2000-2001*. Bristol: HEFCE.

Hurst, A. 1999: The Dearing Report and students with disabilities and learning difficulties. *Disability and Society*, 14 (1), 65-83.

Modood, T. and Acland, A. (eds.) 1998: *Race and Higher Education*. London: Policy Studies Institute.

Morris, J. (ed.) 1996: *Encounters with Strangers: Feminism and Disability*. London: The Women's Press.

NCIHE 1997a: *Higher education in the learning society*. London: HMSO.

NCIHE 1997b: *Higher education in the learning society: report of the Scottish committee*. London: HMSO.

Oliver, M. 1990: *The Politics of Disablement*. Basingstoke: Macmillan

Oliver, M. 1996: *Understanding Disability*. London: Macmillan.

Paterson, L. 1997: Trends in higher education participation in Scotland. *Higher Education Quarterly*, 51, 29-48.

Phillips, A. 1999: *Which Equalities Matter?* Cambridge: Polity Press.

Power, M. 1997: *The Audit Society*. Oxford: Oxford University Press.

Preece, J. 1999: Families into Higher Education Project: an Awareness Raising Action Research project with Schools and Parents. *Higher Education Quarterly*, 53 (3), 197-210.

Priestley, M. (ed.) 2001: *Disability and the Life Course*. Cambridge: Cambridge University Press.

Riddell, S. and Banks, P. 2001: *Disability in Scotland: A Baseline Study*. Edinburgh: Disability Rights Commission.

Riddell, S. and Watson, N. (eds) 2003: *Disability, Culture and Identity*. London: Pearson Education.

Reay, D. 1998: Rethinking social class: qualitative perspectives on class and gender. *Sociology*, 32 (2): 259-275.

Scottish Executive 1999: *Implementing Inclusiveness: Realising Potential* (The Beattie Report). Edinburgh: HMSO.

Scottish Executive 2000: *Social Justice: A Scotland Where Everyone Matters: Annual Report 2000*. Edinburgh: Scottish Executive.

SHEFC 1998: *Funding for the Future: A consultation on the funding of teaching*. Edinburgh: SHEFC.

Shakespeare, T., Gillespie-Sells, K., and Davies, D. 1996: *The Sexual Politics of Disability: Untold Desires*. London: Cassell.

Thomas, C. 1998: Parents and families: disabled women's stories about their childhood experiences. In C. Robinson and K. Stalker (eds), *Growing Up with Disability*. London: Jessica Kingsley.

Thomas, C. 1999: *Female Forms: Experiencing and Understanding Disability*. Buckingham: Open University Press.

Thomas, C. 2004: Developing the social relational in the social model of disability: a theoretical agenda. In C. Barnes and G. Mercer (eds), *Implementing the Social Model of Disability*. Leeds: The Disability Press.

Tinklin, T. and Raffe, D. 1999: *Entrants to higher education*. Edinburgh: CES.

Universities Scotland 2000: *Access to Achievement: A Guide to how the Scottish Higher Education System is Promoting Social Inclusion*. Edinburgh: Universities Scotland.

Williams, R. 1961: *Culture and Society 1780-1950*. Harmondsworth, Penguin.

Williams, R. 1977: *Marxism and Literature*. Oxford: Oxford University Press.

CHAPTER 7

Power, Policy and Provision: disabling barriers in higher education in Wales

Karen Beauchamp-Pryor

Introduction

The Government has recently introduced, for the first time, legislative protection for disabled students in higher education in the form of the Special Educational Needs and Disability Act (SENDA) 2001. In response, Higher Educational Institutions (HEIs) have begun to change policies and practices towards disabled students. This chapter analyses this legislative initiative and the subsequent development of policy and provision towards disabled students.

I will concentrate on three main interconnecting issues – power, policy and provision. The first section of the chapter considers overarching issues of power, drawing on the social and medical models of disability and their potential influence on policy. For example the adoption of a social model implies a focus on rights, because it recognises that disability results from the social, environmental and attitudinal barriers within society. In contrast, the medical model encourages an approach that stresses student's needs rather than rights, because it is aimed at changing or compensating the individual, rather than challenging the barriers that exist. The second section reviews the policy agenda and priorities adopted by the Welsh Assembly towards disabled students in higher education. For example, how far has policy sought to achieve equality and inclusion for disabled people? The final section concentrates on the experiences and views of disabled students in one Welsh HEI of the impact of disability policy and provision.

Power

Definitions of disability powerfully influence the development of policy and provision. It has been argued that the dominant and most powerful model in defining disability has reflected a medicalised/individualised stance (Oliver 1990). From this perspective, disability results directly from individual impairment and functional limitations, with an underlying assumption that human potential and ability are restricted.

This approach has increasingly been contested by disabled people. During the late 1960s and early 1970s the social model of disability was developed and the Union of Physically Impaired Against Segregation (UPIAS) adopted a definition which differed radically from previous approaches:

> In our view it is society which disables physically impaired people. Disability is something imposed on top of our impairments by the way we are unnecessarily isolated and excluded from full participation in society. Disabled people are therefore an oppressed group in society (UPIAS 1976: 14).

From this perspective disability results directly from social, environmental and attitudinal barriers and not individual limitations. Policy and provision developed within a social model will, therefore, be aimed at dismantling the disabling barriers within society, whereas policy and provision developed within a medical model will be aimed at changing the individual.

Those with power are often in a position to define disability as social problems and protect their own self-interests and values. Once defined in this way, individuals become stigmatised and confined to social expectations of ability/dis-ability. This social construction approach accords with an 'everyday' account of social problems where the social problem is individualised and is seen as given, natural and absolute (Hulley and Clarke 1991). The so-called 'objective' criteria of disability are subsequently reflected in the development of policy and provision by those in influential and powerful positions. Therefore, the development and implementation of policy and provision in higher education could potentially be dependent upon who holds the power, defines the problem, and provides the solution.

The dominant approach towards disabled students in higher education has historically reflected a 'needs' led discourse with policy and provision aimed at resolving individual problems (see final section of this chapter.) However, a 'rights' discourse begins to challenge these power relations and practices (Armstrong and Barton 1999).

Closely associated with these power relationships is the use of terminology that transmits dominant ideas and values. Stereotypical images and assumptions are maintained through the use of terms that are potentially stigmatising and might devalue individuals (Thompson 1998). The term 'special needs' was originally adopted to signify a move away from the medical categorisation of disability, but the term is 'now perceived by many as simplistic, pejorative and patronising' (Tomlinson 1995: 7). Nevertheless, 'having special needs' has become embedded in educational discourse and provision (Barton and Armstrong 2001: 704).

Arguably, legislation has also reflected this needs based approach with a medical definition sitting at the heart of the Disability Discrimination Act (DDA). The Act defines disability as:

a physical or mental impairment which has a substantial and long-term adverse effect on a person's ability to carry out normal day-to-day activities (DfEE 1995a: Part 1.1.1)

According to this definition, the 'effect' must be (i) 'substantial' (more than minor or trivial); (ii) 'adverse'; (iii) 'long-term' (likely to last at least 12 months); and (iv) affect 'normal day-to-day activities'. The definition focuses on the effect of impairment and not on the disabling barriers within society. This is reinforced in the DfEE's *Guidance on matters to be taken into account in determining questions relating to the definition of disability* (1995b). Where activities are categorised as 'normal' this means that others are treated as 'abnormal', thus reinforcing the stereotyping and stigmatisation of disabled people.

The Northern Officers Group, an organisation of disabled people involved in local government, has campaigned for the Government to adopt a contrary social definition:

A disabled person is a person with an impairment who experiences disability. Disability is the result of negative interactions that take place between a person with an impairment and her or his social environment. Impairment is thus part of a negative interaction, but it is not the cause of, nor does it justify, disability (Northern Officers Group 2003: 1).

There is a concern amongst disabled people that unless legislation recognises the adverse effect of a medicalised conceptualisation of disability, policy and service provision will continue to view disability as an individual deficit.

The area of higher education was originally omitted from the DDA framework. HEIs were lawfully able to bar a disabled person just because they were disabled. In 1997 the Government set-up a Disability Rights Task Force (DRTF) to address the failure of the DDA. Its report *From*

Exclusion to Inclusion (DRTF 1999) recognised the limitations of the definition of disability contained within the DDA, but retained the medical model approach. Issues relating to the provision of services for disabled students in higher education were considered and the discrimination that exists in post-compulsory education was condemned, but the report ignored claims of indirect discrimination. The DRTF (1999) recommended that higher education should be covered by civil rights legislation either as a separate section of the DDA or as separate legislation focussing solely on post-16 education.

In response the Government implemented the Special Educational Needs and Disability Act (SENDA) 2001, which addresses the exemption of higher education from the DDA and is now included as Part IV of the DDA. Since, September 2002 it has been unlawful to discriminate against disabled people or students on the basis of 'less favourable' treatment and HEIs are required to provide 'reasonable adjustments' where disabled students might be substantially disadvantaged. HEIs are required to change policies and practices, but if the interpretation remains within a medical/individualised framework the danger is that disability will continue to be viewed as stemming from abnormality and lack of ability. Notably, the language of 'special needs' persists and politicians and policy makers have continued to reinforce these stereotypical views of disability in the very naming of the Act.

The voice of disabled people has been largely absent and excluded in the development of legislation and policy (Oliver 1990; Drake 1999, 2002). Consequently, everyday assumptions of disability based on a medicalised conceptualisation and needs approach are mostly reflected in legislation, policy and provision. Admittedly, the Government has increasingly recognised the benefit of 'consultation' and 'participation' from under represented groups in the policy making process and has sought greater representation. However, as Arnstein (1969) argued, citizen participation ranges from non-participation (manipulation and therapy), through degrees of tokenism (informing, consultation and placation), to degrees of citizen power (partnership and delegated power).

The Government is in a powerful position to pick and choose who to include and exclude in the process of consultation and the outcome will be greatly dependent on whose voice is heard. In the past, the Government has turned to traditional charities which are well resourced, powerful and often entrenched in medical model thinking, to represent disabled people. Campbell and Oliver (1996) have distinguished between these traditional charities *for* disabled people and organisations and coalitions *of* disabled people. Research by Drake (1992) demonstrated that the priorities voiced by organisations run by non disabled people *for* disabled people reflected issues of needs, whereas the priorities voiced by organisations led *by* disabled people reflected issues of rights and citizenship.

In summary, disability legislation, policy and provision has, historically, reflected the values and beliefs of those who hold power and the voice of disabled people has remained largely absent from consultation processes. Disabled people and academics have expressed their concern over this failure and argued that legislation and policy needs to accord with the experiences of disabled people. The failure to include a social model definition at the heart of the DDA could potentially result in the formulation of policy and provision aimed at meeting needs and offering compensation, as opposed to reflecting rights and equalising opportunities.

Policy

This section discusses the policy agenda in Wales towards disabled students in higher education and considers the priority and commitment afforded to disability issues by the National Assembly for Wales. It illustrates how the overarching issues of power have influenced the development and implementation of policy in Wales.

The statistics used throughout this section are based on Higher Educational Statistics Agency (HESA) data for 2001/02. Although these statistics provide evidence of low levels of participation in higher education by disabled students and demonstrate inequalities, it is important to remember that HESA data represents and reinforces a medical conceptualisation based on a student's 'disability'.

In 1998 parliament passed the Government of Wales Act, which established the National Assembly for Wales (Transfer of Functions) Order 1999. This enabled the transfer of the devolved powers and responsibilities from the Secretary of State for Wales to the Assembly to take place in July 1999. The National Assembly for Wales (NAW) develops and implements policy within allocated funds received from Treasury. A priority of the Minister for Education and Lifelong Learning, Jane Davidson AM, and the Education and Lifelong Learning Committee was to ensure that a high level of education was available to all the people of Wales. The committee contended that education was the key to liberating talents, extending opportunities and creating wealth (NAW 2000).

In response, a number of high profile investigations and reviews into higher education have taken place in Wales over the last four years. These have comprised a *Policy Review of Higher Education* by the Education and Lifelong Learning Committee (NAW 2001), an *Independent Investigation Group on Student Hardship and Funding in Wales* (Rees 2001), a report on the *Patterns of Higher Education Institutions in Wales* (Ramsden 2002) commissioned by Higher Education Wales (HEW) and the Higher Education Funding Council for Wales (HEFCW), and *Reaching Higher – Higher Education and the Learning Country: A Strategy for the Higher Education Sector in Wales* (NAW 2002).

The Government announced in 1999 its objective of widening participation in higher education to include at least 50 per cent of young people aged below 30 by 2010. Central to issues of widening access, as part of the Welsh Policy Review of Higher Education, two of the major themes were social inclusion and equal opportunities. The Policy Review (NAW 2001: 35) recognised the important link between higher education and employment for disabled people and that higher education provides an opportunity for disabled people to reach their full potential. It further reported that disabled people were seven times more likely to be unemployed than were their non-disabled peers. The number of higher education students in Wales known to have a disability in 2001/02 represented 5.6 per cent of the student population. In order to achieve equality of opportunity and greater social inclusion, the under-representation of disabled students needs be addressed as part of the widening participation policy. The Ramsden Report (2002) contained a section on widening participation and discussed attracting students from non-traditional backgrounds, and referred to qualifications of entry, mature students, ethnicity and social class. However, it made no reference to disability. Welsh Assembly policy also failed to consider the issue of disability among ethnic minorities in their discussions on widening participation, even though HESA data for Wales indicate that only 0.2 per cent of disabled students were from an ethnic minority in 2001/02.

Disabled students were also absent from the written evidence submitted by Higher Education Wales (2001) to the investigation into student hardship and funding. The evidence recognised the conflict between tuition fees and widening access and discussed this in relation to low-income families and mature students, but did not discuss the potential effect on disabled students. The investigation (Rees 2001: 30) did however recognise that disabled students experienced particular financial hardship due to:

(i)   taking 'time out' from studies for health–related reasons;

(ii)   not being able to find work to supplement income;

(iii)   students living in university accommodation (often the most adapted and most appropriate accommodation) not being eligible for housing benefit;

(iv)   delays in receipt of Disabled Students Allowance (DSA) and inconsistencies in its allocation and administration.

The investigation recommended an Assembly review into the anomalies between the support systems and benefits systems affecting disabled students. However, the Assembly felt unable to respond to this recommendation as Welsh policy must comply with overall UK policy.

The conflict between widening access and fees has been recognised by the Assembly and it has been agreed that the variable 'top up' fees announced by the Secretary of State for Education and Skills, Charles Clarke, in the White Paper *The Future of Higher Education* (DfES 2003) will not be implemented in Wales before April 2007 (NAW 2003a). Future responsibility for student support and tuition fees will be transferred to the Assembly in line with policy for Scotland and Northern Ireland (NAW 2003b).

The Policy Review recognised that the fear of debt was a barrier for students from poorer backgrounds and that this was reflected in subtle ways; students were, for example, applying to HEIs closer to home to minimise costs (NAW 2001: 89). The Review failed to consider the likely disproportionate effect on restricting disabled students' choice of courses, institutions and methods of study.

Wales has 13 HEIs and the percentage of disabled students per HEI ranges from the University of Wales College of Medicine with 2.7 per cent to the University of Wales Lampeter at 12.9 per cent. As the Policy Review recognised, more students are choosing to study closer to home because of the fear of debt. This suggests that universities, such as Lampeter which are located in more rural areas are forced to make up their student quota in other ways, including taking increased numbers of disabled students. If this is the case, disabled students will be even more limited in their choice of institution and course of study. These figures also highlight the low level of participation by disabled students at the College of Medicine compared to a higher level of participation (9.7 per cent) at the College of Music and Drama.

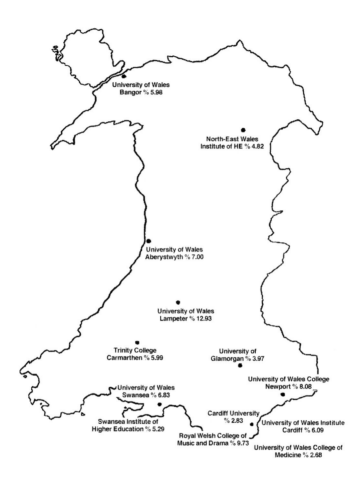

**Figure 1: Percentage of Disabled Students by Higher
Educational Institution in Wales**

The development of disability policy in Wales has appeared to lack the level of expertise found in Scotland and England. The Scottish Higher Education Funding Council (SHEFCE) and the Higher Education Funding Council in England (HEFCE) both established a National Disability Team (NDT) to provide high levels of support. Wales has no such initiative and also lacked the level of financial commitment towards disability provision compared to Scotland and England. The disabled student premium was introduced in Wales in 2002/03 with an allocation of £200 per eligible student (those recorded in HESA returns as full time and in receipt of DSA) (HEFCW 2002). This amount was maintained in 2003/04 at a total cost of £351,400. In addition, a further £148,600 was made available for various disability initiatives (HEFCW 2003). However, in Scotland the disabled student premium represents £591 per eligible student at a total cost of £1,222,000, with a further £250,000 available for disability initiatives (SHEFC 2003). Although in England funding is calculated differently (based on the proportion of students that each institution recruits in receipt of DSA) the allocation for 2003/04 represented £10,317,138 (HEFCE 2003a), with a further £5.48m allocated for 2003/05 towards improving provision for disabled students (HEFCE 2003b). The lack of funding in Wales conveys to HEIs an underlying message that disability provision is not a high priority.

Like the Westminster Government, the Assembly are also in a powerful position to pick and choose who to include and exclude in the process of consultation and representation. The Independent Investigation Group on Student Hardship and Funding in Wales was specifically requested by the Assembly to take evidence from the appropriate interest groups, such as those representing students, providers of education courses and representative bodies (Rees 2001: 3). The 'listen and learn' approach to the consultation process was extensive and 1500 organisations and individuals were invited to present evidence, but arguably the most powerful voices stemmed from the professional bodies. As part of the Policy Review, the Disability Rights Commission, Skill and RNIB Cymru submitted evidence to the Education and Lifelong Learning Committee and were commended for 'eloquently' explaining the 'needs' of disabled students (NAW 2001: 35).

In summary, the Welsh Assembly have recognised the low level of participation by disabled students in higher education and that, as a consequence, disabled people are less likely to reach their full potential. However, despite a number of high profile reports on widening participation, disability policy remains low on the policy agenda. The Welsh Assembly did seek extensive consultation on policy, but the voice representing disabled students appeared to be that of professional bodies and traditional charities, with the focus continuing to be based on meeting needs.

Provision

The final area of discussion examines the experiences and views of students at a Welsh HEI. As part of my PhD research I distributed a questionnaire to all students registered with the Disability Office at a Welsh HEI. From the completed questionnaires I selected twenty students to interview, and it is their views that are discussed here. The students were selected to achieve a representation of impairment categories of impairment as used by HESA, while also reflecting a range of backgrounds and characteristics, such as gender, ethnicity, age, experience of different courses and subject areas and level of study.

For many of these students the first barrier was whether to declare a disability or not when applying to the institution. As Simon explained, 'you are torn between wanting to say and not wanting to say'. Students generally felt a reluctance to 'say' because they felt concerned that they might be labelled, treated differently or even rejected from their choice of course or HEI.

The students interviewed wanted to be independent and not rely on anybody or anything. Independence was important, but in this context was associated with remaining silent. Silence was perceived to create a level playing field, with achievement through individual merit. Students developed their own strategies of coping but when these failed they felt forced to disclose. As Emma stated:

> In some ways I wanted help, but I didn't tell anyone there was a problem, so if I had actually gone and looked for help it would have been better for me.

As a result, she had to suspend her studies in her second year.

The reluctance of students to disclose a disability can result in serious consequences for them. Therefore, how can HEIs encourage students to disclose a disability and address this barrier of disclosure? As long as the focus of policy and provision reflects a medical model and is needs-led, students will feel stigmatised and be reluctant to disclose. If policy and provision encompassed a social model response and recognised a rights focus, this might begin to reduce the stigmatisation experienced by students.

Nevertheless, the majority of the students viewed disability in terms of the medical model. Disability resulted from their impairment, they were at fault and it was their responsibility to adapt and fit in to university life. Students voiced judgements about disability and made comparisons between varying degrees and types of impairment. George, who had a hearing impairment and difficulty talking, but who was able to walk with support, told me that being able to walk meant you could go anywhere and do anything. In contrast, James who had mobility difficulties insisted that communication skills were far more important than anything else. Judgements were also made by the students about the appropriateness of studying various courses. For example, Gareth, a dyslexic student on a mechanical engineering programme, expected departmental attitudes to vary. He thought that not all courses would be appropriate for someone with dyslexia. Students' own perceptions appeared to reflect the everyday assumptions within the HEI setting.

Although students viewed disability in terms of individual impairment, students also recognised that provision had the potential to overcome or reinforce disabling barriers. For Dawn, a visually impaired student, receiving copies of overheads prior to lectures meant being able to follow lectures on the same basis as everybody else. Without them she had difficulty following the lecture and keeping pace with her class.

The learning experience of students was very dependent on how far departments and academic staff listened to, and responded to, their concerns. For instance, James had found his department exceptionally supportive and responsive and felt that his opinion and advice was actively sought on issues of disability. However, in other instances students felt that their views were perceived as insignificant. They also felt daunted in having to inform and remind lecturers about their disability. Some students did not know who they should go and see, or where to go, or found the whole process time consuming and demoralising.

Staff perceptions also varied, not only across the HEI, but within departments. Some lecturers recognised the disabling barriers experienced by students and others continued to see disability as a consequence of individual impairment. Dawn had experienced very different responses from different lecturers. Some lecturers had provided her with extensive notes and directed her to specific reading and other lecturers had told her 'to sort herself out'. Other lecturers had drawn attention to her impairment by their comments and actions and, as Dawn argued, 'they are actually making you different to everyone else'.

During the interviews, students also discussed their relationship with the Disability Office. Some felt a sense of gratitude towards the Disability Office, David, who was having numerous difficulties, told me 'they have done enough already, they didn't have to do what they've done. I'm grateful for what they've done'. The relationship between these students and the Disability Office appeared to be based on meeting needs. Other students had felt very let down, George, who had studied as an undergraduate at the HEI and was currently working towards his Masters, told me:

> They don't care, they don't care at all about the disabled student … they don't have a clue what is going on. … I don't have anything to do with them, so I just sort things out for myself. So that's much better, 'cos it gets things sorted out.

Students often felt that help was promised, but did not always materialise, and that they had to be proactive in ensuring issues were resolved.

A fear of being threatened and bullied by the Disability Office came out in Natalie's interview. Natalie asked me about the number of questionnaires I had received back from students, as she was aware of students who would not complete my questionnaire because of 'a fear' of the Disability Office 'finding out'. Students from special educational backgrounds appeared to be more afraid and lack confidence compared to students from mainstream backgrounds. Where students had raised concerns about the Disability Office they often felt there had been a failure to address these issues.

Central to the student experience was the Disabled Students Allowance (DSA). The DSA was introduced to cover additional costs and expenses incurred by students. It is awarded through the students' local education authority (LEA), with the student required to attend an assessment centre. The students in my research sample experienced long delays in waiting for assessments to be carried out, in equipment and software arriving, and in receiving suitable training in the use of the equipment and software. These delays caused them significant anxiety and affected their coursework. The assessment process was generally disliked and viewed negatively. Students felt disappointed that assessors failed to listen to them and Gareth commented that when he had his assessment he was told 'you need this, this and this, because your symptoms say'. The assessor seemed to have fixed preconceptions within a medical/individualised model and made suggestions that Gareth knew would not be appropriate. When Gareth made alternative suggestions he felt that these were ignored. Gareth had felt quite confident about the assessment process and told me:

> I've played this game for many years now, all the way from assessments in Bangor to assessments in Cardiff. I'm a bit used to it. I wasn't overwhelmed by it.

The assessment for Rachel, however, was difficult and she had felt pressurised into agreeing with the assessor's recommendations. The assessment left her very upset and she told her mother what had happened. Her mother stepped in and the assessment was changed. Rachel's opinion apparently carried little weight.

Two assessors were present at Dawn's assessment and she felt completely ignored, while the jargon used during the assessment reinforced an unequal power relationship.

It was a waste of time ... I was just sitting there and these two blokes were having this discussion like over my head ...all this like computer jargon and I had no idea what they were on about and so even if I did want to say and butt in, I wouldn't have known what they were talking about in the first place.

Assessors were considered to be 'experts' by the students and in most cases students accepted their recommendations. For example, the equipment and software that arrived for James was not adequate and as James told me 'I was told it was the best. I accepted it and it turned out not to be'. Some students had on-going problems with their equipment, and most students I talked to purchased additional software to meet their requirements.

Overall, the assessment process reflected a medical model approach, with the assessors defining the problems and providing the solutions. Students were also unaware of their entitlements and often accepted the word of the assessor as final. Only one student knew he had the right to administer the DSA directly and not through the HEI.

Students viewed disability as isolating, but where they had formed friendships they had found invaluable support. Often when everything else failed it was friends who had stepped in and lent equipment, taken notes, read material and offered assistance. However, not all students found it so easy to 'fit in' and make friends. Some were conscious about using laptops and dictaphones in lectures; others felt excluded as Dawn explained:

You never get any of the other students coming to say hello or anything, or we are going for coffee, do you fancy coming?

Having friends helped to break the isolation and to overcome the feeling of being excluded, but deeply ingrained in students' attitudes was a medical view of disability. Ash et al. (1997), researching colleges of further education, also found that student attitudes were entrenched in a medical model of disability.

Preconceived ideas of disability were also prevalent throughout the Students' Union (SU) and societies. The advice and support offered by the SU was welcomed by students who viewed it as a place to turn to in times of crisis, but did not view it as a body in which they could participate. Events held by the SU were often at inaccessible venues and when James stood for the SU elections he found it difficult to campaign effectively. In my own experience of attending SU meetings, I asked for paperwork in a suitable format and when this request repeatedly failed and I raised my concerns with the General Secretary, I was told that 'I should be grateful for the help I received'.

The SU viewed disability as meeting needs and not in terms of rights. Societies were also seen as exclusive, as Philip found when he approached one of the societies and met with a negative reaction. Attitudes in the SU, as throughout the HEI, appeared to be stuck in a medicalised/ individualised conceptualisation of disability.

Getting involved and having a voice in HEI life seemed beyond the reach of students. Emma expressed an interest in the departmental student staff committee, but felt that those normally elected were 'the ones that might run a club or society, and literally have a fantastic life, and they are into everything'. I asked students their opinion about starting a society/forum where they could share ideas and experiences. This suggestion was welcomed as a way to offer support and to bring about change. Several students said it would have been useful to have known how other students had managed and how they had resolved difficulties. As Emma commented 'it is only when you have experienced something directly yourself can you really understand'. This was linked to bringing about change as Paul argued 'in order to make things work there must be student input, otherwise it's just academic staff and professionals'; and as Marcie commented, 'staff are not aware of problems'.

The students I interviewed wanted to study and do well, but as James commented it is 'sheer damn hardworking determination' that gets disabled students through. Students have to struggle and overcome all the disabling barriers in higher education just to be able to study. Other research has produced similar findings (Preece 1995; Hall and Tinklin 1998; Borland and James 1999).

In summary, my interviews highlighted a range of experiences and views among disabled students within a HEI setting. It was evident from the student's comments that HEI perceptions generally reflected a medical model view. This was illustrated when discussing issues of disclosure, experiences within academic departments, interactions with support and assessment staff and in their relationships with other students. In addition, students often felt their own views were regarded as insignificant or simply ignored. However, students also recognised that, potentially, by sharing their experiences, change was possible.

Conclusion

By examining power, policy and provision, it is evident that the voice of disabled people has remained largely unheard in the development and implementation of policies in the field of higher education. The views and 'representation' of disabled people has largely been dominated by, or taken over by, charities, and professional bodies. This has resulted in the formulation of legislation and policy, as with the DDA, that followed a medical model approach and failed to accord with the experiences of disabled people. However, if a social model interpretation was adopted then this has the potential to bring about radical change within higher education, with the everyday perceptions of disability being challenged and the diversity of all students being valued.

Although, student views and experiences varied considerably from discussions on impairment and disability, relevant courses of study, coping with academic life, claiming allowances, to relationships with HEI staff and other students, it was apparent that students were trying to fit in to HEI life. However, this does not challenge the 'everyday' assumptions of disability. Instead, it is about students negotiating the barriers that exist in higher education. Disabled students now have legal access to higher education, but this is not inclusive while they have to adapt to the existing, exclusionary environment.

The Welsh Assembly has stressed the importance of higher education in creating 'equal opportunities' and acknowledged the specific barriers experienced by disabled people. Nevertheless, little effective policy action has been taken, leaving a strong impression that the social inclusion of disabled people remains a low priority.

Bibliography

Ash, A., Bellew, J., Davies, M., Newman, T. and Richardson, L. 1997: Everybody In? The Experience of disabled students in further education. *Disability and Society*, 12 (4), 605-621.

Armstrong, F. and Barton, L. 1999: Is there anyone there concerned with human rights? Cross-cultural connections, disability and the struggle for change in England. In F. Armstrong and L. Barton (eds), *Disability, Human Rights and Education: Cross-cultural perspectives*. Buckingham: Open University Press.

Arnstein, S. 1969: A ladder of citizen participation. *American Institute of Planners Journal,* 35 (4), 216-24.

Barton, L. and Armstrong, F. 2001: Disability, Education and Inclusion: Cross-Cultural Issues and Dilemmas. In G. Albrecht, K. Seelman and M. Bury (eds), *Handbook of Disability Studies*. London: Sage.

Borland, J. and James, S. 1999: The Learning Experience of Students with Disabilities in Higher Education. A case study of a UK University. *Disability and Society,* 14 (1), 85-101.

Campbell, J. and Oliver, M. 1996: *Disability Politics: Understanding our past, changing our future.* London: Routledge.

DfEE 1995a: *The Disability Discrimination Act.* London: HMSO.

DfEE 1995b: *Guidance on matters to be taken into account in determining questions relating to the definition of disability.* London: HMSO.

DfEE 2001: *Special Educational Needs and Disability Act.* London: HMSO.

DfES 2003: *The Future of Higher Education.* London: HMSO.

Disability Rights Task Force 1999: *From Exclusion to Inclusion: Final Report of the Disability Rights Task Force.* London: HMSO.

Drake, R. F. 1992: *A little brief authority? A sociological analysis of consumer participation in voluntary agencies in Wales.* PhD thesis. University of Cardiff.

Drake, R.F. 1999: *Understanding Disability Policies.* Basingstoke: Macmillan.

Drake, R. F. 2002: Disabled people, voluntary organisations and participation in policy making. *Policy and Politics,* 30 (3), 373-385.

Hall, J. and Tinklin, T. 1998: *Students First: The Experiences of Disabled Students in Higher Education.* Edinburgh: The Scottish Council for Research in Education. www.scre.ac.uk/resreport/rr85/index.html

HEFCE 2003a: *Disability funding 2003-04.*
http://www.hefce.ac.uk/widen/SLDD/grant0304.xls

HEFCE 2003b: *2003-2005 special funding programme: Improving provision for disabled students.*
http://www.hefce.ac.uk/widen/sldd/fund03-05.asp

HEFCW 2002: *Recurrent Grant: 2002/03.* Ref: WO2/18HE, Cardiff: HEFCW.

HEFCW 2003: *Recurrent Grant: 2003/04.* Ref: WO3/18HE, Cardiff: HEFCW.

Higher Education Wales 2001: *Written evidence to the National Assembly for Wales Independent Inquiry into Student Hardship and Funding: From Uncertain Charity to Certain Clarity.* Cardiff: HEW.

Hulley, T. and Clarke, J. 1991: Social Problems: social construction and social causation. In M.Loney, R.Bocock and J.Clarke (eds), *The State of the Market: Politics and Welfare in Contemporary Britain.* London: Sage.

National Assembly for Wales 2000: *Putting Wales First: A Partnership for the People of Wales.* Cardiff: NAW.

National Assembly for Wales 2001: *Policy Review of Higher Education*. Cardiff: NAW.

National Assembly for Wales 2002: *Reaching Higher: Higher Education and the Learning Country – A Strategy for the higher education sector in Wales*. Cardiff: NAW.

National Assembly for Wales 2003a: *No top up fees for Wales*. Press Release. Cardiff: NAW.

National Assembly for Wales 2003b: *Student support and tuition fee regime to transfer to Wales*. Press Release. Cardiff: NAW.

Northern Officers Group 2003: *Defining Impairment and Disability*. http://www.suntimes.btinternet.co.uk/info/disdefine.htm

Oliver, M. 1990: *Politics of Disablement*. London: Macmillan.

Preece, J. 1995: Disability and Adult Education – the consumer view. *Disability and Society*, 10 (1), 87-102.

Ramsden, B. 2002: *Patterns of Higher Education Institutions in Wales*. Cardiff: HEW/HEFCW.

Rees, T. 2001: *Independent Investigation Group on Student Hardship and Funding in Wales, A Report to the Minister for Education and Lifelong Learning at the National Assembly for Wales*. Cardiff: NAW.

SHEFC 2003: *Main grants in support of teaching and research for 2003/04*. Ref: HE/09/03, Edinburgh: SHEFC.

Thompson, N. 1998: *Promoting Equality*. Basingstoke: Palgrave.

Tomlinson, J. 1995: Disability, learning difficulties and further education: the work of the FEFC's specialist committee. In C.Hewitson-Ratcliffe (ed.), *Current Developments in Further Education: The Third John Baillie Memorial Conference*. London: Skill.

UPIAS 1976: *Fundamental Principles of Disability*. London: Union of the Physically Impaired Against Segregation.

CHAPTER 8

Incorporating the Social Model into Outcome-Focused Social Care Practice with Disabled People

Jennifer Harris

Introduction

Social care practice in the UK is routinely concerned with the identification of service users' 'needs' during social services assessments. Local Authorities have had a duty to carry out an assessment of need for community care services with people who appear to need them since the enactment of the NHS and Community Care Act 1990 (Section 47(1)). Previous to that they had duties of assessment of individual needs of everyone who fell within Section 29 of the National Assistance Act 1948 which were enacted through the provisions of the Chronically Sick and Disabled Persons Act 1970 (Section 2). It is asserted here that the focus upon 'needs' has become impractical at both the conceptual and practice levels in recent times.

This chapter begins with an exploration of this move away from the focus on the 'assessment of needs' and offers a more fruitful model of service philosophy. This is the outcomes approach (OCA) that has been used by the author in a research and development project within one local authority area in the UK. The outcome-focused approach is consistent with the spirit of these Acts but challenges the notions of expert power bound up in the framework of assessment in favour of one in which service users utilise the skills and experience of professionals in the identification and achievement of their desired outcomes.

The OCA discussed below incorporates key elements of the social model of disability into routine assessment and review documentation used every day by social care professionals working with disabled people. Social

Service staff receive training in the OCA and the use of newly designed outcomes-focused documentation, which directs the professional to think laterally in assisting the service user to achieve their desired outcome. Thus for the OCA to work properly, the professional must act as a facilitator, as originally envisaged in the NHS and Community Care Act 1990, rather than as a direct service provider or gate-keeper to services.

The project is funded by the Department of Health and is approximately half way through a three-year term. The chapter describes the commencement of the outcomes focus, initial findings concerning successes and problems in its introduction.

Background

The research and development project described here forms the first attempt to change the focus of social care assessment and review from 'needs' to 'outcomes' within a Disability Service. The concept of 'outcomes' as operationalised within the project means that the focus of the work is upon the goals or desired achievements of the service user. The main thrust of direct work with service users for the professional becomes assisting in the identification of these goals (immediate, medium term and long term), and thereafter facilitating their achievement. These processes are documented using newly designed outcome-focused forms that direct and guide the professional in these tasks.

Prior to the innovation of the Outcomes Project, the Social Services department (in common with most other social services nationally) focused its work around the identification of service user 'needs'. There are a number of reasons why focusing upon 'needs' is problematic, both conceptually and practically. The identification of 'needs' is no mean feat, since theoretically these are subjective, potentially endless and relative to one's immediate situation. Direct work with service users is necessarily subjective, the focus being upon their immediate situation, and support requirements. However, to state that the focus of work should be the 'identification of needs' implies a level of objectivity that is rarely present. It also implies that the professional will be working in a 'diagnostic' capacity and contains inherent strict hierarchical implications concerning the relationship between professional and service user (French and Swain 2001: 735).

Focusing upon 'needs' is also problematic because peoples' needs change over time, (often quickly in crisis situations) and there is no specified point at which the work, or a distinct part of it, can be said to have been achieved. In consequence, the work frequently lacks direction and purpose. It is also therefore virtually impossible to know whether resources used have been correctly or fairly targeted. It is similarly almost impossible to measure success or failure.

Another problem with focusing on the identification of 'needs' is that work is structured around a moving goalpost, since once some needs are identified and achieved, there are almost certainly other needs to be met. This way of working engenders a situation where there is no distinct endpoint to the work between professional and service user and the date at which involvement with social services will end is unclear. This scenario leads to situations in which disabled people become 'service users', the point of the work is unspecific, it cannot be judged to have been achieved and involvement with professionals is open-ended over time. Work structured around needs therefore enforces and perpetuates dependency-creation (Oliver 1993; French and Swain 2001: 744). Furthermore, 'needs' are necessarily relative to a particular situation only and their resolution, and therefore the involvement with professionals, can only ever be partial.

Introducing the outcomes focus
In the outcomes project, the challenge set was to change professional practice and documentation used, away from one in which the pro-fessional steers, guides, pronounces the identification of 'needs' and the proposed 'intervention', towards practice driven by the service user, who is encouraged and facilitated to identify their 'outcomes'; a set of immediate, medium and long term goals that they wish to achieve. The focus on outcomes overcomes many of the deficiencies of the 'needs' model described above.

Focusing on the service user's desired outcomes means the work is targeted and specific, with a distinct endpoint in mind. Review dates are set and closely monitored by the service user in terms of achievement of their outcomes. The focus of the work moves away from professional 'assessment of the service user's needs' to the identification and facilitation of desired outcomes, specified by the service user. When the outcomes focus works as it was designed therefore, the service user is in control of the entire process, from identification of outcomes, to participating in their achievement and evaluation of the success or failure of the venture. The role of the professional is to assist the service user in the achievement of their outcomes only. As discussed below, the latter implies a radical culture shift from existing practice.

The research team were concerned to adhere to the social model of disability (Oliver 1990; Barnes 1991) when designing the documentation (particularly in the use of language) and staff training with a view to steering professional practice towards a focus upon 'access' and away from the traditional professional focus upon function and deficit. The new documents also contain a direction to utilise mainstream, instead of segregated, facilities.

The outcome-focused documents incorporated a framework, which was developed in consultation with all stakeholders and from previous research findings (Bamford et al. 1999). This original outcomes framework contained many core criteria that had been found to be of interest and use to disabled service users, but the language used in the framework was old-fashioned and paternalistic, more medical than social model with an acceptance of limitation, functionality and deficit. Our first task was to revise the framework therefore. The revised version of the outcomes framework, devised for the project, contains a much stronger focus on access to educational, training, employment and leisure opportunities, and also focuses upon supporting parenting. The outcomes framework that appears in the new documentation explicitly directs the professional to ascertain the situation as seen by the service user. The spirit of the social model is most evident in the user control aspects of the design and designation of professionals as facilitators/ assistants within the identification of outcomes process.

Experience in this kind of research has shown that one of the best ways of influencing professional practice in particular ways is to design documentation incorporating the innovation and train professionals in its usage. However, it has also been noted that professionals sometimes struggle with the concept of outcomes and their professional and organisational culture militates against introduction of such innovations (Qureshi et al. 1998). Previous research and development work conducted as part of the wider outcomes programme suggested that, once staff have a clear understanding of the outcomes concept, the outcomes focus provides a clearer basis for care planning and briefing providers (Qureshi et al. 2000). Bearing these provisos in mind, in consultation with all stakeholders, we devised outcome-focused documentation structured in such a way that the professional is prompted to assist the service user to express and record their desired outcome.

The OCA assumes the professional has a capacity to act creatively, to put aside the idea of professional as person responsible for arranging services, in favour of acting as a facilitator, enabling the service user to achieve the desired outcome/s. The approach also assumes that the service user is in control of the process. This is however not a new idea at all.

> The modern challenge is to provide alternatives to current practice so that workers and disabled people can share expertise in barrier identification and removal, both at the personal level (for the individual setting their own goals) and at the social level where public facilities need to be made truly public (and not just for able-bodied citizens) (Finkelstein 1991: 35).

Twelve years ago that was seen as groundbreaking and out of reach of most disabled people experiencing social care services. Interestingly, every part of that statement is exemplified in the OCA, but depressingly, the introduction of outcomes is still currently seen as innovative, unusual and difficult to procure in practice.

Beginning work on outcomes

The outcomes focus, as operationalised in this project, locates the service user at the heart of assessment processes and regards their requirements as paramount. The aim and objectives of the work to be done (the outcomes) are identified by the service user through a process of negotiation with professionals from social services. This did not sit easily with current professional practice in the local authority at the project outset. Most specifically, 'expert power' is threatened by the introduction of outcomes as conceptualised in this project (French 1995) since the professional is directed to act as facilitator, ceding control and responsibility for the achievement of the outcome/s to the service user.

All staff in social services that are in contact with disabled service users (senior managers, care managers, occupational therapists, community care workers, sensory impairment workers) were trained in the use of the outcome-focused documents. This comprised an initial training session, group work and discussion with live examples, followed by on-going support meetings over a 6-month trial period – the researched trial implementation (RTI). All outcome-focused documents were collected and assessed by the research team for correct usage of the outcome focus and all staff and participating service users were interviewed. The discussion below concentrates on emerging practice issues to date.

Practice issue number 1: the problem of outcome not 'needs' identification

As noted above, previous to the introduction of the outcome focus, the task of these professionals was the identification of 'needs'. Professionals most often saw the solution to these 'needs' as a 'service' (latterly in-house provision, most recently from a mixed set of statutory and voluntary providers).

The majority of staff from all grades eventually grasped the key differences between focusing on needs and focusing on outcomes. However, some staff experienced difficulty in moving from 'needs' to 'outcomes'. In these cases, practice did not substantially change and staff continued to record 'needs' on the outcome-focused documents. This was obviously occurring and it looked most peculiar. Thus, where the outcomes are to be recorded we had examples under 'health' stating 'to use the toilet' and the planned action to achieve the outcome being 'raised toilet seat'. This restricted and restrictive mode of working that was being used by these professionals prior to the project proved singularly impervious to the introduction of the outcomes focus.

Depressingly, staff in these instances failed to grasp the difference between the identification of a need and an outcome. To be clear, the research team were not disputing that functional items are important to service users and therefore must be recorded as important in cases where they are required. The staff in these instances however, were making these functional items the whole focus of their work and this reduces the possibilities of exploring the whole context of the service user's aspirations (their outcomes), demeans service users by focusing solely upon bodily functions in this way and reinstates (and in many ways reinforces) the expert power of the professional over the service user. These facets of this type of working also compound each other. Reducing interaction with service users to the resolution of functional items is the antithesis of the OCA, since it limits, rather than expands, service users' aspirations.

Practice issue number 2: problems with width and breadth of the OCA

The concepts underpinning the framework were purposefully 'wide' in orientation, to facilitate the broadest possible consideration of the options available. Professionals struggle with both the width and breadth of the framework in several ways. Firstly, in using the new care plan, some feel a need to cover all the items in the framework (despite instruction to the contrary). However, obviously not all items are appropriate for all service users. One professional raised at a monitoring meeting that the documents are inappropriate because she worried about feeling obliged, (when working in this cover-all manner), to raise the issue of 'employment' with a terminally ill service user. In this case, the professional's decision was therefore not to use the outcome-focused documents with terminally ill service users on a point of principle. This, it was claimed, was because the only 'outcome' they could see was the service user's death and they considered it morbid to discuss this. Despite support and encouragement by the research team this professional singularly failed to make the leap of imagination to consider that terminally ill people may have outcomes they wish to achieve and that working in this way can still prove to be useful.

Practice issue number 3: falling back into provider of service mode

Another feature of the old 'needs-led' system was that professionals appeared to rush to reach a service solution. This continued under the outcomes project when, instead of conducting a dialogue on the service user's desired outcomes, the professional 'leaped into the fray' – cutting short the conversational element in a rush to identify a solution that is a service (generally a service that can be readily accessed by the professional only). This was found to sometimes result from an over-developed sense of responsibility on the part of the professional, but was also sometimes linked to pressure of work and burgeoning case-load.

Cases were noted where the professional clearly does act as facilitator and the service user does identify their desired outcome. However, at this point, sometimes the professional 'forgets' that all stakeholders have both a duty and a responsibility to work towards this outcome and moves back into provision mode rather than enacting their envisaged role. An example of this is a case that was adhering to the outcomes framework at first. The service user identified a need for training in computer/IT skills that the professional noted. The professional however, then identified a class (which should have been done more appropriately by the service user) and set about identifying transport to the class. However, when this proved problematic (no accessible buses were available), the professional then took the service user there every week, acknowledging to the research team that this was not actually part of their job description, or a good use of their time. This example demonstrates that there are various places within the process at which the professional can 'revert' to the type of traditional practice that assesses, codifies and provides for identified 'needs'. It is interesting to consider what ought to have happened in this example; should the professional have joined forces with local disabled people campaigning for an accessible bus service; should they have used information resources to identify funding sources to enable the service user to arrange transport? Both of the latter would adhere to the spirit of outcome-focused social care practice.

Practice issue number 4: 'asking for the moon'

Professionals were concerned that service users would ask for outcomes that could not be supported and that, given resources available, it was impossible to provide. Experience of using the outcome focus with other service user groups however, has proved that service users rarely do this, (Qureshi et al. 2000).

Under the OCA, we told the professionals in training, you are *not* wholly responsible for the achievement of the desired outcome. The outcome-focused documents support this as there is space to record the part being played by other stakeholders, crucially, the service user themselves, informal carers, professionals from housing departments and so on. On the whole, this was welcomed by professionals, who, under the 'needs' approach had felt pressured to meet them all, and invariably, inadequate when this was unachievable. This did not wholly dispel professional anxieties however, although it should be noted here that these were more hypothesised and voiced as concerns than actually experienced in practice by the professionals in question.

Practice issue number 5: reluctance to move outside of narrow service solutions

Professionals demonstrated a reluctance to move practice outside of a range of 'safe' narrow, clearly delineated, service solutions. This has been noted before in previous studies (Harris and Bamford 2001). It would be easy to apportion blame for this at the feet of the professional, however, we have some initial evidence that service users may approach social services with a narrow service solution in mind, often because they know someone who has obtained that service through this means. So for example, a service user may know someone who has obtained stair rails and approaches social services with this in mind for themselves. Under this circumstance, the outcome-focused approach, which assumes that the service user would start from first principles by identifying a desired outcome of 'access to all areas of the home' before discussing creative solutions, can fail to get off the ground. Thus, both the professional, through the rush to reach the service solution stage and the service user through limiting requests to functional items or discrete services, may prematurely close off avenues to the pursuit of the desired outcomes.

Practice issue number 6: inability to grasp/reluctance to accept the outcomes concept

Not all professionals find it easy to understand the concept of outcomes. Some, as discussed above, struggle with the differences that come when moving away from 'needs' especially when they have been trained in and have used for many years, a very different style of working. Some professionals with a health background (particularly occupational therapists) struggle to accept the framework and in particular dislike the width and breadth of its coverage for two reasons. Firstly, they expressed a preference for 'assessment instruments' that permit the explicit inclusion of 'functional categories' such as 'toileting' and 'feeding'. This issue arose on a frequent basis in support sessions and the OCA was declaimed for its deficiencies in this area. In actual fact, the core activities underlying all these concepts could easily and appropriately be encapsulated on the outcome-focused documents, under categories of 'health' and 'nutrition'. Whilst the process of including all stakeholder comments into the design and approach was protracted and wide-ranging, the research team refused to incorporate functional categories that focus on deficiency within the outcomes framework since we consider the terms in the outcomes framework to be both more respectful to service users, more egalitarian in approach and more in line with the spirit of the social model of disability.

Secondly, the outcome-focused documents contain on the first page a direction to the professional to write within a box titled 'summary of presenting situation *as seen by service user*' (italics added). The notion of the service user's priorities being delineated and expressed prominently as the focus for all later work, caused a few professionals considerable anxiety. Many problems were anticipated and proclaimed with both the prominence and shift in power relations inherent in the directive, although the vast majority were, in actual work situations with service users, unfounded.

Practice issue number 7: relinquishing expert/professional notions of power

Some professionals proved unwilling to allow service users to sit in the driving seat – not always for the reasons of 'fear of becoming redundant within the profession' either. Power struggles ensued, particularly with the group of occupational therapists. These objections were couched in terms of issues of 'professionalism' (for example, giving excuses for not using the new documentation and approach as these would diverge from those approved by the professional membership organisation of occupational therapists). 'Expert power' is threatened by the introduction of outcomes. This is because the outcomes focus as practiced in this study, directs the professional to place the identification and achievement of the service user's desired outcomes as paramount.

The research team heard several excuses for not adopting outcomes. For example, one excuse was that the service user was 'not able to engage fully due to impairment'. This was said about a service user who has Multiple Sclerosis and who has fluctuating cognitive impairment. In these cases the research team found it difficult to understand why the identification of outcomes cannot take place at a time when the service user feels well and is not done when they do not. This could be another example of the rush to reach a service solution, but is more likely to denote that the timing of work is still more convenient to the professional than to the service user. Either way, it appears that the notion of the centrality of the service user's role is lost in such cases.

In one outcome-focused document the professional is prompted to record the desired outcomes of the service user. The document includes the outcomes framework with a column at the side for descriptive information. One problem noted however was that documents were returned with insertions such as, 'Mr. X wants to be able to do Y' rather than 'to do Y' (as would be the case if the service user had been steering the interaction). These instances were early indications that some professionals were struggling to 'convert' to the outcomes focus and were reverting to their former practice of expressing their expert judgement as to what should happen, or be provided.

The outcomes framework, training and documents were designed upon the premise of equality between service users and professionals, with the in-built assumption that professionals would act as facilitators in the service user achieving their desired outcome/s. Some professionals in the study have so far proved unwilling to allow service users to enact this role. Notably these professionals are mostly occupational therapists, implying that training and practice in medical settings does not sit easily with the outcomes ethos. Interestingly, care managers, community care workers and sensory impairment workers, whose professions are more influenced by the social work tradition did not appear to experience such conflict over their professional standing. A number of 'excuses' are given for the failure to shift practice in this way. For example, the researchers were told that the service user would 'not be able' to engage with outcomes fully due to the nature of the impairment. In these circumstances, professionals appear to feel honour-bound to 'take over' rather than seek a creative solution that would adhere to the spirit of the outcomes focus.

Practice issue number 8: fear of 'Big Brother'

Some professionals were concerned that their employers will use the OCA, and the greater accountability it affords, to 'check up' on staff performance. In other words, they fear that assisting service users to detail outcomes and documenting these in depth may highlight professional inadequacy in either recording or professional practice. As the project continued over an extended period of time, both the use of the new documents and practice were subjected to regular assessment by the research team and scrutiny by the management level of the local authority.

In the majority of cases, staff had high levels of professional competence at the outset of the project and these staff did not register disquiet. However, some staff who had remained resistant to innovations over a considerable period of years, were clearly threatened by being placed in the limelight by the outcomes project. Some staff were not using the officially sanctioned documentation at all, as they preferred other forms that, at some time in the past, had been allowed. These professionals particularly struggled with the new outcomes documentation, because although it was built on the officially sanctioned forms, they had to struggle with two innovations. In many cases, criticisms levelled at the outcomes documentation in such cases, proved to be at items on the officially sanctioned forms (that had not been changed by the researchers). All professionals are accountable to their employers, and those in the provision of public services also have a duty to react responsively to their customers. The researchers found it somewhat curious to have to point this out.

Conclusion

The intellectual puzzle for future stages of the project is to disentangle which of the practice issues identified are caused by staff misunderstanding the outcomes focus, misunderstanding the social model (or both) and the extent to which any of these problems are intentional or accidental. Without doubt, the practice issues identified in this chapter demonstrate that enacting the OCA is challenging for professionals and forces them to reconsider a number of assumptions about their daily practice with service users.

Some professionals appear to have a problem in moving from the identification of 'needs' to 'outcomes'. Partly this appears due to entrenched patterns of working with service users, in which professional practice has built up over a number of years. Moving outside of the parameters of these patterns causes professional anxiety. When this occurs it is generally professionals such as occupational therapists with health service training who experience most anxiety. At least some of this anxiety (and consequential reluctance to operationalise the OCA) appears to be caused by reluctance to relinquish expert power. Interestingly, this is not always due to a wish to retain employment, but seems more bound up with a fear of the consequences of failure to achieve the more aspirational items that service users identify when using the OCA. Under the social model, we should of course expect that any challenge to professional power and status will be resisted (Oliver 1990) but the form this resistance takes, appears to change over time in response to local circumstances.

Some professionals fall back into provider of service mode instead of thinking and acting creatively with service users to generate solutions to social problems. Some professionals also appear to show reluctance to move outside of narrow service solutions. This again is caused by the explicitly aspirational tone of the OCA. It does not appear to be directly related to any tenets of the social model of disability but is caused by professional habituation in relying upon sets of 'safe' service solutions. Assisting professionals to step outside of these narrow service solutions and engage with disabled people's aspirations is an on-going objective for the research team.

Although some professionals claim an inability to grasp the outcomes concept, this is not always wholly believable, since it is often the least trained, less professionally educated staff who manage to operationalise the OCA with the least amount of tribulation. Undoubtedly, the outcome-focused documentation confronts some notions of professionalism and the right to practice within certain professional codes, head-on. The research team and management view these conflicts as areas for further work.

The professional fear of 'Big Brother' that the OCA appears to stimulate may be well founded. Although this was not an intentional aspect of the project remit, the OCA could certainly be used for this type of purpose by social services management. For this reason, although not designed for this purpose, staff may see outcomes as supporting this intention.

The research is incomplete, as noted previously, but the omens are good to date. This chapter has concentrated upon issues arising to date and many of these concern conflicts of interest and notions of professionalism. However, it should be noted that even at this early stage, service users appear to value the OCA and appear comfortable with setting goals and working towards them. Several service users of long standing contact have noted in surprised and delighted tones that this is the first time they have been asked for these types of views, or that professionals have discussed a distinct end product in working with them. Service users also appear to welcome the greater accountability and personal control afforded by the OCA. The challenge of introducing an outcomes approach that incorporates elements of the social model of disability has raised a number of professional practice issues that the research team will continue to address and consider.

Bibliography

Bamford, C., Qureshi, H., Nicholas, E. and Vernon, A. 1999: Outcomes of social care for disabled people and carers. *Outcomes in Community Care Practice No. 6.* York: Social Policy Research Unit, University of York.

Barnes, C. 1991: *Disabled people in Britain and discrimination: A case for anti-discriminatory legislation.* London: Hurst and Company.

Finkelstein, V. 1991: Disability: An administrative challenge? (The Health and Welfare Heritage). In M. Oliver (ed.), *Social Work, Disabled people and Disabling Environments.* London: Jessica Kingsley.

French, S. 1995: Visually impaired physiotherapists: their struggle for acceptance and survival. *Disability and Society*, 10 (1), 3-20.

French, S. and Swain, J. 2001: The relationship between disabled people and health and welfare professionals. In G. Albrecht, K. Seelman & M. Bury (eds), *Handbook of Disability Studies.* Thousand Oaks, CA.: Sage, 734-753.

Harris, J. and Bamford, C. 2001: The Uphill Struggle: Services for Deaf and hard of hearing people; issues of Equality, Participation and Access. *Disability and Society*, 16 (7), 969-980.

Oliver, M. 1990: *The Politics of Disablement.* Basingstoke: Macmillan.

Oliver, M. 1993: Disability and dependency: a creation of industrial societies? In J. Swain, V. Finkelstein, S. French and M. Oliver (eds), *Disabling Barriers – enabling environments.* London: Sage, 49-60.

Qureshi, H., Patmore, C., Nicholas, E. and Bamford, C. 1998: *Overview: Outcomes of social care for older people and carers. Outcomes in*

Community Care Practice No.5. York: Social Policy Research Unit,
University of York.

Qureshi, H., Bamford, C., Nicholas, E., Patmore, C. and Harris, J. 2000:
*Outcomes in Social Care Practice: Developing an outcome focus in
care management and user surveys*. York: Social Policy Research
Unit, University of York.

CHAPTER 9

The Implementation of Direct Payments: issues for user-led organisations in Scotland

Charlotte Pearson

Introduction

Since the implementation of direct payments in April 1997, there has been a concerted drive to increase the number of disabled service users across the UK. Having been initially introduced as enabling legislation, local authorities in Scotland, England and Wales are now required to offer direct payments to all eligible persons. Recently this was extended to include older people, 16 and 17 year olds, parents of disabled children and 'carers' in England and Wales. Over the next few years in Scotland, implementation of the Community Care and Health (Scotland) Act 2002 will see direct payments broadened to cover children's services and all persons defined as community care users. These include persons who are: frail, receiving rehabilitation after an accident or operation, fleeing domestic abuse, a refugee, homeless, or recovering from alcohol or drug dependency (Scottish Executive 2002). Such a move clearly marks an important policy shift and has significant implications for the disability movement, which has fought a long campaign to secure direct payments for disabled people.

Whilst in many areas of England and Wales, there are increasing numbers of direct payment users (Department of Health 2002), six years after implementation in Scotland policy remains largely marginalised (Pearson 2004). The first major study into direct payments in Scotland carried out by Witcher et al. (2000) confirmed this limited availability with only 13 out of the 32 local authorities having fully operational or pilot schemes and a total of 143 users. Although more recent figures show a rise to 534 users (Scottish Executive 2003a), this represents only a fraction of the total in England and Wales (Pearson 2004). The reasons for this delay centre on an anti-market discourse (Pearson 2000) whereby many local authorities view direct payments as a privatisation tool to erode key social services. In addition, weak disability activism has also contributed as an important constraining factor. As such, the basis for policy expansion in Scotland differs from England and Wales in that direct payments have been far less popular as a mainstream service option for disabled people across many areas.

Throughout this time, the role of support organisations has been identified as being critical in the successful development of direct payments across the UK (Hasler et al. 1999; Witcher et al. 2000). Whilst Centres for Independent/ Integrated Living (CILs) have traditionally been viewed as the main centres of expertise for user support, there has also been a growth in other local support groups over the past few years. However as Morgan, Barnes and Mercer (2000) have observed, these services have assumed a number of different forms, many of which have not developed from a 'user-led' framework promoted by the disability movement. Drawing on a small study of support organisations in Scotland, this chapter explores some of these challenges. It is argued that the shift to widen direct payments raises both a series of concerns and challenges for CILs and the wider disability movement. On one level, as the move to integrate new users gathers pace, CILs are increasingly seen as the main centres of expertise. Alternatively, they could be left in an increasingly precarious position, whereby there is an assumption that they are willing and able to support these new groups without additional resources. At the same time, the increasing presence of direct payment support services with limited user involvement and affiliation to local authorities may equally serve as a threat to the longer-term role of user-led support for disabled people.

The research study

This chapter reports on a small study carried out for Direct Payments Scotland (DPS) over summer 2003. The research was designed to provide DPS with information on how support needs could be best met as new changes in Scotland are implemented. With this in mind, the study set out the following objectives:

- To explore the current roles of user-led organisations in supporting the needs of direct payment users.

- To examine the capacity of these organisations to provide additional support for a more diverse direct payment user population.
- To examine the capacity of representative organisations of new user groups to offer specialist direct payment support.

For the study, fifteen semi-structured interviews were carried out with a range of groups representing current and new direct payment user groups (as determined by the Community Care and Health (Scotland) Act 2002). Discussion in this chapter focuses primarily on interviews with organisations undertaking an existing support role for direct payment users. This covered the two main CILs in Edinburgh and Glasgow, the Scottish Personal Assistance Employers Network (SPAEN) and two other (non user-led) direct payment support services. However, additional commentary is taken from interviews with personnel with responsibilities for direct payment planning from five local authorities (selected to reflect geographical diversity and including two urban and three rural areas). The views of three new user groups, covering the parents of disabled children, homeless persons and drug users are also referred to, together with three groups from minority ethnic communities, where direct payment take-up has been particularly poor. Interviews were semi-structured, lasted between 20 and 40 minutes and were carried out between May and July 2003. Questions were framed around the role and remit of the organisations and their capacity and willingness to adapt to changes in response to the new legislation. Data from the interviews were analysed with the aid of NUD*IST through a framework of themes developed from the interview schedule.

Direct payments and the independent living movement: issues in Scotland

Since the campaign for independent living began over twenty years ago, direct payments have represented an integral goal for the disability movement. Over this time, the emergence of CILs in the UK has helped instigate the shift in realising this goal through the development of community based support controlled by disabled people. An important basis for the transition to direct payments came in the mid–1980s from the demands of small groups of disabled people in areas such as Hampshire, Essex and Edinburgh. This began with the emergence of indirect payment schemes, whereby cash is paid through a third party (usually a local voluntary sector organisation) to the individual (Pearson 2000). These early cash payments represented an important initial challenge to rigid and paternalistic modes of service provision offered by local authorities to disabled people.

As mentioned earlier, since the initial implementation of direct payments in April 1997, there has been a marked difference in take-up across the UK. Figures released by the Department of Health (Department of Health 2002) for England and Wales show a total of 7882 users. (It should be noted that this figure represents a combined total, although in practice the overwhelming majority of users live in England, with less than 200 direct payment users in Wales.) Whilst numbers in many areas still remain relatively low with fewer than 50 users (Hasler 2003), individual authorities like Essex and Hampshire have over 600 users. This is in marked contrast to the overall total of 534 users in Scotland.

Since 1997, the more widespread use of direct payments in England has also been supported by a faster pace of legislative change (Pearson 2004). This began with the extension of direct payments to older people from February 2000 in England and Wales (Department of Health 1998) and six months later in Scotland (Scottish Parliament 1999: col. 1119). Subsequent changes south of the border also included those set out in the Carers and Disabled Children Act 2000, which gave payment access to parents or guardians who look after disabled children, 16 and 17 year olds and carers. A later announcement in the Health and Social Care Act 2001 made direct payments mandatory in England and Wales from 2003, although by this time most areas had schemes in place.

In response to the limited use of direct payments in Scotland highlighted in Witcher et al.'s (2000) research, the Scottish Executive has promoted a number of measures in an attempt to encourage greater uptake. In line with the rest of the UK, the enabling feature of legislation has now been removed so that from June 2003, local authorities across the country have been obliged to offer direct payments to all disabled people requesting them. In addition to the expansion of user groups through the Community Care and Health (Scotland) Act 2002, a focus has also been made on the role of information access and service support through the establishment of DPS in 2001. An initial allocation of £530,000 was made by the Executive to set up the project, with renewed funding to support work until 2006. The remit of the project covers three main areas. Two of these include increasing awareness of direct payments amongst users, local authority staff and service providers and identification of training needs amongst key personnel. The third area focuses more specifically on establishing and developing user-led support organisations. Consequently,

DPS has worked closely with the two Centres for Independent Living in Edinburgh and Glasgow and has sought to promote their approaches to direct payment support as a model for service development across the country. Indeed, the importance of this type of organisational support was underlined by DPS in their 'Five Steps' guide to implementing direct payment schemes (DPS 2002). This has also been acknowledged by the Scottish Executive and highlighted as good practice in their policy and practice guidance published in June 2003 (Scottish Executive 2003b). As DPS suggests to potential organisations, the type of structure promoted is one that should be flexible enough to incorporate a range of user interests within each organisation's constitution:

> You should ensure involvement in your support organisation of people from client groups to whom direct payments will start to become more widely available – e.g. people with learning disabilities, or housing support needs, mental health users, people from ethnic minorities (DPS 2002:3).

As the discussion so far has suggested, for the two main CILs in Scotland, the emphasis on user-led support has been a key goal from the outset. In 1991, the first Scottish CIL opened in Edinburgh followed by the Glasgow CIL in 1995. Both the Edinburgh and Glasgow centres offer a range of services focused around the independent living needs of disabled people and together with Scottish Personal Assistants Employers Network (SPAEN), form the major centres of user-led expertise for direct payments north of the border. Whilst support for direct payment users through training and advice work forms a key part of CIL work, their remits extend to include far wider aspects of independent living through which a range of additional training opportunities and peer counselling services have been developed.

Given the symbolic importance of direct payments in the history of the independent living movement, it was unsurprising that concerns were raised by CIL representatives over the policy shift in Scotland to include other groups as defined by the 1990 NHS and Community Act. As one respondent commented, there remained anxieties over the wider position of CIL control through the extension of direct payments and the expectations of providing service support associated with this change:

> We wouldn't ever loose ownership of the organisation. Direct payments and independent living came out of the disability movement and we wouldn't sell out on that   (CIL representative).

Yet despite this unease, each of the interviewees acknowledged the importance of making direct payments more widely available to other groups. As another respondent commented:

> Everything has a history and something that has preceded it. If direct payments have come out of the disability movement and [they're] going to benefit lots of people in the long term then it must be a good thing (CIL representative).

In contrast, for one local coalition of disabled people involved in the development of a new direct payment support service, the extension to new groups was seen as largely unproblematic. However, it was important to focus on the social model as a basis for inclusion and not rigidly categorise individual identities:

> Direct payments are primarily given to disabled people but looking at the social model [of disability] that's going to widen out – disabled people can also be refugees, homeless, drug users or whatever. You can't draw a hard line and say it's only disabled people (Local coalition of disabled people representative).

Keeping up with demand: shifting patterns of support for CILs

Underpinning these broader philosophical concerns relating to the 'ownership' of direct payments, however, was a more practical concern from the CILs with regard to meeting new demands within their budgets. As one of the CIL respondents commented, 'we are willing to work with anyone as long as we have the experience and resources to cope with their demands'. To date, both CILs and SPAEN have already experienced an increased workload, as more local authorities have referred users to their service. This has extended their service provision over a much wider geographical area and has put considerable pressure on staff as they have sought to meet the needs of an increasingly dispersed user population. Indeed, one case was described where staff based in Glasgow had been supporting users in the north of the country since the local user-led support service had folded six months earlier. Whilst the local authority was seeking to tender for an alternative service provider, in the meantime no payment was made for this role.

As the respondent outlined, the reasons for this increased caseload stemmed from the limited pool of expertise around direct payment support in the country:

> Because of the lack of user-led support groups in local areas, we have been approached by numerous local authorities [for direct

payment support] and we've said, 'we can't do it' and then
they're approaching [the other main CIL] who say 'we can't do
it either' (CIL representative).

As Morgan et al. (2000) reported from their study, funding for CILs is
a major problem with most income short term and limited to particular
services. Moreover despite the widespread recognition of the importance
of support organisations in facilitating direct payment packages, local
authorities are not obliged to meet these costs as part of individual
assessments. Indeed the CILs and SPAEN reported considerable variation
in local authority willingness to cover payments for these services. These
ranged from councils who core funded support services to those which
made limited or no contributions. One instance was described where one
of the CILs discovered that a local authority had been advertising their
services on information leaflets despite only making token annual
payments. Other examples were cited where, despite attempts to contact
the local authority and formalise an agreement, no response had been
made and the council continued to spot purchase services as and when
they required them.

This type of sporadic funding basis is clearly unsustainable in the longer
term. Given that CILs and other user-led support services rely on this
income as a key part of their funding, the variation in local authority
funding clearly makes service planning very difficult. Even with local
authorities that had made more substantial payments, there remained
difficulties in defining longer-term goals:

> We were trying to anticipate demand and draw up a business
> plan for ourselves that looked at the increase in the client group
> and extra staff we need. But the social work [department] are
> saying 'we have to look at what's needed just now'... there's just
> no forward planning (CIL representative).

Developing new support networks: user-led or user consulted?

Whilst CILs have been widely seen as the main providers of independent
living support and expertise around direct payments, over the past few
years a number of designated support organisations for direct payments
have been established across the UK. In promoting these, key proponents
such as DPS and the National Centre for Independent Living (NCIL) have
emphasised the importance of developing these as user-led (DPS 2002).
However, it is clear that many of these organisations have promoted only
a limited role for users – which to date have mainly been disabled people.

Indeed, this difference was clearly reflected in the organisational structure of the two direct payment support services interviewed for this study. In both cases, support services were staffed mainly by non-disabled, local authority employees. Although each organisation stated that they had disabled people on their management committees, it was clear that the overall direction of the services remained outwith the disability movement. Moreover in contrast to the CILs and SPAEN, both respondents generally welcomed the extension of direct payments to a wider user population as a positive move and envisaged no conflict of interests with their existing roles. In terms of future funding, the picture was perhaps more optimistic than the CILs, where one of the support services thought that any requests for additional funding from the local authority would be unproblematic. However, like the CILs there was a sense that they would have to prove the need for increased resources for specialist training as demand from new users emerged, rather than having new structures in place prior to change.

Likewise for local authority planners seeking to develop direct payment support services, concerns appeared to focus primarily on offering users choice and for them to adapt and include any new user group. Indeed in one area, this issue had come to a head in the planning stages of the support organisation. Whilst the local coalition of disabled people had taken a leading role in drafting the constitution, the remit proposed was considered to be too narrowly defined and was subsequently redrafted. As the planner described:

> It [the constitution] was very focused on disability and so I said 'you've got to widen it so that regardless of who comes in on a direct payment has the option of being user-led and is able to be involved in the service' (Local authority policy planner).

Accommodating new user groups

So far, discussion has highlighted two main concerns for CILs, firstly, the increasing work-load for direct payment support without adequate resources being made available and secondly, the increasing popularity of non user-led direct payment support services amongst many local authority planners. It is, of course, unclear whether in the long-term these type of support services will emerge as a real challenge to CILs as service providers, but there appears to be evidence at this stage that some local authorities may favour service support outwith the disability movement. As local authorities in Scotland move to widen policy access, the next section of this chapter explores some of the support options under consideration and questions the impact on CILs and user-led organisations within the disability movement.

As detailed, CIL support for direct payment users forms part of a network of independent living services offered by the centres. Faced with the extension of direct payments, staff interviewed for this study had been considering how this role might develop over the longer term. Given the concentration of direct payment expertise in the CILs, the idea of offering consultancy to new user groups and local support organisations has been raised as a possible framework for proceeding with change. Through this approach, new groups would be invited to work with the CILs to develop their skills and training for support until they are able to establish their own support group. This would encourage the development of more locally based user-led services but without altering the overall management and control of CILs by disabled people.

However, questions were raised about the appropriateness of providing direct payment support to other groups. Whilst it was acknowledged that individual identities do not fit easily into unitary categories, there remained unease about the relevance of the experiences of disabled people as a basis for wider support:

> I think we should prepare ourselves for people saying 'well your expertise is as a disabled person and the difficulties experiences by other disabled people, but what do you know about being an asylum seeker or drug user?' (CIL representative).

Another option raised was to employ specialist workers for the new user groups within the CILs. In doing this, direct payment support would be specifically framed around the different user groups and would provide a 'one-stop shop' for all groups. However although this would perhaps provide a more specialist level of knowledge for more diverse user needs as part of CIL structures, concerns were raised over the implications of this type of shift for the management and constitution of CILs. Indeed, this pushes CILs further towards the designated direct payment support service model favoured by some local authorities.

Discussions also took place with three organisations representing users from minority ethnic communities. These included two groups from the Chinese community and one from the Jewish community. One of the groups – representing the needs of older Chinese people – conceded that they had never heard of direct payments. In the case of the group representing the children and families, also in the local Chinese community, the development worker said that she had some knowledge about policy but suggested problems such as language and bureaucracy had acted as the main barriers to publicising direct payments and had therefore prevented any potential users coming forward. Likewise for the worker representing the needs of the Jewish community, knowledge about direct payments was fairly limited although there was said to be some interest from individuals. However, none of the groups interviewed had had any contact with the local CIL and were unaware of its existence. As such, each of the organisations stated that both service provision and/or support would be organised through their groups if users came forward in the future. Whilst it is acknowledged that this only presents the experiences of two communities in one Scottish locality, findings mirror some of the broader problems surrounding basic information access for direct payments highlighted by other black minority ethnic groups in the UK. This is illustrated in studies of, for example, the experiences of young black disabled people (Bignall and Butt 2000), and of Asian disabled people (Vernon 2002). Furthermore, the concentration of both provider *and* support roles within these organisations also suggests that there is a clear need to provide culturally appropriate direct payments support.

Groups interviewed for the study representing new users (as defined by the 2002 Act), also reported a lack of knowledge about the forthcoming changes. Indeed, in one case a major organisation representing refugees turned down a request for an interview because it was stated that 'direct payments will not affect our services in any way'. For the others although there was some awareness of forthcoming changes, the issue of support had not been addressed. However, the work of the local CILs was generally acknowledged and welcomed as a possible framework for service development. As the respondent from a group representing drug users commented:

> Many of the barriers faced by disabled people are very much the same as those with drug problems...I think we could learn a great deal from them in terms of person centred services and human rights (Drug support group representative).

This type of partnership was also broadly welcomed by the group working with homeless persons. However for staff working with parents of disabled children, the appropriateness of the CIL in its current form was questioned in that its focus to date has centred on adult needs. As such, this underlined the need to develop more specialised training in order to meet new support needs.

Indeed, it was evident from the interviews undertaken with local authority planning representatives for direct payments that very little had been done in the way of preparatory work for taking on additional roles. Moreover, concerns remained over the impact of policy extension and clearly this type of change in the culture and organisation of services needs to be made in reasonable time to ensure good access and continuity across all user groups. At the time of interviewing (July 2003), no guidance had been produced by the Scottish Executive. However in light of the type of concerns outlined in this chapter around the capability of local authorities to diversify policy at this stage, the Executive announced a deferment of policy expansion until April 2005 (Scottish Executive 2004). Whilst planners remain committed to expanding policy to new user groups and therefore changing the pattern of uptake, there seems to be some recognition that this will need to be done gradually.

Review

As highlighted in this discussion, direct payments are about to move into a new era as they become more extensively used and accessible to a more diverse user population. For CILs and the wider disability movement, this clearly has important implications both in terms of practical support and representation of disabled people at a local level and through the overall policy direction. It was argued in an earlier study (Pearson 2000) that direct payments should be viewed as an appendage to the 1990 NHS and Community Care Act. In these terms, policy was promoted initially by the Conservative Government through a market discourse. Central to this idea has been the use of direct payments as an instrument for accessing choice and diversity in service provision.

Seven years on from its initial implementation, it is clear that this route has also influenced the Scottish Executive in its decision to extend policy to all user groups defined in accordance with the Community Care legislation. At the same time, although some elements of the social justice origins of policy (Pearson 2000) remain in evidence, as an increasing number of people gain access to direct payments, there remain fundamental concerns. Indeed for the disability movement, a prerequisite for social justice rests on the premise that individuals should not be passive recipients of services, but in control of when and how they are delivered. As support services are recognised as being central to successful direct payments schemes, it is clear that the experiences of disabled people need to be drawn upon in this area of service provision. At this transient stage, it is vital that CILs gain appropriate recognition for their expertise in this area and are utilised as the framework for user-led support. But in taking on this enhanced role in providing knowledge and expertise for new direct payment users, adequate resourcing must be made available in order to allow centres to employ more staff and maintain other interests.

However, it is clear from the wider pattern of direct payment support services developing in Scotland (DPS 2003) that many local authorities are favouring use of generic support services with limited user involvement and close affiliation with social service departments. Whilst many of these organisations promote an active role for users in their constitutions, interpretations of this involvement vary considerably and often include almost any kind of engagement. As a recent study into user involvement in voluntary organisations found (Robson, Begum and Lock 2003), users only really value 'user-centred involvement' where service users objectives and priorities become the focus of the organisation's work. Any shift away from this framework will inevitably push direct payments away from its independent living roots and towards a more welfarist model of service provision. Indeed, the failure by some local authorities to invest in support services serves to underline the on-going gaps in understanding about the role of direct payments. Furthermore, findings reported in this chapter replicate earlier research in highlighting gaps in providing information and support for direct payment access to black and minority ethnic communities. It is evident, therefore, that work still needs to be done to emphasise the function of policy as a means of promoting independent living and the social model of disability, rather than simply a re-organisation of cash limited community care services.

As more diverse user groups access direct payments over the next few years, it is clear that these new interests will need to be represented by support services. Whilst the CILs are increasingly recognised as centres of excellence for user-led support, they require additional resourcing in order to meet new demands. In the context of the social model, this need not be incompatible with a disability rights agenda. However, change does need to be carefully considered to ensure that the rights and interests of disabled people are at the forefront and that support roles are independent and user-led.

Bibliography

Bignall, T. and Butt, J. 2000: *Between ambition and achievement: young black disabled people's views and experiences of independence and independent living*. Bristol: Policy Press.

Department of Health 1998: *Modernising Social Services*, London: HMSO.

Department of Health 2002: *Direct Payments Totals as at 30 September 2002*. London: Department of Health, available from: www.doh.gov.uk/directpaymentsautumnstatement2002.xls

DPS 2002: *Five Steps: A Guide for Local Authorities Implementing Direct Payments*. Edinburgh: Direct Payments Scotland.

DPS 2003: *DP News*, Issue 9.

Hasler, F. 2003: *A summary of the Department of Health Figures for Direct Payments Users in the UK in 2002*, Report to the European Network for Independent Living Board Meeting, 8 March 2003, www.independentliving.org/doc6/hasler200303.html.

Hasler, F., Campbell, J. and Zarb, G. 1999: *Direct Routes to Independence; A Guide to Local Authority Implementation and Management of Direct Payments*. London: Policy Studies Institute.

Morgan, H., Barnes, C. and Mercer, G. 2000: *Creating Independent Futures: An Evaluation of Services led by Disabled People*. Leeds: The Disability Press.

Jones, R. 2000: *Getting going on Direct Payments*. Trowbridge: Wiltshire Social Services on behalf of the Association of Directors of Social Services.

Pearson, C. 2000: Money talks? Competing discourses in the implementation of direct payments. *Critical Social Policy*, 20 (4), 459-77.

Pearson, C. 2004: Keeping the cash under control: What's the problem with direct payments in Scotland. *Disability and Society*, 19 (1), 3-14.

Robson, P., Begum, N. and Lock, M. 2003: *Developing user involvement: Working towards user-centred practice in voluntary organisations*. Bristol: Policy Press.

Scottish Executive 2002: *Social Work (Scotland) Act 1968: Sections 12B and 12C Direct Payments: Policy and Practice Guidance*, Circular No: CCD8/2002. Edinburgh: Scottish Executive.

Scottish Executive 2003a: *Statistics Release: Direct Payments 2003*. Edinburgh: Scottish Executive National Statistics Publication.

Scottish Executive 2003b: *Direct Payments Social Work (Scotland) Act 1968: Sections 12B and C: Policy and Practice Guidance*. Edinburgh: Scottish Executive Health Department, Community Care Division.

Scottish Executive 2004: *Phased roll out of direct payments to new community care groups from April 2005*, Circular No: CCD 1/2004. Edinburgh: Scottish Executive.

Scottish Parliament 1999: Pensioners debate, *Scottish Parliament Official Report,* 2 December, 3, 12.

Vernon, A. 2002: *User-defined outcomes of community care for Asian disabled people.* Bristol: Policy Press and Joseph Rowntree Foundation.

Witcher, S., Stalker, K., Roadburg, M. and Jones, C. 2000: *Direct Payments: The Impact on Choice and Control for Disabled People.* Edinburgh: Scottish Executive Central Research Unit.

CHAPTER 10

Social Model Services: an oxymoron?

Dave Gibbs

Changing fortunes of social model praxis

This chapter examines the application of a social understanding of disability to the development of practical supports for disabled people's goals – the job of a Centre/Coalition for Independent/Inclusive Living (CIL). It provides a brief 'status report' on a programme that has been underway for twenty years at one CIL, in Derbyshire (where we are a 'Coalition for Inclusive Living', but the name variations need not concern us here), then looks at obstacles to their further development and to effective extension into the mainstream of public services.

The usual language of a CIL's work is one of the refinement of models by a process of practical application, rather than of theory. Opportunities like this seminar series, however, encourage a brief detachment in which to examine issues that underlie daily concerns. The ones I will focus on here are primarily issues of *relationships* – those between ourselves, as a development unit working to a mandate from disabled people, and the authorities that implement statutes and deliver mainstream services.

Concerns about these relationships are not new. The capacity to work together in a strategic way, as was possible in Derbyshire CIL's (DCIL) early years, was effectively lost more than ten years ago. Profound changes of relationship between central and local government and the voluntary/ community sector went along with the intense centralised control needed to introduce 'internal markets' in public services. More recent changes stress an increased role for voluntary and community organisations, but for all the emphasis on their 'added value' the role envisaged is as auxiliary service providers within an essentially hierarchical structure. A core role of grassroots innovation, which may go on as much as a generation ahead of anything operating within that structure, is likely to remain in jeopardy.

Others have offered pointers on ways to understand these changes in examining another relationship – that between the academic discipline of 'disability studies' and the disabled people's movement (Barnes et al. 2003). After noting effects on this relationship of 'the increasing marketisation of academic life', the authors distinguish three approaches applicable to the relationship. These are: an 'inside out' approach giving primacy to direct experience (as in a general statement that 'personal is political'); an 'outside in' approach led by analysis ('political is personal', if you like); and an 'outside out' approach embodied in the reductive mode of thought which dominated the modern era and still goes unchallenged much of the time.

In my understanding of how our work as a CIL has developed, there has been a 'phasing' of the first two approaches. It might be expressed simply as: model + praxis = theory. For this to become a fully developed alternative to reductive thinking, we will need to add an 'inside in' approach too. This will be a 'whole systems' one focused on connections rather than on a reduced state of things connected. Wide applications of this thinking began to be introduced by writers like Bateson (1972), but we can recognise it in a basic form in the original framework that disabled people put forward for a CIL – the 'Seven Needs' (Davis 1990).

Statutory authorities are, by and large, 'outside out' entities: the way they have conducted their relationships is highly reductive. I have noted elsewhere (Gibbs 1999) that applied social sciences have held on to this thinking long after the 'hard' sciences have begun moving away from it. Here I want to go further and identify specific traits – underlying *errors of thought* – that may account for what I believe is a permanent failure in the theoretical base of 'social care' services. Then I will try to come forward with more 'connected' alternatives by which social model praxis may gain the mainstream.

A status report

There is no consistent format for those organisations of disabled people variously called Centres or Coalitions for Independent/ Integrated/ Inclusive Living. In response to local circumstances, something with the essentials of a CIL can be produced by several different routes:
- one that starts with a core service and adds on others;
- one where several existing services are brought together under a new management structure;
- one where a range of services and projects are managed in a loose association;

- one where a range of closely linked projects are set up from the start.

A recent study (Morgan et al. 2000) found no distinct boundary for what might be defined as or define itself as a CIL. My own list of essential features would be:

1. an underlying principle of peer support, in which disabled people come together and support each other;
2. disabled people's control on the governing body;
3. an applied social understanding of disability; and
4. an integrated approach to support needs, recognising that a social model cannot be applied by services that meet needs in isolation.

This is enough background for a brief review of the current status of the main activities in an early organisation of disabled people such as Derbyshire CIL (DCIL) that has its origins in the fourth mode listed above.

Information
The network of Disablement Information & Advice Lines (DIALs) began as a handful of local peer-support lines set up by disabled people in the late 70s. A national body to promote the network, DIAL UK, was formed early on and has done much to set standards for a professionalized service. DIAL-Derbyshire was absorbed into DCIL as its Information Section. Despite 26 years continuity as a service developed by disabled people, it remains essentially a development project: ultimately, the goal is for mainstream public information services to be fully inclusive.

Peer counselling
Disabled people began to qualify as counsellors in the mid 1980s. Defining support that was about developing confidence, rather than 'coming to terms with disability', and was not easy to begin with in terms of standards set by established counselling associations. More recently some affinity of approach has been recognised with the highly effective 'MindFields' courses associated with the European Therapy Studies Institute. This has helped to support the counselling team's interest in strengthening the professional basis of their service.

Independent living advice
In 1995 DCIL contracted with the Social Services department as a 'community care provider'. The context of this development, and the issues of resolving different approaches, are fully analysed by Priestley

(1999). Even after the difficulties were overcome, this contract on its own was an insufficient arrangement to deliver outcomes of independence, but it was linked with a National Lottery funded development project. This project both employed disabled people as 'integrated living advisers' (giving status to what had been a voluntary peer support role) and began an 'education programme' by which a qualification at NVQ Level IV would be developed for this role. A local organisation lacks the infrastructure to market and deliver such a programme on its own, but when that structure is in place it will be an important adjunct to 'disability equality training' as a means to professionalize training developed from peer support.

Mentoring

When independent living arrangements are secure and under the disabled person's control, possibilities open up to go on to community participation in a fuller sense. The principle of peer support, by which people pass on their experience, can be extended to any of the transitions during the life-course, where added obstacles are in the way of disabled people. Ways are being found to train disabled people as mentors in transitions like those from 'special schools' to adulthood, from 'day care' to community alternatives, and from 'welfare' to training and employment opportunities.

Community development

Support to individuals has to be matched by improved access in communities, to meet changing expectations of a full active role. Community development functions can add value by networking in many ways, but problems in getting sustained resources for this arise because its benefits have been difficult to measure. Simple measures DCIL has used, however, touch on fields that are developing rapidly. Estimates we have made of economic impacts at a District level anticipate ways economists are beginning to evaluate social welfare (Sefton 2000). Simple 'quality circles' to evaluate change in progress apply 'theory of change', and member participation programmes develop 'social capital'. Consolidating these connections will in time provide an evidence base to 'professionalize' community development functions.

Errors of thought in the provider–user relationship

In this section I want to distinguish the main barriers in thinking which, in my view, continue to defeat goals of the disabled people's movement and the effective application of a social understanding within mainstream services. They may be best thought of as residues from a culture of welfare paternalism, and are:

- an insistence on categorising people instead of issues and support needs;
- a management culture of control, assessment and prescription to which concepts like peer support and self-definition of outcomes are anathema;
- a relationship of 'helper and helped' which is locked into a mentality of 'us and them'.

Arising from these, and on another level, is an emergent culture of target-setting, measurement and monitoring which is dehumanising and contrary to human rights. Its detrimental effects on public services is being recognised (Audit Commission 2002), hopefully before it reaches a point where its stresses will implode and render existing models of public service unworkable.

For each of the three relics of welfare paternalism that create the obstacles, there is a well-defined train of new thinking that leads beyond them. These alternatives cannot be presented, I suggest, as any viable reforming programme, but only as an indivisible replacement model of support provision. I will try to describe and understand each of the obstacles, and then propose corresponding solutions.

Errors of categorisation

By errors of categorisation I mean a process in public administration by which attention to support needs and outcomes is continually distracted by a compulsion to classify people. It has two main expressions, which present great barriers to delivery of useful practical support: the 'silo mentality' – dividing people up for administrative purposes; a converse process of lumping people together, e.g. 'sick and disabled'.

Perhaps one of the best illustrations of the process is in attempts to measure 'quality of life'. This has entered the problematic setting of prioritising who receives support, and of course that has made it controversial. I think it only became problematic, though, because of distraction from its proper terms of reference. The first measures of 'quality of life' did not refer to people's personal characteristics at all; they referred to environments (Marks 1999: 38ff), that is, to:

- air – how free is a community's air from pollution;
- water – how much untainted water does a community have access to;

- then shelter, and an adequate varied diet;
- then freedom from conflict and persecution; and
- then freedom to learn and apply learning, to gain independence and earn a living, to raise a family – to make the natural transitions of a life's course.

By these criteria, you have a good quality of life if neither your environment nor your society fetters your development – if neither of them disable you, in other words. These environmental measures are obvious and can be understood by anyone, yet this does not prevent their diversion in various areas of health and public administration into preoccupation with quite bizarre farragoes of personal characteristics. The first stage in addressing barriers to employment, for example, is to sort people into categories like 'musculo-skeletal', 'respiratory' and 'mental'.

Errors of response

By errors of response I mean the system of assessment and prescription for 'social care' services. It contains several elements:

- a summary invalidation of an individual's own perceptions;
- a default to basic maintenance like home-care rather than outcome-based support, for example mentored transition;
- a confusion of short-term and long-term considerations.

Service 'modernisation' and the new training behind it are full of declaration and invocation with an appearance of addressing the worst effects of one or other part of this system. But as Finkelstein (1999:6) points out, in much of it '"assessment of needs" and "empowerment" have been abandoned in favour of verbiage'. What it lacks is overview and strategy, displaced or tokenised by hierarchical management structures in which 'users' views' are reduced to a part of what is to be managed. Words like 'empower' and 'enable' (even 're-able', which has entered the modernisation programme like a mystery virus) are used in a sense of something that can be prescribed. This usage must be flatly refuted: from the moment someone presumes to prescribe and manage another's 'empowerment' they prevent it; from the moment they ask 'how can I empower this person?' they begin to do the opposite.

Despite the key role of an assessment function in the training and role identity of many practitioners, large sectors of it have in fact come about by default. These are the countless means of 'gatekeeping' resources by some form of quasi-medical endorsement. Disabled people have had provision for their needs firmly under medical supervision throughout the industrial era, so this medical model is very deeply bedded. Doctors are involved in all kinds of things that do not obviously call for medical qualifications: deciding if you can drive or where you should be educated; prescribing wheelchairs; requirement for personal assistance; measuring work capability; benefits entitlements. In earlier times, doctors' associations appear to have resisted having bureaucratic gate-keeping jobs off-loaded on to them – an interesting piece of history that I don't believe has been properly documented. Of course power, once handed over, is seductive and self-enhancing: new consultancies in Rehabilitation Medicine soon arose from systems to gate-keep supply of basic equipment.

Errors of perceived relationship

By errors of perceived relationship I mean a perception that difference between the provider and user of a service, which may be temporary and to do with stage of the life-course, is permanent and inherent. Put more simply, it tacitly assumes a distinction of 'us and them'.

This error is supported by a social theory that is primarily mechanistic and reductionist. Cause and effect explains the difference between 'us and them', and reductive analysis informs the interventions by us in the lives of them. I suggest that this method of thinking does not explain the division of 'us and them' but creates it. In an alternative view of the service relationship, we all occupy a matrix with multiple scales of empowerment in different life faculties, and we move up and down various scales at different times in our lives. Such a relationship is not amenable to reductive analysis, and methods of intervention that assume an unchanged 'us' can be an agent for changing 'them' so that they become part of the problem.

As with errors of response, this third kind is self-perpetuating. Once a system is in place that manipulates people to accept subsistence on the outer fringes of society, there is no clear demarcation from more drastic modes of exclusion – institutions, withholding of treatment, and ultimately assisted exit.

Where do the errors come from?

It is necessary to ask if what I am calling 'errors' are specific to a particular stage of transition from welfare paternalism, or if their social, cultural and political context extends more widely. If it is the latter, new analytical tools may need to be found in order to ground the search for alternatives. These tools might be sought in two quite different ways.

1. Historical. Both the beginning and end of the 'modern' era – the Enlightenment era of science – saw attempts to analyse the 'hard-wired' errors that thought is prone to. In the seventeenth century Francis Bacon defined his four 'idols of the mind'; early in the twentieth century Bertrand Russell in the 'Principia Mathematica' set out his highly formalised concept of 'logical typing'. Bacon's 'idols' are predispositions to perceive something in terms of reference to which it does not belong. The four he proposed grade from specific and personal (like assuming others perceive things in the way we do) to general and cultural (like those bedded in language or traits we put down to 'human nature'). Russell's system of 'logical typing' resides in the field of formal logic, and caution is needed to map it onto more day to day concerns. Its purpose is to keep thoughts that apply to a particular thing strictly separate from thoughts about any 'class' that the thing might belong to. I suggest that a formal error of logical typing has been made when certain kinds of individual difference are: a) seen apart from the rest of someone's personal equation, and b) made to define a class in which varied individuals are treated in homogenised ways. This error contributes to creating what I earlier called an 'error of perceived relationship'.

2. Global. The concept of social exclusion, along with its under-standing and solutions, has rapidly extended in the last few years to a global setting as part of the complex debate on 'globalisation'. Analysis of the social injustice, waste and destruction associated with a dehumanised global economics led by uncontrolled finance networks (Capra 2002) suggests the same pattern on a different scale as the obsessive centralised control led by 'targets' which public services have been encouraged into by 'errors of thought' like those identified above. Equally, the co-ordination of regular actions against the World Trade Organisation from 1999 onwards has been by global networking of highly diverse interests. The voluntary and community sector may learn to respond to its own 'colonisation' in a broadly similar way.

A framework for solutions

In the above analysis of disabling obstacles in public service relationships, I have suggested they arise from structural 'errors' which are more 'hard-wired' than may have been recognised. The introduction of alternatives, therefore, will be correspondingly difficult. It may not be enough to have a clear-sighted alternative model and pilot projects to demonstrate its practical applications. An 'outside out' mode of thinking, serving the interests of a hierarchical power base, can be countered only by one that is 'inside in' – an alternative system.

A framework robust enough for alternatives outlined below will provide safeguards against reductive ('outside out') modes of thought which 'objectify' people and their needs. It will be one that is systemic: that is to say, it will replace a disposition to see the world in terms of dualities – subject and object, observer and observed, producer and consumer – with a recognition of interrelations, feedback, and learning exchange. Diverse applications of systems thinking, advanced for example by Bateson (1972), have been taken up by writers like Midgley (2000), who follows systems thinking through from philosophy to the 'politics of social inclusion' and operational issues of interventions in community development work. At least one university based unit promotes applications of systems thinking primarily in health-related research (http://www.uwe.ac.uk/solar/index.htm).

An indivisible social model

In 2001, the World Health Organization (WHO) published the *International Classification of Functioning, Disability and Health* (ICF). This substantially revised its original *International Classification of Impairments, Disabilities and Handicaps* (WHO 1980). The ICF refers to a 'dialectic' of 'medical model' versus 'social model', and claims that its new classification is 'based on an integration of these two opposing models' (WHO 2001: 20). It withdraws the term 'handicap' as redundant while extensive sections on measures of 'participation' illustrate its acknowledgement of the social dimensions of both disability and health. The revision may appear at first to be a substantial step to adopting a social understanding, even moving towards what might be called a 'social model of health'. I would argue that, to the contrary, no progress can be based on its notion of 'integration'.

When reflecting on how the 'social model' might develop, it must be recognised how widely it continues to be subverted. Even social work practitioners now sometimes claim that their departments 'work to the social model'. The relics of welfare paternalism located in statute and in working practices mean that such claims rest on unacceptable distortions or, at best, admit only what I would call an 'individual' level of social model. In a fully integrated programme, however, two other levels are applied. A 'collective' level extends to broader issues of access to communities and to experience shared with other excluded groups. A further, 'historical', level identifies and challenges active processes of exclusion at their source. These goals are not addressed as a natural consequence of meeting needs at the individual level.

The impact of the social model has come from its clarity and simplicity, which has two immediate effects:

- on the self-esteem of individual disabled people who see, gradually or by a dramatic change of awareness, that 'disability' is not in them but in their surroundings;
- in a switch to very direct practical solutions, after befogging complexities of classifications, assessments, pressure to 'come to terms with' the things that most need to change, and deferral of attention pending 'cure'.

In order to fully operationalise these impacts, however – to fully 'cash out' their benefits, maintain progress, and guard against distortion – a further point has to be recognised. For the social model to work, you have to buy in to the whole thing. The social model is a 'paradigm': its application shifts the whole framework in which something is thought about. Because the whole framework has shifted, it is no longer reducible – parts of it cannot be combined with other models in a process of *bricolage* (or 'pick and mix').

There are several questions that might be asked to test this 'hard' interpretation of what the social model means. I would simply like to present them here for critics to scrutinise – whether activists, academics, or people with vested interests in different models altogether. A 'yes' to any question will mean the model is 'reducible' and can compromise with other models; the absence of 'yes' responses means our task is to develop the social model till it joins up with other new and unfamiliar ways of looking at the world.

The questions I would suggest are:

- Is there a 'percentage' angle – are there situations that only can be understood using, say, one part social model and two parts something else?
- Is there a 'point of view' angle – the social model works from one viewpoint on a given situation, but not from another?
- Are there 'intermediates' between social and individual models?
- Does the social model work on one level but not on another – for example between personal, social and historical points of reference?

'Professions Allied to the Community'

The idea of 'Professions Allied to the Community' comes from Vic Finkelstein, who set it in direct contrast with 'professions allied to medicine'.

He expressed a view that:

> Centres for Integrated Living (CILs) are one structure created by
> disabled people to service (self-defined) aspirations and, in my
> view, workers in these centres are an embryonic PAC. This
> professionalisation process exactly replicates the progress made
> by women when they created their own midwifery service
> (Finkelstein 1999:6).

In my 'status report' earlier, I tried to give some sense of how far the
various functions of one CIL have begun to 'professionalize'. Clearly, the
process is still far off from what most people would think of as a
'profession' – a high status calling rooted in intensive training. I think it
fair to say that professional training has become increasingly dominated by
acquisition of technical skills and knowledge – a focus on learning about
things rather than their connections and relationships. The new alignments
of skills needed for PACs would need to include a corrective to this – a
'didactic framework', shall we call it – that has structured in to it safeguards
against the errors we've identified and guidance towards the
complementary new faculties.

In a recent article (Gibbs 2003) I made a very tentative sketch of some
characteristics and content for this framework:

- It will be defined not only by its knowledge base but also by its
  purpose: to reverse long-term cycles of disempowerment.
- It follows that its theoretical base will be a developed historical
  understanding of destructive imbalances of power.
- It will be cross-cultural, because it must deny sustenance to aspects
  of a global economy that most threaten progress towards social
  equality and sustainability.
- It will combine personal support and community development
  skills.

Coming to specific 'modules' that might be included, there might be on
the personal support side:

- uses of information and systems of information,
- models developed from peer support,
- something from the pragmatic end of counselling theory, such as
  'human givens' (Griffin and Tyrell 1999);

and on the community development side:

- infrastructure of public service provision,
- purposive monitoring and audit of social capital,
- models of system intervention (Midgley 2000).

A life-course framework

Mark Priestley (2003) has recently examined aspects of disabled people's exclusion within a framework of the 'life course'. His aim was to explore the life-course as 'a useful analytical frame for understanding current disability debates', but it also may be useful as a strategic framework. When DCIL responded this year to local consultation about eligibility criteria for access to 'social care' services, we tried to apply that approach: the process may have taken us a little way towards proposals for practice that would guard against the third 'error'.

Problems in deciding eligibility include:

- A conflict between meeting basic maintenance needs of as many people as possible and the substantial support needed to establish independence, where this is the only appropriate outcome.
- An expectation that younger disabled people might be service consumers for 30-40 years, so are a resource 'problem' because most service use for the adult population as a whole falls within a few years late in life.
- A stress on preventing negative change may impair support for positive change. Review focuses on checking if provision can be reduced or withdrawn, rather than monitoring whether it is working or needs to change direction.

Proposed adjustments are:

- That focus on transition – as already applied in young disabled people's transition to adulthood – is extended to all other stages of the 'life course'.
- That the 'standard' support pattern becomes one of support at a stage of transition: transition from education; transition from family or institutional dependence; transition from illness or injury; transition to supported old age.
- That the overall model then becomes one of many people passing through supported periods, rather than a lot of people maintained at a subsistence level and a few supported to greater independence as resources allow.
- That standard working practice 'defaults' to focus on outcomes, and reverts to maintenance only by active choice.

Effects would be:

- More people using services for shorter periods (as a stage towards a longer-term outcome where use of 'social care' services is fully integrated with use of any other kind of public service).

- A better chance to pass on from a first stage outcome (support with personal care and domestic needs is safe, secure, and under the user's effective control) to a second stage where support is with goal setting and possibilities of moving on in life.
- Linking with trends to multi-sector provision. Closely related supports towards employment, for example, may be found in public, voluntary/ community, and private sectors. The perceived aims and daily language of different sectors may differ widely, but partnership structures are needed to bring them together on common ground.

The key benefits of focus on transition are:

- It provides a common framework for different levels of intervention – acute health interventions, 'care' solutions, and support programmes in the voluntary/community sector.
- It minimises transfer of choice and control out of an individual's life-course to someone else.
- It puts service interventions in a context that everyone shares.
- It draws 'social care' interventions into a closer proximity to other public and private support interventions that a citizen calls in as and when required to supplement their own skills, such as a solicitor, architect, or plumber.

Mainstream applications?

The social policy context

It remains to link the analysis and proposals in this chapter to the wider social policy setting. Modernisation of public services is, of course, a very active area of social policy just now. For disabled people, however, this high level of activity is a source of some bewilderment. There seems so much opportunity to support full inclusion, yet so little specific strategy to bring it about. Two linked interpretations might be ventured:

- disability policy remains predominantly within a corral of 'health and social care';
- the high cost of maintaining this corral means that the cost constraints of disability policy always come before anything else.

Both the policy and those who must implement it, therefore, are in a classic 'double bind': 'we can't afford to help you out of the corral because it costs too much to keep you in the corral'.

One commentator on the wider policy context offers as explanation for recent Government conduct a dominance of neo-liberal over social democrat thinking at the policy centre (Hall 2003). This would certainly tend to make invisible any product of thought outside the fundamentalist dogma of 'market forces', but it seems so incredible that there could be such a degree of drift from social democratic origins that more specific evidence ought to be found.

The current Home Office incumbent, David Blunkett, has written rather more analytically than is usual for Ministers while in office. In *Politics and Progress* (Blunkett 2001) he sets out a vision for reviving 'excluded communities', but this takes a view of 'communities' which seems to leave apart issues relating to excluded constituencies. Specifically, disabled people's inclusion is conflated with what he calls the 'challenge of incapacity' – security for 'those who cannot work'. Neither here nor in other statements of policy thinking is there any clear separation between prevention of work by illness and by disabling obstacles placed in people's way by their environment. Certainly, there is no recognition that self-definition might be the way to make this separation, rather than some form of quasi-medical assessment. It has to be concluded that the kind of errors identified earlier extend from the policy centre, and have to be analysed on a similar basis. Solutions too would be of the same broad type: in this example, the concept of 'incapacity' should disappear, subsumed in a general policy of inclusion and support with transition.

Meantime, the chimerical co-existence of neo-liberalism and relic welfare paternalism would seem to provide a particularly toxic environment for disabled people's inclusion. Strung between defunct ideologies, the meaning of 'inclusion' may cease to relate to communities at all, but promise instead a corral for everyone within a single management hierarchy. With no 'third way' on offer beyond the even worse option of charitable 'trickle-down', there is one basic principle to fall back on: needs and solutions are defined within the excluded constituencies where they arise.

Social model services?

My title signals some wariness at the notion of social model services, and I should indicate why I think the line taken above makes it problematic. To use my organisation, DCIL, as an example: it is not to be seen definitively as 'a service' because provision of a personal service is only one of the responses that might be required to meet a mandate from disabled people. The people it supports are not to be constructed as 'users', because such a role has constraints on what people might want to say about the purpose, direction and inclusiveness of public services. And it does not purport to 'involve users', because historically it's an organisation in which disabled people 'involved workers'.

Because the social model is non-reducible, it cannot be implemented by any programme of services that is separate from other functions. Even within the disabled people's movement, it is commonly believed that 'service provider' and 'lobbying' functions are incompatible in a single organisation. To the contrary, the social model cannot be applied by either on its own. The duality is false, and a social model is applied by a continuous series of responses, geared mainly to the degree of resistance mounted by established modes of working.

The word 'services', moreover, does not have the same meaning in relation to disabled people as 'public services' does in relation to the general population. To use the concept cited earlier, its reference is of a different logical type. 'Public services' are specific operations that support the social infrastructure, like transport, housing, and public recreation; disabled people's services are a class of operations that places additional controls on a sector of society. To admit disabled people to public services, the outcome of an applied social understanding of disability must be the disappearance of that class of operations. 'Social model services', then, is an oxymoron.

Bibliography

Audit Commission. 2002: *Recruitment and Retention: a public service workforce for the 21st century*. London: Audit Commission.

Barnes, C., Oliver, M. and Barton, L. 2003: Disability, the Academy and the Inclusive Society. In C. Barnes, M. Oliver and L. Barton (eds), *Disability Studies Today*. Cambridge: Polity, 250-60.

Bateson, G. 1972: *Steps to an ecology of mind*. Chicago: University of Chicago Press.

Blunkett, D. 2001: *Politics and Progress: Renewing Democracy and Civil Society*. London: Politico's.

Capra, F. 2002: *The Hidden Connections: a Science for Sustainable Living*. London: Harper Collins.

Davis, K. 1990: A Social Barriers Model of Disability: Theory into Practice (the emergence of the 'Seven Needs'). Derbyshire Coalition of Disabled People (http://www.leeds.ac.uk/disability-archiveuk/index.html)

Finkelstein, V. 1999: Professions Allied to the Community (PACs), I, II. (http://www.leeds.ac.uk/disability- archiveuk/index.html)

Gibbs, D. 1999: Disabled People and the Research Community. ESRC funded seminar series, 'Theorising Social Work Research'; seminar 2, 'Who Owns the Research Process'.

Gibbs, D. 2003: Welfare Reform and a Social Model of Health. *Coalition* (Greater Manchester Coalition of Disabled People), February 2003: 26-30.

Griffin, J. and Tyrell, I. 1999: *Psychotherapy and the Human Givens.* Hailsham: The European Therapy Studies Institute.

Hall, S. 2003: New Labour has picked up where Thatcherism left off. *The Guardian*, 6 August.

Marks, D. 1999: *Disability: controversial debates and psychosocial perspectives*. London: Routledge.

Midgley, G. 2000: *Systemic Intervention: philosophy, methodology and practice*. New York: Kluwer/Plenum.

Morgan, H., Barnes, C. and Mercer, G. 2001: *Creating Independent Futures: an evaluation of services led by disabled people. Stage Two Report.* Leeds: The Disability Press.

Priestley, M. 1999: *Disability Politics and Community Care.* London: Jessica Kingsley.

Priestley, M. 2003: *Disability: A Life Course Approach.* Cambridge: Polity Press.

Sefton, T. 2000: *Getting Less for More: Economic Evaluation in the Social Welfare Field.* Paper 44. London: Centre for Analysis of Social Exclusion, London School of Economics.

WHO 1980: *International Classification of Impairments, Disabilities and Handicaps.* Geneva: World Health Organization.

WHO 2001: *International Classification of Functioning, Disability and Health.* Geneva: World Health Organization.

CHAPTER 11

The Dynamics of Partnerships and Professionals in the Lives of People with Learning Difficulties

Deborah Phillips

Introduction

Building on my own recent research and utilising the narrative accounts of women participants, this chapter sets out to explore some of the inherent power dynamics evident in cared-for and the carer relationship. Many of the women involved in this investigation related negatively to the impact of professional judgements in the planning of their daily routines and health needs. However, there was also evidence of strong alliances between women and the female support staff who worked with them. This chapter argues that the role of professionals, and the emphasis on multi-agency partnerships and 'participation' in relation to health and welfare practices, continues to ignore real partnerships with people labelled as having 'learning difficulties'. Meanwhile, at the grass roots level, changes are being witnessed in the introduction of non-medicalised, alternative health practices as well as through a social model understanding of learning difficulties.

'People don't usually listen to me; they just tell me what to do'

This statement was made by Beccy (a pseudonym as with all the names of research participants), the first person I interviewed as part of my research project. It highlights the controlling role of professionals in the everyday lives of people labelled as having 'learning difficulties'. When I met Beccy in her home, the table and floor were covered with piles of papers, letters, files and so on that she had gathered together to show me. Her life, she said, 'was laid out in these papers...all the details you need to know.' She was nervous and repeatedly asked if I was a social worker. Beccy seemed surprised that someone may be interested in what she had to say, her side of the story, as opposed to 'telling her what to do', and organizing her life.

Beccy's history, told in her own way, is probably somewhat different from the mound of literature she had spread out before her. She is a woman in her mid-thirties who lives independently in a small coastal village but also cares for her father who is nearby. She is physically disabled as well as being labelled as having learning difficulties. Beccy claims she has learning difficulties because she cannot cope with life like other 'normal people'. She is mother of two children, both of whom, she says 'were taken from me at birth by Social Services'. During the two year communication I had with Beccy, her life experiences consisted of a series of upheavals and transitions; parental problems, violent relationships, a planned then cancelled marriage, struggles with the benefit system and finances, plus the constant anxiety of her adopted children.

Beccy identified herself in a number of roles: as a mother, a daughter and a grown woman about to be married. However, these roles remain ambiguous. As a mother she is without children, as a daughter she is treated like an eternal child yet also positioned as carer of her father. As a woman, her sexuality is misplaced; from the 'crippled prostitute' to the victim of violent relationships and failed partnerships. Nonetheless, Beccy is also politically active and a strong campaigner for disabled people's rights. Her aim, she insists, is to get decent wheelchair access into all the pubs and places she likes and needs to go. Far from being a woman with learning difficulties it became clear that Beccy, like many other women interviewed, were in fact struggling with, negotiating and managing some very complicated life situations. Similar to Walmsley's (1994: 273) research, I also found participants who:

> presented images of themselves which were complex and multi-faceted, a rounded picture of human beings struggling to make sense of their situations and relationships.

The 'learning difficulty' label, professionals and provision

However, this certainly is not the image generally associated with women labelled as having learning difficulties. In a historical context, prejudice and discrimination against such people has been deeply ingrained in society. Attitudes based upon psychological fear, superstition and notions of 'abnormal' or 'feebleminded' have evoked practices which promoted the 'systematic removal of disabled people from the mainstream of economic and social life' (Barnes 1991: 27). Silencing and segregating people in isolated institutions also led to them being labelled and studied as a 'separate category of human beings' (Atkinson 1997: 14), with their histories recorded by others and identities constructed within medical and educational discourses (Gilman et al. 1997). Institutionalisation also brought about methods of classification in relation to a notion of 'normality'. This social construction, based on a concept of personal 'competence', relates to intellectual ability, but also extends to include normative and rational ways of behaving (Jenkins 1998; Dowse 2000; Goodley 2000). People are not only judged by their cognitive impairment, the label also incorporates assessments of 'challenging' or 'difficult behaviour.' Goodley claims these judgements are reflected in peoples' personal activities, stating that 'when they are allowed into the community; perfection is demanded' (2000: 43). Davis (1998: 103) sums this up by asserting that people with learning difficulties actually challenge Western conceptions of autonomy and individualism, and because of their 'difference' they are considered a threat to the basic social order. To put it simply, people labelled in this way have been, and continue to be, defined by what they cannot do, rather than what they can.

Medical intervention, the labelling process, 'special needs' educational assessments and the use of specialised terminology used in these programmes, play a predominant role in carving out notions of learning difficulty (Dumbleton 1998; Simpson 1999). A person is labelled in the terms of their pathology – what is wrong with them – as well as being allotted a particular grade or category. Impairment then becomes localised as the individual's problem, which in turn fulfils the classic 'personal tragedy' syndrome highlighted by Oliver (1996: 120). While it is not denied that some people who experience these conditions may require aid and support, this medical framework suggests the cause of learning difficulty is clear cut and definable. Ryan and Thomas, for example, argue that,

> ... in very many instances the type of mental handicap is simply unknown ... in even fewer cases is it possible to identify a precise cause, or describe the causal mechanisms involved in such a way that curative measures can be devised (1980: 16).

There is no overarching reason why these impairments are medically conceptualized or considered within the remit of professional control. Indeed, these boundaries falter when some impairments, like cerebral palsy or epilepsy, occur in people who are not labelled as having a learning difficulty, while other people labelled in this respect do not experience a specific impairment. In fact, the medical and nursing needs of people with learning difficulties are really no different from the rest of the population (Hattersley 1987). Nonetheless, the powerful networks of biomedical control also extend to the production of 'new' medical knowledge (this can be witnessed in the increase in genetic technology), thus remaining a dominant influence in the lives - and potential lives - of people with learning difficulties.

This dilemma is evident in service provision. Although community care initiatives have placed emphasis upon developing needs-led and user-led services - an approach where the social model of disability is seen to override the medical - care assessment and planning procedures still remain predominately in the professional domain (Aspis 1997, 1999; Ramcharan 1997). This situation can be linked to New Labour's social policy programme where 'social justice' is now redefined in such terms as 'participation' and 'community' (Blair 1997,1999). The 'third way' for social care is based on moves away from those who provide the 'care', to the receivers of care: the individual, their carers and their families (Department of Health 1998: section 17). Such strategies have been criticised by public sector social workers, where the introduction of multidisciplinary agencies and partnerships (with voluntary and community sector) has marginalized and reduced social work to crisis management (Jordan 2001).

However, this marginalized position also applies to people labelled as having learning difficulties, where policies, and the emphasis on 'partnerships and inclusion', has also failed, thus remaining rhetorical as opposed to realistic. An example of this can be seen in the White Paper *Valuing People: A New Strategy for Learning Disability in the 21st Century* (Department of Health 2001). Not only have the proposed aims been under financed (Leason 2003), but according to Race (2003a) there is ample evidence that the medical model is alive and well, despite the White Paper recommendations. This conclusion transpired from a review of the position of learning difficulties in both academia and in professional training programmes for health and social workers (Race 2003b). Furthermore, criticism from user-led organisations involved in service planning remains problematic. Despite some exceptions, the practice seems to pivot on user involvement being regarded as a 'requirement' imposed by government, and thus another burden to contend with. The reality of creating real partnerships and hearing the voice of people with learning difficulties therefore remains locked in the traditional confrontational approach between service user and provider (Beresford 2003a).

An unequal situation consequently continues, where people who are caught up in this system are judged by professionals on their abilities or 'competences', whilst being encouraged to express needs and 'become' independent. It is also a position that fails to recognize the diversity between people labelled as having learning difficulties. This is particularly evident for women, where issues concerning gendered differences continue to be unrecognized and relatively low on the agenda of service provision (Clements 1995; Brown 1996; Scior 2003). In view of this situation, this investigation set out to record some of these life experiences, or what Goodley (2000) calls the 'lives that exist beyond the label'. Rather than relating to a label that has been constructed through medical and welfare discourses, I wanted to know how women themselves told their own stories, and understood their lives, as opposed to the case histories recorded by others including carers, families and professionals. However, what soon became clear in this study were the relationships and the intrinsic power dynamics that existed between the women and caring professionals.

Challenging behaviour?

For many of the women included in the research there was little doubt that certain aspects of government policies, community care plans and the more recent policy for direct payments had indeed improved their lives. On a political front, the success of self-advocacy groups and organisations like People First promoted a sense of solidarity and self empowerment. Yet relations with social workers, care managers and staff remained tense. To illustrate some of these dynamics, I return to the narrative of Beccy and also draw on the accounts of Hanna and Jacky.

Beccy has experienced a number of conflicts with care professionals but perhaps the most detrimental experience, in relation to her mental health and well being, has concerned her two children. Both were adopted, although Beccy has been allowed to keep in touch with the 'new' parents. Around her home Beccy has photographs of her children and during the time of my contact she often spoke of her turmoil regarding them. The son, now aged nine had expressed a wish to see his mother. Beccy finds this difficult to cope with as she believes the child will hate her, claiming:

> Why does he want to see me? He must hate me. I left him as a
> baby, he must know that? But I didn't leave him, Social Services

took him, but he's not to know that. It wasn't my idea to have the children adopted. You know, one minute I had 'em and the next I had a safety order slapped on me.

Beccy has been advised that she can write to her son but the letter should not contain anything emotional and she should not mention her love for him (Beccy asked me 'how' she could write such a letter). Reflecting on her life experiences and the loss of her children, Beccy says: 'I was nothing more than a surrogate mother. I've been used ... to give kids to someone else'.

Beccy's insight into her own situation and how she now feels used by Social Services and other professional agencies, demonstrates a degree of ingenuity that reaches far beyond the deterministic label of learning difficulty. Such understanding is also evident in Hanna's life history. Like Beccy, Hanna also has a deep mistrust of social workers. Hanna quizzed me thoroughly over my role as researcher, convinced I was a social worker in disguise and out to: 'trip me up'. Once reassured, Hanna related a string of events, which illustrated the huge influence that professionals had, and continue to exercise, in her life. She claims she has been 'passed from pillar to post with no respect'. Her life consisted of a series of moves from institutions, residential homes, hostels and day centres. For a period Hanna was homeless and lived on the streets. There were also experiences of sexual abuse and a terminated pregnancy, although Hanna asserts that she was coerced into having an abortion by her parents and doctors. She related how one social worker had later accessed these data in her medical records, without her consent, and used the information in a manner that breached confidentiality. Indeed, during the period of interviewing, Hanna's wrangling with her new social worker became apparent. Often appointments were cancelled at the last minute, leaving Hanna annoyed and disappointed. She may have taken the morning off working in the local pub in order to meet the social worker. The irony is that Hanna is relatively independent, yet remains dependent on the social worker for certain requirements.

In contrast, Hanna has very good relations with the Day Centre manager, the office and care staff. The centre that Hanna attends works on 'social model' principles rather than within a medical model. Emphasis is placed on the removal of disabling social and environmental barriers. The centre, which has evolved into a 'drop-in' point, has established good relations with the local community as well as focusing on employment prospects. Finding suitable housing and the chance to engage in further education is high on the agenda for service users. There is also opportunity to join alternative or complementary therapies and take courses in health and exercise routines. Hanna does yoga, has a healthy diet, regular exercise and goes for aromatherapy sessions. She says: 'after a "do" with her (social worker) its nice to have a relaxing massage'. In effect, Hanna's decision to seek out such alternative support is part of her resistance to the system she is caught up in with the local Social Services. This is a situation where she feels powerless. On the other hand, her relations with the people in the Day Centre and the chance to exercise her choice in health care do provide a sense of autonomy. Unfortunately, this situation does not apply in all cases.

Jacky, who lives in a very different environment, in another part of the UK, does not have access to many services other than the Day Centre and her 'new' social worker. Unlike Hanna's situation, the Day Centre remains in the rather traditional model of 'caring' for its users as opposed to promoting empowering activities. This pattern had been replicated by Jacky's parents who continued to treat her as the eternal child, even though Jacky is a woman in her mid-thirties. However, the sudden death of her mother placed Jacky unexpectedly in the role of caring for her father. Like the interdependent relationship between Beccy and her father, Jacky's dad strives to maintain her in a manageable, child-like position. This is a position that her mother sustained over the years in her role of carer for Jacky and also carer for her husband. Her death had a profound effect upon them both. Yet the fact that Jacky is taking on more of her mother's role in the home increases her independence but also creates conflict with her father.

This is further complicated by her desire to form a more permanent relationship with her boyfriend Terry, although her father is unprepared to accept such an arrangement. The extra support Jacky and her dad requested resulted in Jacky being placed in weekend respite care, in order to give her father a 'break'. Jacky was outraged by this and claimed that 'me and dad just need a bit of help in the house and someone to talk to'. She feels that the social worker brought in to assist the situation is actually 'interfering not helping'. Jacky did indeed spend time in a range of respite care units and spent the whole time worrying about her father, who requires practical assistance in the home. However, with careful planning, Jacky managed to turn these events to her and her boyfriend's advantage. They realised that by careful negotiation they could arrange to spend the weekend in the same respite care unit, and thus see each other in relative privacy. Both Jacky and her boyfriend understood this liaison and the clandestine planning involved as a rebellious act against those in control of their lives, but also a situation they were forced into.

These brief snapshot accounts provide some insight into the disturbance women experience in their day-to-day lives with professionals and service provision. Conflicting opinions and drastic interventions made by professionals, particularly concerning parenting and sexuality, have been documented by other researchers (for example, McCarthy 1999; Boxall, Jones and Smith 2003; Olsen and Clarke 2003). Participants in this study spoke of these conflicting opinions and the attitudinal barriers professionals present that further compound the social and environmental barriers they also face. Beccy, for example, spoke at length about the disapproving attitudes she encountered, not only with health and welfare professionals, but also to a certain extent with her neighbours. The fact that she is a disabled woman and a mother appears problematic, even threatening. Beccy concluded her account by stating that 'now I've had the hysterectomy...they might get off me back'.

With all the professional advice Beccy has received over the years there seems little evidence of appropriate emotional support. Beccy's experience of grief and loss, which accumulates as a mental health 'disorder', seems to have gone unnoticed. Instead, Beccy, like Hanna and Jacky, are considered to exhibit 'challenging behaviour'. In Jacky's case her 'behaviour' emerged from the failure of service provision and social workers to understand and recognise the period of transition she was undergoing. A reworking of these power dynamics and the controlling interventions made by professionals would indeed raise the question of 'whose behaviour was challenging?' However, the narratives also exposed another area where participants encountered problems in daily life. This concerned the right to be in control of their own bodies.

Bodily integrity

Bodily integrity is a term borrowed from Williams (1999: 680), who uses it to define the 'right of the individual to protect his/her body against external or internal risk'. This right is considered the fundamental factor in the sustenance of the autonomous welfare subject. Here, I use the term to describe how women claimed their right to control their own bodies and to protect themselves, and others, from risk. Part of this risk stemmed from the need to maintain their personal health as well as to be safeguarded from the threat of physical or sexual abuse. This 'bodily integrity' is also applied to negotiate the constraints experienced within service provision. For example, it has been described how Jacky expressed her bodily integrity by exercising her right to engage in a relationship with Terry. By manipulating their circumstances, Jacky managed to meet Terry while they we both 'in care' in respite units. Although Jacky may be victim of an oppressive system, she also demonstrates the ability to partially disrupt that system. Likewise, Hanna guarded her right to choose alternative methods of healthcare when she favoured aromatherapy as a means to relax, as opposed to prescribed medication. In part, this was an act of resistance against the established 'norms' of traditional medical services, but I would suggest that it was also the desire to maintain control over her body and who had access to it. Hanna, as with the majority of female participants interviewed in this study, had been subjected to sexual and physical abuse in the past. As a result, the possibility of entering into a conventional male / female relationship posed the greatest risk and threat to her bodily integrity. Hanna now claims friendships, as opposed to relationships, are important to her, as well as being in control of her own health and well being.

The question of who has access to bodies, and who makes choices for bodies, was highlighted in the narratives of Yvonne and Shona. Yvonne attends the same day centre as Jacky, and also spends weekends in respite care. Yvonne claims these weekends 'make me ill.' She relates stories of being given her tablets too late, or outside the normal routine, which results in her having a 'do' (epileptic seizure). She also used the word 'disgusted' to describe her bathing experiences in the care unit. Apparently, Yvonne had been left in a bathroom for some time without towels or a bathrobe. This resulted in her getting cold and having to walk naked through a corridor in order to get to her room. The experience had a marked effect on Yvonne, who felt humiliated and reported that staff failed to show respect. Indeed Yvonne's account corresponds with participants in McCarthy's (1999) study, who related similar incidents concerning lack of personal privacy when bathing. Not only did Yvonne feel embarrassed, she felt her body had been neglected by those designated to care for it.

It is also apparent from the participant's accounts how they felt their bodies were contained and policed through a system of institutionalised discourses. On a macro level the structure of educational and welfare provision intersecting with medical and social work practices bears down upon them, recording every action. These pressures filter into the minute activities of day-to-day lives. Case notes, daily logbook accounts, personal programme plans and reviews, all document patterns of behaviour and personal bodily functions. Visits to the doctor or dentist, dates of menstruation, times of baths, personal hygiene recommendations and so on, are all noted down for women who live in residential care. Many women spoke of their lack of choice concerning dress, or how keyworkers would select clothes on their behalf or recommend a certain style. Shona, for example, reported how her keyworker, who was roughly the same body size as her, would try clothes on in the shop so that Shona could see how they looked, although Shona did not try the clothes on herself until she got home. Shona says that she would like more opportunity to shop and select her own things as she feels she 'looks a bit like her' (the keyworker). Yet despite her lack of choice regarding clothes, Shona states that she gets on well with her keyworker and other staff in the house, and regards her social worker as 'a friend, my advocate'.

The 'turn' to embodiment

As stated earlier, Hanna also gets on with staff members at the Day Centre. In addition, a significant number of other participants also shared common experiences with female care workers. This commonality centred on bodily matters and mainly focused on diets, exercise, health issues – particularly the menopause, and clothes. Many of the participants were members of women's groups that had been organised by female support workers. From my attendance and observations made during some of these sessions, plus the accounts provided by other participants and support workers, it was evident that the desire for 'bodily integrity' also applied to female staff. The attention to bodily matters therefore indicates a move away from the biological / medical model to a more social understanding of the body.

There are a number of factors that have encouraged this shift, although the influence of the disabled people's movement and impact of feminism has accelerated this change (Phillips 2002). As Williams (1999) explains, professional (medical, social work and education) control of the 'body' came under threat during the 1960s when a wide range of campaigns began to resist professional judgements. Many of these campaigns were spearheaded by feminists who sought to reclaim bodies from abusive relationships, rape and sexual violence as well as actively campaigning against ECT (electric convulsion therapy), abortion and reproductive rights. Evident in this study has been the 'filtering down' of these earlier campaigns and the changes they produced. For example, there was recognition and increased awareness of violence and abusive relationships, plus knowledge of campaigns (like Zero Tolerance) and legal procedures to challenge these harmful practices. Additionally, concerns about health and well being were high on the agenda, with a move away from medical or drug intervention to that of alternative practices like aromatherapy, yoga, massage and attention to diet.

Part of this reconfiguration of social relations includes the notion of an 'embodied identity'. In this context, the body is a channel through which social and cultural meanings are inscribed, and thus a site of identity and knowledge (Bourdieu 1990; Turner 1992). The attention to bodily matters and the 'turn' to complementary medicine, as opposed to allopathic, are part of this transformation. The participants who engaged in these practices experienced a sense of 'embodied agency'; a means of controlling their own body through their choice of methods. In this context, the 'demystification of professional knowledge and techniques' (Williams 1999: 680) presented an opportunity where women, who have been subjected to a range of medical and social controls, can become relatively autonomous. One of the main influences in this shift, in relation to the participants in this study, has been the input from support staff. It was evident that several female care workers possessed knowledge of heath and personal safety issues and extended this information to the women they supported. However, on the negative side, media and cultural representations of the female body also placed importance on body image and dieting, and in some situations this conflicted with bodily integrity. For example, eating disorders, anorexia and self-abuse among women with learning difficulties are areas that deserve greater attention and research.

Obviously, several other factors underpin the above shift and are worthy of inclusion at this stage. First, the impact of community care arrangements that promoted a shift to smaller group homes and then to independent living or shared housing was an important factor in the life-quality of the participants. More recent emphasis on education, and policy drives to encourage inclusion in mainstream further education colleges, were particularly beneficial to the younger women; whereas women like Hanna and Beccy who attended 'special school' now claim 'not to have been educated'. Equally, recent policy changes leading to direct payments assist recipients to make informed choices, and challenge traditional notions of 'care'. For example, organisations like Values Into Action (VIA) provide clear guidelines for people with learning difficulties who wish to access the Direct Payment scheme in order to buy and manage their own personal assistants. Williams (1999, 2001) also highlights the influence of local self-help and support groups, as well large-scale organisations like the British Council of Disabled People (BCODP) and People First, who have not only provided greater access to information but also challenge assumptions of dependency and medical labelling. Additionally, the demands of these groups to have a say in the organisation of services and to be recognised and respected for their differences have 'raised important questions about the social relations of the organisation and delivery of care services' (Williams 2001: 471).

Review

This chapter has sought to explore the impact of professional health and social care systems in the daily lives of women labelled as having learning difficulties. From the brief narrative accounts it is evident that dynamics of power relations between women and these networks of care are somewhat strained. Running parallel to these practices however, is evidence of health and support needs being met, albeit not through traditional medical services or professional agencies. As stated previously, the demystification of these professional knowledges and techniques has, in turn, produced strong alliances between female support staff and the women they support. Thus the emergence of a 'social body' as opposed to a 'medicalised body' has created an opportunity for women to exercise their bodily integrity. These shifts of power relations, I suggest, are evident in comparatively small, yet significant changes in non-medicalised, alternative health practices, as well as through a social model understanding of learning difficulties.

Earlier, this chapter referred to New Labour's ideology on social care, particularly the significance of 'partnerships' and 'inclusion'. The issue of 'partnerships' remains a contentious and controversial area of debate. Even though some professionals may feel undermined, my argument and indeed the narrative voices in this research project, illustrate that 'real' partnerships between people with learning difficulties and professionals are not being made. It appears that although some 'hands-on' support staff have embraced and promoted positive attitudes, these changes are not visible on a higher professional level. This is perhaps most obvious in the failure of professionals to recognise people with learning difficulties in a holistic context. Life style adjustments, periods of transition and issues concerning parenting and sexuality are all areas that require greater understanding. These understandings will not come about while professionals continue to relate to learning difficulties as a purely medical / behavioural condition. This approach not only fails to listen to people with learning difficulties themselves, but also excludes the potential for professionals to seek awareness in alternative directions. Meanwhile, the dilemma is further extended by recent government initiatives based on 'evidence-based' practice (participatory and user-led research) and how this can influence policy and public services (Beresford 2003b). Although this may be an innovative proposal it could prove difficult to facilitate when professionals are still locked in medical discourses and where the policing of bodies still prevails.

Bibliography

Aspis, S. 1997: Self Advocacy for People with Learning Difficulties. *Disability and Society*, 12 (4), 647-654.

Aspis, S. 1999: What they don't tell people with learning difficulties. In M. Corker and S. French (eds), *Disability Discourse*. Buckingham Open University Press.

Atkinson, D. 1997: *An Auto/Biographical Approach to Learning Difficulty Research*. Aldershot: Ashgate.

Barnes, C. 1991: *Disabled People in Britain and Discrimination: A case for Anti-Discrimination Legislation*. London: Hurst and Co / BCODP.

Beresford, P. 2003a: Fully Engaged. *Community Care*, 1498, November, 38-41.

Beresford, P. 2003b: *It's Our Lives: A Short Theory of Knowledge, Distance and Experience*. London: Citizen Press & Shaping Our Lives National Users Network.

Blair, T. 1997: Why we must help those excluded from society. *The Independent*, 8th December 2002.

Blair, T. 1999: Speech to the Institute for Public Policy Research. London, 14th January 2003.

Bourdieu, P. 1990: *The Logic of Practice*. (trans. R. Nice), London: Routledge.

Boxall, K., Jones, M. and Smith, S. 2003: Advocacy and parents with learning difficulties: even when you've got an advocate Social Services still always do what's easiest for them. In D. Race (ed.), *Learning Disability – A Social Approach*. London: Routledge.

Brown, H. 1996: Ordinary women: Issues for women with learning disabilities. *British Journal of Learning Disabilities,* 24 (4), 47-51.

Clements, J. 1995: Real Men, Real Woman, Real Lives? Gender issues in learning disabilities and challenging behaviour. *Disability and Society*, 10 (4), 425–35.

Davis, C. A. 1998: Constructing other selves: (in)competences and the category of learning difficulties. In R. Jenkins (ed.), *Questions of Competence: Culture, Classification and Intellectual Disability*. Cambridge: Cambridge University Press.

Department of Health 1998: *Modernising Social Services: Promoting Independence, Improving Protection, Raising Standards*. Cm 4169. London: HMSO.

Department of Health/ Home Office 2000: *No Secrets: Guidance on developing and implementing multi-agency policies and procedures to protect vulnerable adults from abuse*. London: HMSO.

Department of Health 2001: *Valuing People: A New Strategy for Learning Disability for the 21st Century*. London: HMSO.

Dowse, L. 2000: Contesting Practices, Challenging Codes: self-advocacy, disability politics and the social model. *Disability and Society*, 16 (1), 123–141.

Dumbleton, P. 1998: Words and Numbers. *British Journal of Learning Disabilities*, 26 (4), 151–153.

Gilman, M., Swain, J. and Heyman, B. 1997: Life Histories or Case History: the objectification of people with learning difficulties through the tyranny of professional discourse. *Disability and Society*, 12 (3), 254–294.

Goodley, D. 2000: *Self-Advocacy in the Lives of People with Learning Difficulties: the politics of resilience*. Buckingham: Open University Press.

Hattersley, G.P. (ed.) 1987: *People with Mental Handicap: perspectives in intellectual disability*. London: Faber and Faber.

Jenkins, R. (ed.) 1998: *Questions of Competence: Culture, Classification and Intellectual Disability*. Cambridge: Cambridge University Press.

Jordan, B. 2001: Tough Love: social work, social exclusion and the third way. *British Journal of Social Work*, 31, 527–546.

Leason, K. 2003: Who gets to Decide? *Community Care*, 1481, July, 28–30.

McCarthy, M. 1999: *Sexuality and Women with Learning Disabilities*. London: Jessica Kingsley Publishers.

Oliver, M. 1996: *Understanding Disability: from theory to practice*, Basingstoke: Macmillan

Olsen, R. and Clarke, H. 2003: *Parenting and Disability: Disabled parents' experiences of raising children*. Bristol: Policy Press.

Phillips, D. 2002: Women, Learning Difficulties and Identity: a study through personal narratives. Unpublished PhD, University of Leeds.

Race, D. 2003a: Cinderella in the Lion's Den – reflections on the place of learning disability in Disability Studies. Paper presented at *Disability Studies: Theory, Policy and Practice* Conference, Lancaster University, 4-6th September.

Race, D. (ed.) 2003b: *Learning Disability – A Social Approach*. London: Routledge.

Ramcharan, P., Roberts, G., Grant, G. and Borland, J. (eds.) 1997: *Empowerment in Everyday Life: Learning Disabilities*. London: Jessica Kingsley.

Ryan, J. and Thomas, F. 1980: *The Politics of Mental Handicap*. London: Free Association Books.

Scior, K. 2003: Using Discourse Analysis to Study the Experiences of Women with Learning Disabilities. *Disability and Society*, 18 (6), 779-795.

Simpson, M. 1999: Bodies, brains, behaviour: the return of the three stooges in learning disability. In M. Corker and S. French (eds.) *Disability Discourse*. Buckingham: Open University Press.

Turner, B. 1992: *Regulating Bodies: Essays in Medical Sociology*. London: Routledge.

Walmsley, J. 1994: Gender, Caring and Learning Disability. Unpublished PhD thesis. Milton Keynes: Open University.

Williams, F. 1999: Good-enough Principles for Welfare. *Journal of Social Policy*, 28 (4), 667-687.

Williams, F. 2001: In and beyond New Labour: towards a new political ethics of care. *Critical Social Policy*, 21 (4), 467-493.

CHAPTER 12

De/Constructing 'Learning Difficulties' in Educational Contexts: the life story of Gerry O'Toole

Dan Goodley

Introduction

Education is an ideological battlefield for disabled people (Apple 1982). For people with 'learning difficulties', child and adulthood involves participation in education and training contexts that are full to bursting with professionals. This chapter examines those educational and training cultures, occupied by people with the label of 'learning difficulties', that remain oppressive and disabling, even in the current climate of new disability policy and legislation. Firstly, I will present the life story of a person with the label of 'learning difficulties' – Gerry O'Toole – in order to explore his and his peers' experiences of education and training contexts. Secondly, to allow for an examination of the story I will draw upon some ideas from a theoretical arena (poststructuralism) and an approach to analysis (discourse analysis). Third, I will examine Gerry's story in terms of what it can tell us about education and work contexts. Three findings from this analysis will be discussed: (i) education creates 'learning difficulties'; (ii) education regulates and governs; (iii) education can be resisted and challenged. In order to bring together theory and practice in the social model of disability, it is argued that much can be gained by turning to the stories of people who occupy educational places and the poststructuralist analyses that accompany their experiences.

The term 'learning difficulties' is used in this chapter to describe people who have been labelled at some point in their lives as requiring specialist 'mental handicap services' (Walmsley 1993: 46). This term is chosen instead of other synonyms such as 'mental handicap', 'mental impairment' or 'learning disabilities', because it is the term preferred by many in the self-advocacy movement. As one self-advocate puts it: 'If you put "people with learning difficulties" then they know that people want to learn and to be taught how to do things' (quoted in Sutcliffe and Simons 1993: 23). Moreover, this chapter suggests that the very phenomenon of 'learning difficulties' is constructed by institutional practices, such as education.

> What should concern us is the mystifying fact that so many social scientists ... do not regard mental retardation [sic] as a social and cultural phenomenon. I say mystifying, because nothing in the probabilistic world of social scientific reality is more certain than the assertion that mental retardation [sic] is a socio-cultural problem through and through (Dingham 1968: 76).

A narrative: the life story of Gerry O'Toole

In this chapter, I will be drawing upon the narrative of a person with 'learning difficulties'. This story is the product of an ethnographic approach in which the story of the primary narrator (Gerry O'Toole) is supplemented by narratives of significant others – comrades with 'learning difficulties'. The methodological, ethical and analytical considerations are dealt with in more detail in Goodley et al. (2004). But suffice to say, 'Gerry' is a person I got to know over the years through my voluntary work and research. He has always intrigued me. Here was a person who boasted a rich and varied life. Unlike many of his peers, Gerry dipped in and out of educational and training settings. While many people with 'learning difficulties' inhabit these contexts from group home, to Day Centre, to MENCAP organised disco on a Tuesday evening, Gerry entered these places only from time to time. His life appeared to say something to me about existing differently to his welfare-located peers. Maybe he appealed because his ordinary life of family, friends and work seemed so extraordinary in view of the years of institutional living experienced by so many of his friends. Crucially, his story – and those of his peers – said some dramatic things about the educational / training cultures that they were involved in. As we consider the contemporary policy, professional and political context of disabled people, and the social model of disability's response, it is worth keeping in mind the lived realities of people with learning difficulties. By turning to one story we are reminded of the very real implications for many.

Gerry O'Toole's life story (abridged from Goodley et al. 2004: 3-14)
Here are some of my precious stories – events that shaped me. *You* won't
have heard of them. Its time to start listening to what *we* have to say.
Sooner or later, you'll listen. *You* will have to. Its difficult to explain to
you about places you may have never experienced. You have seen people
like me, though. In the shopping malls. In fast food restaurants. In
minibuses with steamed up windows. In small groups, shadowed by senior,
more competent adults; middle aged women or young trendy blokes with
goatee beards. Our cultures sometimes cross swords. You have words for
people like me. Retard, Joey, defective, idiot, spaz, mong. You might not
use these words now but if pressed you would shamefully recall a
childhood vocabulary that flourished with such insults.

> *'Frog', Paul shouted, 'Frog'. The gang fell about, giggling. ('Frog'
> was all Paul really said, that and 'I love Jonny Vickers', much to
> Jonny's embarrassment. He once spent the day spray painting 'I love
> Vickers' on lampposts around the town. He was one of only two lads in
> our secondary school who had support workers around them at all times.
> He was a minor celebrity but people laughed at him.)*
>
> *Then Paul pulled down his pants and asked us, 'Do you want to
> see it wee?' 'Yeah – ha, yeah. I want to see it wee!' shouted Tez. And
> so Tez did – Paul neatly peeing into the drain. And we all laughed, all
> eight of us in Litton Close, a cul de sac near our primary school –
> recalling a place where our prejudices weren't so vicious.*

Now, things are more subtle, I guess. You will feel it inappropriate to
catch my eye, to smile or to acknowledge me. And if you do clock me,
you'll probably wonder afterwards if it was the right thing to do. You can't
win and neither can I. We are – how do they put it – always batting for
different sides?

> *I am a resident. You reside.*
> *I am admitted. You move in.*
> *I am aggressive. You are assertive.*
> *I have behaviour problems. You are rude.*
> *I am noncompliant. You don't like being told what to do.*
> *When I ask you out for dinner, it is an outing. When you ask
> someone out, it is a date.*
> *I don't know how many people have read the progress notes people
> write about me. I don't even know what is in there. You didn't speak
> to your best friend for a month after they read your journal.*
> *My case manager, psychologist, occupational therapist, nutritionist*

*and house staff set goals for me for the next year. You haven't decided
what you want out of life.*

Someday I will be discharged ... maybe.

You will move onward and upward. (Extract from 'You and Me',
an anonymous poem publicised by Values into Action, London,
http://www.viauk.org/)

What do you feel when you see us? When you saw that 'mongey guy'
in the street? Is it pity, sadness, a sense of fortune? Well, you might be right
in having those feelings of concern. But the reason you feel like you do is
less to do with my 'condition' and more down to the world that creates
me in its own vision. In spite of or because of these difficulties we have
in relating to one another, people like me – my comrades and I – we have
been quietly getting on with changing things. You just never knew
anything about my story and all the others that have come from this new
burgeoning, exciting, radical movement called People First. But our
successes are never easily achieved. Some difficult terrain has been tread.

*It was freezing and as I entered the outdoor market, Gerry was, as
always, conspicuous. Red, white and black bobble hat that just hid his
long straggly thinning hair. A greying stubble made him look 10 years
older than the 39 that he actually was, though lovely warm piercing
green Irish eyes ensured that you were charmed. A beige canvas bag full
to bursting with papers and documents weighed down Gerry's left
shoulder to the point that he worked with an uneven gait. Scruffy green
combat jacket, brown waistcoat, cream shirt, brown trousers and new
white trainers completed the 'vision'.*

'How are you Gerry?'

*'Fine. There is this chap who wants to come to the People First
meetings'*

'Who is he?'

'I don't know'

'Is he a member of staff from the centre?'

'I don't know'

'Is he a researcher wanting to find out about self-advocacy?'

'I dunno'

'Is he a person with 'learning difficulties'?'

'Dunno – didn't ask him'.

My father was a tall, strong, vocal man. He smoked Woodbines and
loved a pint in the local working men's club. He was funny and imposing.
When I was 18 he took me and my older brothers to the club to celebrate.

I am now a paid up card-carrying member. The Friday after my dad died I went in. At the bar, Clive the secretary tells me that I need to pay for my membership. 'You're a member in your own right now Gerry. Now your dad has gone, God rest his soul, you can't be his guest, you need to be a proper member'. I asked him how much it was. '85 to you'. 85 quid I thought, 'can I pay in instalments like me Mam does with the washing machine?' '85 pence you daft bugger!' laughed Clive. They often get me like that.

Somehow, there was always someone around. If my Mam and Dad were at work then there was an older sister there to make my tea, run my bath, tickle me until I burst. Every morning when I was young my Dad walked me to school. We would stop at the dual carriageway across from the school and watch as my schoolmates were ferried past in ambulances. When they finally arrived at school, they were sick as dogs from the rough journey. Jeremy would crease me up, telling me how they'd have to hang onto the stretcher that was kept between the rows of seats. Of course, when they went round a corner the stretcher would move and they'd be pulled to the back of the bus, scattering those that stood up, kids flying into one another. Once in school, things were never so bad for me. I have friends now who never had a family, a safe haven. Sophie's mother couldn't cope. Sophie was ordered off to hospital when she was young.

I was in and out of special school and eventually left at 15. They were strange places, funny buildings, you were labelled as soon as you got there. Lessons were boring, colouring-in books that were already covered with the crayon scribbles of previous years' students. Class after class with the headmaster playing piano. Asking us which piece of classical music he was murdering. Keen, lively, young teachers joining us straight from teacher training college only to promptly leave by the end of their first or second term. Broken people. Students sound asleep in class, drooling onto the desks where they rested their heads. My mother would complain, 'Why can't Gerry be taught proper mathematics and English', she would tell the teachers. They told her I was struggling so much that I wouldn't be able to do the things my brothers and sisters were doing. Daft really, because when I worked with my Dad on the markets I was really good at counting up the change people needed. One teacher said to my mother that I would never be able to read and write. I did, though. At home. It wasn't the best of places. One day, I broke into the caretaker's office. I nicked a spade. Some time later, the teachers caught me trying to dig myself out of the school – I was trying to escape under the fence. I got into trouble a lot at school for talking or having a laugh in class. Some big lads off the estate eventually burnt down the school. After I had left, some of my mates managed to get themselves into the 'normal schools'. They told me that they had loads of parties, drinking with the other kids in the pubs in town.

The 6th form had some new members – 12 people with 'learning difficulties' from the Day Centre. Kevin – Down Syndrome lad was the only one who was school age. Kevin followed Bant around, much to the amusement of Bant's fellow sixth formers. Bant was popular – stupid but popular. And then when Bant got bored he would play to the crowd.

'Whose your favourite, Kev?'

'Bant'

'Who do you love?'

'Bant'

'Course yer do'.

And then Bant would run out of the classroom for a ciggie. Too quick for Kevin, who would bury his face in the seat – sobbing his heart out.

Others joined the special needs group at the 'tech'. I was never going to be packed off to some 'life skills class'. As a teenager, school meant little to me. Well, I was on the market stalls at the time, so it wasn't really interesting. I really started to get into the market stall work. Some of my mates either went to the Day Centre full time or, if they were lucky, got a job (if that's what you can called not being paid to work) farming, t-shirt printing or decorating old people's houses. My brother jokes that we are part of the Irish Catholic mafia. A job was always going to be there for me.

The boys' toilets. Lunchtime. Brid [18 yrs, small in stature, long hair, eyes too small for his face], Jano [20 years, large frame, short haired, piercing brown eyes] and David [short, overweight, mouse like, scared, thick rimmed glasses.]

Brid: So, twatter – is it true? Is it true, then? 12 toes 'ave ya? Ya freak.

[Brid pushes David into the cubicle, David covers his face with his lower arms.]

David: No ...

Brid: Jano, shut door, man.

[Jano firmly closes the door and rests against the door. He is laughing.]

Brid punches David hard in the stomach, and struggles with David's shoes, eventually prising them off, as he forces David to sit on the toilet seat. David is howling. Awful screams echo.]

Brid: Fucking hell [laughs] look at this Jano, look – it's the elephant man! Jesus, that's horrible [laughs]

[Jano moves into the cubicle and squeals with delight. Brid and Jano catch each other on and run out of the toilet, their laughter echoing in the toilet while ringing out over the factory floor.

David pulls himself up from the seat by the door and stoops down to collect his shoes and socks. As he moves out of the toilet we catch a reflection of him in the mirror. We can make out the mirror image of chalk marks scrawled on the back of his long grey coat 'I am a knobhead. Kick me!']

David was bullied for two years. He had a meeting with his mother, his keyworker, an occupational therapist and the work supervisor. The occupational therapist asked him if he wanted to take a holiday. He said yes. He hasn't worked since, that was 12 years ago. I heard that David has spent the last three years at home. He never leaves the house, even though his Mum and sister want him to get out, to make friends. He stays in bed, all day, every day.

For me work has always been a laugh with my cousins, my brothers, and our pals. Five am start, breakfast in the market café at eight and back in time for the punters. Lots of 'craic'. Weekends we get off somewhere different – York, Newcastle, Glasgow, Rotherham, all the different markets. I am well known, always asked if I need more work. From time to time I collect glasses in Mulligans, which is a really cool Irish pub. A trio plays rebel songs every Friday night and it is packed with regulars as well as students nursing a pint or two. One Saturday night, Trevor the landlord asks if anyone knows of a right wingback that could play for the pub football team. I overheard him. So did my brother Callum. 'Our Gerry's got a sweet right foot, you want to ask him'. I am now a regular. Scored two last match.

Last Wednesday I rushed down to the Day Centre. Quick coffee. Then, we spent ages helping each other with our aprons – Steve's difficult to dress in his wheelchair. Then June, whose staff, bakes a cake. Mixing up the ingredients, adding dried fruit, whisking away, talking us through her handiwork. She does it all. Always has done. We are her willing audience. We wait in relative silence watching the cake rise through the glass of the oven door. Rebecca asked me why I even bother – 'can't cook, won't ever be allowed to bloody cook' she mocks. I tell her – I come to see my mates. Questions?

Making sense of Gerry's life story: poststructuralism and discourse analysis

Gerry's story allows an insight into educational and training cultures. But how do we make sense of it? In this section, I will introduce an approach to analysis – discourse analysis – which has its roots in the theoretical arena of poststructuralism.

Postmodernism and poststructuralism

Poststructuralism has finally entered the paradigm of disability studies (Hughes and Paterson 1997; Allan 1998, 1999; Corker 1997; Shakespeare 2000; Corker and Shakespeare 2002). Poststructuralism has been viewed as a methodology for capturing the workings of late capitalism, post-fordism, the knowledge society or postmodernity (Bell 1973; Jameson 1984). Postmodernism – the study of postmodernity – is a term ripe for social scientific debate. It continues to receive passionate support and scathing criticism. In *The Postmodern Condition*, Lyotard (1979) challenges what he terms the 'grand narratives' of modern societies. These narratives have three features:

1. They aim to be overarching – so scientific narratives on 'learning difficulties' aim to understand and treat all people so-labelled.

2. They boast foundationalism – they desire to base knowledge on claims that are 'known' with certainty, such as scientific measurements of intelligence.

3. There is an optimistic faith in progression – 'truths' progress the world, and people with learning difficulties are rehabilitated or, 'at best', cured.

For Lyotard, grand narratives are increasingly open to question. Following Assiter (1996: 17), how can we still unquestionably cling to the progressive qualities of grand narratives – enlightenment projects such as 'science' – that foundered on the rock of tragedy that was Auschwitz? Grand narratives are not and never were benevolent offerings for all. Poststructuralism, the methodology of postmodernism (offered by writers such as Judith Butler, Michel Foucault, Jacques Derrida and Jacques Lacan), interrogates the workings of grand narratives in a number of ways.

- Grand narratives are viewed with scepticism as they reflect the manipulative powers of 'discourses' (which serve particular societal and institutional functions).

- The universalising theorises of grand narratives are rejected because they actually marginalize certain social groupings to the status of 'other'.
- The main aim of modernist narratives – understanding human beings – is viewed critically; there is a price to be paid in understanding human beings.
- Institutions and knowledge disciplines – such as psychology, education, rehabilitative disciplines – aim to know but also control.
- Individual human beings are viewed as creations and constructions of institutions, power and discourses – 'the individual, with his identity and characteristics, is the product of the relation of power exercised over bodies' (Assiter 1996: 9).

If we take Marx's (1845) argument that human essence is the ensemble of social relations, then poststructuralism can be viewed as a methodology that is in tune with contemporary knowledge societies of late capitalism. There are people out there who are constructed by society and its institutions (such as education). Our job as disability thinkers is to challenge disabling visions of personhood owned by those institutions.

A poststructuralist method: discourse analysis

Discourse analysis provides a social account of subjectivity – of how we understand and see ourselves and others (Burman and Parker 1993). Rather than viewing subjectivity as in the heads of individuals, discourse analysts turn to the texts, practices, knowledges, documents, experiences and stories – discourses – by which subjectivity is accounted for and constructed From this position, then, Gerry's story is viewed as a text that contains a whole host of discourses of disability, 'learning difficulties', education, employment, competency and adulthood. Discourse analysts have problems with the notion of the 'individual' and 'the body' and their modernist association with the natural. In a seminal paper, Hughes and Paterson (1997) introduce a poststructuralist gaze on the body. Following Donna Haraway (1991) they note that neither our personal bodies nor our social bodies may be seen in the sense of existing *outside* of human behaviour. While the classic social model distinction of 'impairment' and 'disability' is politically useful, the former remains a biological, individual and embodied phenomenon (e.g. Thomas 1999). In contrast, discourse analysis turns attention to the ways in which *bodies are made*: how surfaces of the body are monitored and how the body is regulated (Hughes and

Paterson 1997: 330). Regimes and truths about disabled bodies have been central to their governance and control:

> Meaning follows the name (or diagnostic label) … The power of the name penetrates the flesh and maps out for it a performance (Butler 1993; cited in Hughes and Paterson 1997: 333).

Poststructuralism and its method (discourse analysis) critically examines those discourses that create particular views of objects (the label of 'learning difficulties'), subjectivity (having 'learning difficulties') and the human subject (a person with 'learning difficulties'). Such discourses can be found in educational contexts (Ball 1990).

Education in the life of Gerry O'Toole: de/constructing 'learning difficulties'

Discourse analysis allows us to make sense of the ways in which human beings are constructed, shaped and moulded via the power of discourses and how these very discourses are used to make sense of ourselves and others. With Gerry O'Toole's story in mind, we will turn to three discourse analyses.

Education creates 'learning difficulties'

Gerry's narrative opens up possibilities for viewing the ways in which disabled people are regulated. Following Wilkinson and Kitzinger (1995: 3), the aim is to explore what it means to be a person with 'learning difficulties' in this postmodern tale, by interrogating those discursive practices that constitute versions of self. 'Learning difficulties' tends to be viewed as an objectified, naturalised phenomenon (Goodley et al. 2004). Yet, this 'thingification' of the world, persons and experience produces a phantom objectivity and denies and mystifies the body's fundamental nature as a *relation between people* (Titchkovsky 2002: 105). People with 'learning difficulties' are formed through the binding of complementary discourses: such as 'medical', 'psychological' and 'individual'. These discourses are especially conducive – and become almost commonsensical by nature – to specialist institutions of group home, day centre, special school, learning support unit, segregated or supported workplace. Crucially, people with 'learning difficulties' are objects. If we take the stories of Bant and David we can see the person with 'learning difficulties' as plaything and object of abuse: not as active person or human subject, but passive object. People with 'learning difficulties' are aware of this process of objectification, hence, the move towards the label of 'People First'. The former speaks of a history of being viewed solely as an object of ridicule, control and disposal. The latter – People First – collectively identifies people as subjects rather than objects.

Impairment construction, through objectification, has contributed markedly to the exclusion of people identified as those objects (Tremain 2002). For people with 'learning difficulties' the very construction of their impairments – and associated notions of 'incompetence', 'maladaptive functioning', 'low intellect' – is at the heart of their experiences of disablement: the constant social (re)construction of 'learning difficulties'. Education creates the passive object of 'learning difficulties' rather than the active human subjects that may exist behind the label.

Education regulates and governs

Gerry's story is also about regulation and governance (Foucault 1973a, 1973b, 1977, 1983; Burman and Parker 1993). Michel Foucault illustrated the ways in which discourses and practices mascarade as 'truths'. These practices are particularly noticeable in what Rose (1985) terms the 'psy-complex' – seen most vividly in welfare and knowledge systems that have contributed to practices and treatments associated with the rational treatment of the irrational mind / body. There is a sense that Gerry is very much aware of the psy-complex in institutions such as special schools – 'funny buildings, strange places, labelled as soon as you got there'. However, the psy-complex does not remain in professionalised institutions. From Reality TV, to self-help books, therapy and increased reflecivity, domineering discourses of our 'selves' – and how our selves should be – are felt and experienced in everyday life. People with 'learning difficulties' are 'village idiots', 'the funny backwards chap', the weird guy in the working men's club. Understanding ourselves – a key progressive aim of a civilised, modern society – allows us to 'know' a 'handicapped person' just from looking at them.

This knowing of self – and how self should be – has been termed governance. This can range from governing others (such as gazing at the abnormal with David's story), through to more elusive self-governance ('now things are a lot more subtle'). David was free to make a choice, to go on holiday, which then resulted in long-term exclusion. In making sense of ourselves, we draw upon discourses, which may give us a sense of agency. However, we are free only to govern ourselves. As Kurtz (1981: 14) puts it, 'acting like a retarded person [sic] can soon become second

nature' – governance is often about self-restraint. The modern human
subject is provided with discursive resources that allow them opportunities
for making sense of themselves in particular ways. The end of this process
is subjectification; experienced as an inner consciousness, created by
drawing upon available discourses. While common sense may have us
believe that an increased knowledge of ourselves – and resultant
subjectification – results in enlightened individuals and developed
societies, there is a price to be paid. Subjectification may render bodies
docile: perhaps most graphically captured when students fell asleep in
Gerry's class.

Gerry knows his place in the cooking class at the day centre, excuses
it as an opportunity to see friends – but is this a knowing acceptance? For
many people with the label of 'learning difficulties', their daily lives are
regulated and controlled by professional intrusions. Education is
increasingly multi-layered in terms of the increasing forms of
professionalisation:

> While the ambulances and large-scale institutionalisation of
> Gerry's childhood might have disappeared, the advent of a
> whole host of specialist services (psy-complex), discourses of
> self-knowledge   (governance)   and   their   application
> (subjectification) create a new horrific realisation: at least when
> slammed up in the old hospitals inmates' minds had wings
> (Goodley et al. 2004: 128).

Education can be resisted and challenged

Narrative has had an uneasy relationship with disability studies. For some,
personal stories re-emphasise old enemies of case file understandings of
disability and impairment (Finkelstein 1996). Similarly, Barnes (1998)
states that most of this writing represents either sentimental biography. A
post-structuralist narrative / reading does not have these naturalised hang-
ups. Discourse analysis is a resistant approach to analysis: resisting static,
structuralist and immovable views of discourse while embracing resistant,
performative acts of human subjects.

Foucault (1977) suggested that where there is power there is also
resistance. A poststructuralist discourse analysis understands the categories
of 'person' and 'learning difficulties' as phenomena formulated in power
relationships of language. Now, 'man-made' things can often be
demolished and rebuilt. Although certain people have more access to the
raw materials of discourse than others, opportunities exist for all to

reconstruct versions of personhood. One key area of resistance lies in the multiple identities of a discursive world (Goodley et al. 2004: 128-29). During the day you may move between the different subject positions of parent, partner, colleague, consumer, player and lover. Each of these positions has power connected to it. Gerry's narrative is characterised by the many different subject positions – from day centre user, to worker, to key family member, to membership of the working men's club. The character of this narrative is someone allowed to move in and out of institutionally created subject positions. Often, there are very direct acts of resistance with tremendous symbolism – like when Gerry wanted to dig himself out of school! Other characters in Gerry's narrative find that external (material) barriers challenge their subject movement. It is therefore even more remarkable to see people who are so objectified by the professional gaze finding spaces to escape subject positions – such as Gerry O'Toole. For some their new subject positions might have to take place away from the professional gaze. Perhaps, this is key to Gerry's narrative – to enter contexts away from the professionally populated spaces of learning difficulty services.

Gerry is a remarkable character. He slips in and out of service settings. His life is rich and varied. Many of his friends do not enjoy such freedoms. We are reminded that modernist projects such as professionalisation have not been eclipsed with the diversity, tolerance and liberty of postmodernity (Hughes 2002). But, rather than rejecting educational professionals, we should be aware of professional resistance. When Gerry talks of 'broken teachers' he demonstrates how professional subject positions are not all encompassing. Professionals are also often caught up in the disabling world of the psy-complex (Parker et al. 1995; Parker 1997). It is no surprise then that members of the self-advocacy movement have spoken about those members of staff who have broken the professional mould to offer support (Goodley 2000). Gerry's story, therefore, is as much about professionals of the disability industry as it is about people with learning difficulties.

Conclusion

A pressing concern for disability studies (and the developing social model) is to take seriously the ways in which many work and educational contexts, by their very nature, contribute to the exclusion of people through their institutional practices and discourses which are so compelled to construct versions of subjectivity and with them the objects of disabling discourses. Educational and training zones are symptomatic of a late capitalist society that values, promulgates and divides knowledge and access to knowledge. In order to promote enabling theory, practice and politics, much can be gained through a turn to the texts of narrative and discourse.

Acknowledgements

I would like to acknowledge the support of the Economic and Social Research Council (Grant No. R000237697) which allowed me the opportunity to consider some of the debates raised in this chapter.

Bibliography

Allan, J. 1998: Theorising special education inside the classroom: a Foucauldian analysis of pupils' discourses. In P. Haug and J. Tossebro (eds), *Theoretical perspectives on special education*. Kristiansand: Norwegian Academic Press.

Allan, J. 1999: *Actively seeking inclusion: pupils with special needs in mainstream schools*. London: Falmer.

Apple, M. 1982: *Education and Power*. London: Routledge & Kegan Paul.

Assiter, A. 1996: *Enlightened women: Modernist feminism in a Feminist Age*. London: Routledge.

Ball, S. (ed.) 1990: *Foucault and Education: Disciplines and Knowledge*. London: Routledge.

Barnes, C. 1998: The Social Model of Disability: A Sociological Phenomenon Ignored by Sociologists? In T. Shakespeare (ed.), *The Disability Reader: Social Science Perspectives*. London: Cassell.

Bell, D. 1973: *The Coming of Post-industrial Society*. London: Heinneman.

Burman, E. and Parker, I. (ed.) 1993: *Discourse Analytic Research: Repertoires and Readings of Texts in Action*. London: Routledge.

Butler, J. 1993: *Bodies That Matter: On the Discursive Limits of Sex*. London: Routledge.

Corker, M. 1997: *Deaf and Disabled, or Deafness Disabled? Towards a Human Rights Perspective*. Buckingham: Open University Press.

Corker, M. and Shakespeare, T. 2002: *Disability/Postmodernity: Embodying Disability Theory*. London: Cassell.

Davies, J. and Watson, N. 2002: Countering Stereotypes of Disability: Disabled Children and Resistance. In M. Corker and T. Shakespeare (eds), *Disability/Postmodernity: Embodied Disability Theory*. London: Continuum.

Dingham, H. F. 1968: A Plea for Social Research in Mental Retardation. *Journal of Mental Deficiency*, 73 (1), 2-4.

Finkelstein, V. 1996: Outside, Inside Out. *Coalition*, GMCDP, April, 30-36.

Foucault, M. 1973a: *The Birth of the Clinic: An Archaeology of Medical Perception*, (trans. A. M. Sheridan). New York: Pantheon Books.

Foucault, M. 1973b: *Madness and Civilisation: A History of Insanity in the Age of Reason*, (trans. R. Howard). New York: Vintage/Random House.

Foucault, M. 1977: *Discipline and Punish: The Birth of the Prison*, (trans. R. Howard). New York: Pantheon Books.

Foucault, M. 1983: The Subject and Power. In H. L. Dreyfus and P. Rabinov (ed.), *Michael Foucault: Beyond Structuralism and Hermeneutics*. Chicago: University of Chicago Press.

Goodley, D. 2000: *Self-advocacy in the Lives of People with Learning Difficulties*. Buckingham: Open University Press.

Goodley, D., Lawthom, R., Clough, P. and Moore, M. 2004: *Researching Life Stories: Method, Theory and Analyses in a Biographical Age*. London: Routledge Falmer Press.

Haraway, D. 1991: *Simians, Cyborgs, and Women: The Reinventions of Nature*. Routledge / New York.

Hughes, B. 2002: Bauman's Strangers: impairment and the invalidation of disabled people in modern and post-modern cultures. *Disability and Society*, 17 (5), 571-84.

Hughes, B. and Paterson, K. 1997: The Social Model of Disability and the Disappearing Body: Towards a Sociology of Impairment. *Disability and Society*, 12 (3), 325-40

Jameson, F. 1984: Postmodernism, or the cultural logic of late Capitalism. *New Left Review*, I/146, 53-92.

Kurtz, R. A. 1981. The Sociological Approach to mental Retardation. In A. Brechin, P. Liddiard and J. Swain (eds), *Handicap in a Social World*. Sevenoaks: Hodder & Stoughton in association with the Open University Press.

Lyotard, J. 1979: *The Postmodern Condition*, Paris: Minuit.

Marx, K. 1976/1845: Theses on Feuerbach. In *Karl Marx Frederick Engels. Collected Works, Vol 5*. London: Lawrence & Wishart.

Parker, I. 1997: *Psychoanalytic Culture: Psychoanalytic Discourse in Western Society*. London: Sage.

Parker, I., Georgaca, E., Harper, D., McLaughlin, T. and Stowell-Smith, M. 1995: *Deconstructing Psychopathology*. London: Sage.

Rose, N. 1985: *The Psychological Complex*. London: Routledge and Kegan Paul.

Shakespeare, T. 2000: *Help*. Birmingham: Venture Press.

Sutcliffe, J. and Simons, K. 1993: *Self-advocacy and Adults with 'learning difficulties': Contexts and Debates*. Leicester: The National Institute of Adult Continuing Education in Association with Open University Press.

Titchkovsky, T. 2002: Cultural Maps: Which way to disability? In M.Corker and T. Shakespeare (eds), *Disability/Postmodernity: Embodying Disability Theory*. London: Continuum.

Thomas, C. 1999: *Female Forms: Experiencing and Understanding Disability*. Buckingham: Open University Press.

Tremain, S. 2002: On the subject of impairment. In M. Corker and T. Shakespeare (eds), *Disability / Postmodernity: Embodying Disability Theory*. London: Continuum.

Walmsley, J. 1993: Explaining. In P. Shakespeare, D. Atkinson and S. French (eds), *Reflecting on Research Practice: Issues in Health and Social Welfare*. Buckingham: Open University Press.

Wilkinson, S. and Kitzinger, C. 1995: *Feminism and Discourse: Psychological Perspectives*. London: Sage.

CHAPTER 13

Independent Living and the Road to Inclusion

Gerry Zarb

Introduction

This chapter examines the significance of independent living to social inclusion, the links between independent living and the social model of disability, and the barriers to independent living that disabled people face. It also discusses independent living as a civil and human rights issue, and outlines the prospects for achieving legally enforceable rights to independent living for all disabled people.

The discussion is set in the context of the Disability Rights Commission's (DRC) ongoing work on establishing a right to independent living. The Commission is working closely with a wide range of disabled people and other organisations on trying to achieve this objective. These include the European Network on Independent Living and the National Centre for Independent Living. The DRC's overall strategic vision is to bring about a society in which all disabled people can participate fully as equal citizens. A lot of the Commission's work is taken up with dealing with specific acts of discrimination that are defined by existing laws. But the DRC's remit also includes identifying and challenging other forms of discrimination and exclusion – including those that, at this point in time, have no legal remedy. Barriers to independent living currently fall into this category.

In 2002 the DRC formally adopted the following general policy statements in relation to independent living:

> *There should be a basic enforceable right to independent living for all disabled people.* Policy objectives for social care services need to include guaranteed minimum outcomes, backed up by a right to

independence. The provision of social care must extend beyond functional 'life and limb' support to include support to enable participation in social and economic activities.

All social care support services should be based on the principles of independent living. All organisations commissioning and providing services should be aware of the social model of disability and be fully committed to delivering services that enable choice, control, autonomy and participation (DRC 2002).

Why is independent living a rights issue?

The concept of independent living is a very simple one, and mirrors the essential principles of the social model of disability. Basically, independent living means disabled people having the same choice, control and freedom as any other citizen – at home, at work, and as members of the community. Any barriers to independent living can therefore be viewed as having a direct bearing on disabled people's freedom to exercise their human and civil rights. In other words, full participation and inclusion can and must be built on the foundation of independent living.

As Finkelstein (2001: 6) points out, the essential principle of independent living – that disabled people should have control over their own lives – was also central to the social model solutions to end exclusion and segregation proposed by the Union of the Physically Impaired Against Segregation (UPIAS) in the *Fundamental Principles of Disability* (UPIAS 1976). Following on from the basic distinction between the individual and social models of disability, UPIAS stated that:

> disability is a situation, caused by social conditions, which requires for its elimination, (a) that no one aspect such as incomes, mobility or institutions is treated in isolation, (b) that disabled people should, with the advice and help of others, assume control over their own lives, and (c) that professionals, experts and others who seek to help must be committed to promoting such control by disabled people (1976: 3).

Similarly, there have always been strong links between the political organisation of the disability movement, its re-definition of the 'problem' of disability and the collective challenge to discrimination:

> Indeed, it was the idea of independent living which gave a focus to the struggles of disabled people to organise themselves, initially in the United States and subsequently elsewhere, including Britain (Oliver 1996: 15).

There is little understanding (outside of the disability movement itself) however that independence could, or should be, established as a basic universal human or civil right. Even in countries like the UK where there has been considerable expansion in availability of resources like direct payments, access to independent living is still essentially granted on a discretionary, rather than mandatory basis. There are also considerable restrictions on both the levels of resources people can receive, and on the ways in which they are allowed to use these resources to organise their support systems (Zarb 1999; Morris 2004).

One of the main reasons for these restrictions is that removal of all of the barriers to disabled people's full social and economic participation requires practical action across a variety of social and economic sectors such as education, transport and employment (Zarb 1995). Public support systems on the other hand typically have great difficulty linking all of these actions together and, instead, tend to have different administrative functions to deal with them separately. So, for example, disabled people might be eligible to receive services to enable them to access personal assistance at home, but not at work. Similarly, assistance with travel might be available for certain activities (going to school or to the shops, for example), but not for participation in social or leisure activities. In practice this often means that, instead of being able to participate freely in the full range of community life, disabled people have to organise their lives around whatever kinds of practical support are available. This might tackle some of the practical barriers they face but rarely all of them. And, in a lot of cases, the minimum support people can expect to receive does not guarantee much more than simply being able to stay alive.

This almost universal problem is not just about the inefficiency of public support systems. More important still is the issue of controlling public expenditure and the negative impact this has on older and disabled people. Put crudely, removing all of the barriers to disabled people's full social and economic participation is considered to be simply too expensive when compared to meeting the costs of other social and economic priorities. In practice, this means that needs are defined by what public support systems are able, or prepared, to afford rather than the actual barriers that disabled people face in their day to day lives (Zarb 1999, 2001).

Eligibility for community care, for example, is mainly determined by the level of risk to people's functional independence. Assistance is only guaranteed if there is a substantial risk to people's health or functioning (if someone is unable to feed themselves for example). Anything beyond that is largely dependent on availability of resources and the spending priorities of different local authorities (some of whom, to be fair, are much more progressive than others in terms of promoting independent living). As a result, practically all of the existing support systems place some kind of ceiling – either in terms of cost or eligibility criteria, or often both of these – on the level of resources at which independent living is considered to be cost-effective. This means of course that people for whom independent living is considered to be too expensive are faced with a stark choice between struggling to maintain their independence in the community, or entering institutional care. Effectively, this amounts to putting a price on people's freedom.

Establishing independent living as a human or civil rights will of course mean much more than simply removing the barriers in existing support systems – although that objective remains absolutely crucial. Ultimately, even more fundamental rights of citizenship would need to be established in order to invert (or subvert) existing common sense understanding of disabled people's excluded and segregated position in society. The problematic nature of this challenge can be illustrated by consideration of how the concept of rights to independent living might compare to existing rights of citizenship, as these are commonly understood. Existing debates about civil rights imply an important distinction between what might be called 'essential' and 'conditional' rights. Essential (or immutable) rights are those that relate to barriers which no reasonable person could view as acceptable as a normal condition of citizenship (such as the freedom to develop social relationships, and engage in family life). Conditional rights on the other hand relate to barriers which, potentially, all citizens might face at some point – albeit not necessarily as a consequence of disabling social structures, institutions, and attitudes. Examples include the restricted freedom of choice over type or location of housing or financial insecurity.

However, in reality, it is probably fair to say that very few rights of citizenship are unconditional in the sense that they are associated with guaranteed material outcomes. Thus, the Human Rights Act 1998 states that all citizens have the right to work but in practice that only confers a right of opportunity to work (not a guarantee that work will always be available). In the context of the right to independent living, the implication is that there might be a distinction to be made between rights to services, resources and other entitlements that enable equality of opportunity and equality of access and those that would, if enforced, guarantee certain material outcomes.

People who are not convinced about the need for a right to independent living might argue that, by advocating the social model of disability, we sometimes stray over the line between equality of opportunity and guaranteed outcomes by advocating complete removal of barriers over and above those faced by all citizens. But, in some cases guaranteed material outcomes are essential precisely because of the fact that, without them, disabled people cannot have equality of opportunity or access. Obviously we could argue that things like personal assistance, facilitated decision making and the removal of material access barriers fall in to this category. But something like the right to a completely secure living environment might be less clear-cut on the basis that, arguably, this is not something that any citizen can be guaranteed.

Such equivocation is potentially very dangerous as it opens up the possibility of independent living being seen as a conditional rather than an essential right of citizenship. Full inclusion cannot be achieved without the level playing field that removing barriers to independent living would create. It is essential therefore that we are able to clearly demonstrate what the barriers to independent living are, as well as the practical impact they have on disabled people's lives.

Dependency, segregation and discrimination

There are numerous ways in which disabled people are discriminated against as a result of not having any basic rights to independent living. Just a few examples illustrate this point.

i)   *Enforced admission to institutions and cuts in services*

Disabled people have very few guarantees about being able to live in the community and there is no legal protection against people being forced to live in institutional care against their wishes.

Indeed, despite an overall slowdown in the rate of permanent admissions to residential and nursing care, for some groups of disabled people, the numbers are still on the increase. Between 1997 and 2002 the number of people with physical and sensory impairments in local authority supported residential and nursing care showed a modest decrease from 10,356 to 9,755. For people with learning disabilities, on the other hand, there was an increase of nearly 20 per cent from 25,446 to 30,345 while the figure for people with mental health problems rose by more than 40 per cent from 7,965 to 11,275 (Department of Health 2003).

There has also recently been an increase in reports of disabled people being threatened with enforced admission to institutional care as a result of cuts in social services budgets and the limits this places on public expenditure on disability services. As budgets come under pressure some local administrations are also raising the threshold for eligibility for services with the result that, in some cases, disabled people are being denied access to essential support for basic activities like washing and eating. For example, in one case the DRC has dealt with in the past few months, disabled people were told that they could only be guaranteed to have a bath or shower once a fortnight and, even then, only if there is a substantial risk to their health. There are also no guarantees about continuity of support if people want to move from one local authority area to another, which is a significant obstacle to social and economic mobility.

ii)   *Restrictions on opportunities for training and employment*
Opportunities for economic participation are an essential part of independent living. However there are many examples of people being prevented from participation in training or employment as a result of not having access to personal assistance or other resources necessary to maintaining independence. Again, this is as much to do with a failure to understand what independent living is supposed to be about. For example, disabled people do have various entitlements to practical assistance at work as well protection under the DDA against discrimination in employment. But, if you are not guaranteed the support you need to get up in the morning so you can actually get out to work, these rights are in reality of limited use.

iii)   *Restrictions on access to direct payments and personal assistance*
Direct payments to arrange personal assistance are also an absolutely crucial resource for enabling independent living. However, there is significant inequality of access to direct payments on the grounds of discriminatory assumptions about disabled people's capacity to manage their own affairs and the lack of any rights to support systems for people who need assistance to manage their own support arrangements.

For example, according to the latest full year figures, out of 7,882 people receiving direct payments only 736 (less than 10 per cent) are people with learning difficulties. The figures for mental health service users are even worse at only 132 (less than 2 per cent), with over 60 per cent of local authorities reporting no mental health service users supported via Direct Payments at all (SSI 2003: 37)

iv)   *Lack of rights to advocacy and communication support*
There are very few rights for people who require assistance with communication. Similarly the provision of advocacy to enable people to make real choices about what services they receive and how they are delivered is almost always on a purely discretionary basis. Often the people who most need this kind of support are the least likely to get it.

The DRC believes that all disabled people should have a right of access to advocacy if they need it. All disabled people should also have a right to support to meet their access, information and communication needs. These services are not only vital for maximising opportunities for independent living. For many disabled people, they are also essential to enable them to exercise their basic human and civil rights.

v)   *Restricted access to appropriate health care*
Access to appropriate health care when you need it is also vital to enabling independent living. However, a combination of physical, organisational and attitudinal barriers mean that many disabled people have restricted access to basic health care facilities. For people who are assumed to have limited capacity there is further discrimination in terms of compulsory treatment that, again, can often mean people being forced to go into institutions against their wishes. Most serious of all perhaps is that disabled people are sometimes denied essential health care because of the medical profession's judgement about the value and quality of disabled people's lives. At present there is no legal protection against this happening.

vi)   *Attitudinal barriers*
A related problem is that disabled people's aspirations for independence are too often undermined by over-protective or negative attitudes about disability amongst both service professionals and the general public. Most disability services are based on the belief that disabled people are 'vulnerable people' who need to be protected and 'cared for'. This is extremely damaging to the development of independent living as it only serves to reinforce perceptions of disabled people as passive 'recipients of care', rather than active citizens facing practical barriers to participation in the social and economic life of the community. By refusing to acknowledge

any other legitimate role for disabled people in society, such beliefs are fundamentally discriminatory.

vii) *Regulatory barriers*
Discriminatory attitudes about the value of disabled people's lives are further reinforced by other areas of policy and legislation such as health and safety regulations and Mental Health legislation. Much of the existing legal and policy framework for social care adopts a particularly restrictive approach to the assumed 'vulnerability' of disabled people and the potential risks, either to themselves or others, which are presumed to be associated with extending independent living. Again, in many cases, this effectively provides a legal justification for denying disabled people's rights to independent living.

Negative attitudes linking risk and disability also impact on other aspects of disabled people's lives such as education. Cognitive or emotional impairments are often interpreted and labeled as 'behavioural problems' with the result that a need for social support is translated into a need for exclusion (Russell 2003). A recent study by the Audit Commission for example found that, in the 22 Local Education Authorities visited, 87 percent of exclusions at primary level and 60 percent at secondary level were of pupils with Special Educational Needs (Audit Commission 2002). Needless to say, this kind of response does little to enhance opportunities for independence and self-determination.

Transforming dependency
The pervasive categorisation of disabled people as 'vulnerable people' in the context of public support systems is a major obstacle to independent living. Such categorisation is based on a reductionist and individual model of disability that is both muddled and damaging. It is muddled because external barriers are seen purely in terms of problems for individuals requiring atomised, individual solutions, thereby leaving the underlying structural source of disabling barriers unchallenged. This failure to link individual needs to structural barriers is both discriminatory and damaging because it effectively leaves disabled people in a state of dependency. It can be likened to a roundabout where services based only on partial solutions simply recycle dependency while at the same time closing off the exits that would re-route disabled people towards empowerment and inclusion.

As Finkelstein argues, there are clear parallels with the social model analysis offered by UPIAS in the context of reductionist responses to other kinds of barriers faced by disabled people, such as those related to exclusion from economic activity:

> We also felt, given the background of that time where the popular concern was to campaign for a national disability income, that this, incomes approach, is basically a compensatory approach. What people are asking is that disabled people, because they are disabled (because through no fault of their own they are impaired), should be provided with a statutory income to compensate for their personal defects – it's a compensatory approach. The UPIAS argument, however, was that the central issue is one of oppression not compensation. We don't want to be compensated for being oppressed! We want people to stop oppressing us! The logic of these different perspectives is very simple. The former interpretation of disability places us in a permanently dependent relationship to able-bodied society for handouts – what we called state charity. The latter approach says that the able-bodied society's got to change, it's an oppressive society (Finkelstein 2001: 4).

The impact of this 'compensatory approach' to disability in the context of independent living can be illustrated very clearly by the process of assessment for community care services which is narrowly focused on personal 'activities of daily living' or 'self-care'.

From April 2003, local authorities in England are supposed to undertake assessments and reviews according to a unified set of criteria designed to evaluate eligibility for support based on the risk to people's independence. The new assessment guidance (Department of Health 2002) proposes that eligibility should be assessed according to the degree of 'risk' ('critical', 'substantial', 'moderate' or 'low') to a person's independence in terms of the following factors:

- *autonomy* – which refers to the extent of choice and control people have over their own lives;
- *health and safety* – for both disabled people and others;
- *managing daily routines* – including practical support people need to meet their responsibilities to family members or other dependents;
- *involvement* – as well as involvement in work, education and learning, family life, social and community activities this also includes recognition of individual's broader social roles and responsibilities.

In theory, assessments should now look at all of these aspects of independence in the round and assess the degree of risk – both currently and longer-term – attached to failing to meet an individual's needs. However, the assessment process is also used as a rationing device and there is evidence indicating that, in practice, eligibility for support is only guaranteed when there is a 'critical' or 'substantial' risk to health or functioning (Prasad 2002).

So, for example, where failure to provide support would pose a risk to health or prevent somebody from carrying out 'vital' personal care or domestic routines, this would be defined as a 'critical' risk. Inability to maintain involvement in several aspects of work, education or learning, and/or social support systems and relationships, on the other hand, is classified as only a 'moderate' risk to independence. In an environment of competing resources eligibility thresholds tend to be set high, with the result that the overall balance between the various risk criteria remains heavily skewed towards a functional 'life and limb' approach. Factors such as health and safety and daily routine are given greater emphasis than autonomy and involvement in community life whereas, in reality, these are interdependent and are all equally important to disabled people themselves.

As Morris points out, truly enabling assessment should be about human and civil rights:

> Assessments should identify: what someone wants to achieve, and what is getting in the way. Instead of asking 'What is wrong with this person', a needs-led assessment asks 'What is wrong for this person?'
>
> Assessments should ask: which human and civil rights are being contravened? Which need to be promoted, improved, or extended? (Morris 2002: 4–5).

The differences in approaches to assessment that Morris outlines echo the distinctions between dependency and independence and between compensating for and challenging exclusion. Developing support systems to enable independent living implies the need for a significantly different approach to assessment and the organisation of support systems focusing on barriers and outcomes that would enable disabled people to participate on the same basis as other citizens. However, as already discussed, there are significant barriers to achieving the kind of root and branch transformation that meeting this objective would require. The final part of this chapter examines how this challenge could be met.

Prospects for achieving a right to independent living

There are going to be many obstacles to overcome before the right to independent living is a reality for all disabled people. There are also opportunities for challenging the denial of this right, and these must be pursued if full inclusion is to be achieved.

First, one of the most important challenges will be to overcome the differences in people's understanding of what independent living means, and why it is so important. We need to be clear that, when we talk about disabled people having a right to independent living, this covers <u>all</u> groups of disabled having the right to whatever kind of support they need to make their independence possible. It also means that we have to adopt a truly inclusive definition of independent living. Different individuals and groups need different kinds of practical support to achieve freedom, choice and control. For example, access to communication support for deaf people and advocacy or supported decision making for people with learning difficulties is just as essential to achieving independent living as personal assistance. Any definition of independent living that does not explicitly acknowledge the different ways that disabled people define and achieve independence will not be fully inclusive.

Second, although making the concept of independent living broad enough to embrace all disabled people has many positive benefits, it also creates new challenges. The biggest will be to find ways of transforming and extending existing models of independent living without diluting the essential philosophy and principles on which it has been built. For example, concepts like choice, control and self-directed personal assistance – both in the way they have been conceptualised and applied in practice – have not fully embraced the needs and experiences of people with learning disabilities or mental health problems. Making choice and control possible for these groups would mean that the concept of independent living needs to be broad enough to include different ideas about things like how we define capacity for decision making and the role of advocates in enabling people to communicate their own choices and aspirations.

There are also challenges associated with the extension of independent living options to older people as we are seeing for example with direct payments. Again, some groups of older people will have slightly different ideas about what independence means to them, and how they want to achieve it. This could create new opportunities for building alliances but there are also concerns about the possibility of diluting the concept of independent living if the boundaries are extended too far. At the same time, it is important to realise that making the concept independent living fully inclusive also demands a proper analysis of the ways in which disablement and other forms of exclusion – particularly ageism – interact to enforce and maintain segregation and dependency.

A key issue will be to develop forms of analysis that can link disabled people's experience of discrimination and exclusion with the disabling institutions and processes that help to create that experience in the first place. We need to find a way of making visible the process by which subjective experience becomes a material and practical reality. There are already some pointers to achieving this goal, such as the work by Beresford and others on developing a social model of madness and distress, but this has yet to be fully integrated into the core activity of disability studies (Beresford et al. 1996; Beresford 2000).

Another important challenge we are going to face is how to find the right kind of legislation to support a right to independent living for all disabled people. There will almost certainly need to be changes to existing legislation to secure specific rights to resources that would enable independent living (a right to independent advocacy for example). However in order to make this possible we first need to establish the general principle that independent living is a basic and universal human and civil right.

One vehicle that offers positive potential for establishing this principle is the European Convention on Human Rights (Clements and Read 2003). In the UK we have recently seen some success in using the Human Rights Act 1998 to support disabled people's right to independent living which gives some positive encouragement for the future. For example, in one case recently supported by the DRC, the courts ruled that organisations providing community care services must take proper account of people's dignity, independence and human rights and respect their rights to participate in the life of the community. Another landmark case in 2002 (Bernard vs. London Borough of Enfield) involved a woman who, because of unsuitable housing could only use the downstairs rooms in her family home. In this case the courts ruled that the local authority's failure to provide adequate housing adaptations created a breach of her right to privacy and family life under the Human Rights Act.

These cases are potentially very encouraging. In its present form the scope of the Human Rights Act is nowhere near broad enough to fully protect people's right to independent living, but cases like this can go a long way towards establishing the case for such rights. As we have seen in the UK, the Human Rights Act can also help to establish benchmarks about what degree of independence disabled people have a right to expect, and to highlight deficiencies in national legislation that can be used as a basis for lobbying and campaigning.

Are rights enough?

The discussion in this chapter explicitly links the right to independent living with general and universal citizenship rights. But it is debatable however whether legalistic remedies on their own would be sufficient to overcome the denial of citizenship rights experienced by disabled people.

First there are reservations about the efficacy of anti-discrimination legislation generally for the most excluded groups (for example, people who have spent all or most of their lives in institutions). Because rights within the kind of legalistic framework provided by, for example, the Disability Discrimination Act 1995 are dependent on people having the necessary resources to exercise them, those who have the most to gain or who are in most need of legal protection are often the least likely to benefit (Zarb 1995). The deep-rooted (and often internalised) exclusion associated with institutionalisation and segregation may effectively disenfranchise whole groups of disabled people, thereby creating a hierarchy of access to any rights to independent living that may be achieved in the future.

Second, some commentators (Finkelstein 1999, 2001; Oliver, 2001) have questioned whether any solutions that are, essentially, based on individualised rights can be seen as compatible with the social model of disability and the collective emancipation of disabled people. One of the central arguments in this critique is that the civil rights approach is still, essentially, based on 'compensating' disabled people for the various forms of disadvantage and exclusion they face, rather than structural change aimed at removing the causes of exclusion. As Finkelstein contends:

> Since such disadvantages are no fault of its own, a 'caring' society, the argument goes, will humanely concede 'rights' and provide compensatory services and benefits. This not only frees people with abilities from all responsibility for our predicament but the compensatory approach encourages a feel good-factor for being charitable. A complete inversion of social reality! Indeed this illusion about what are in practice 'compensatory' civil rights being a big idea is so enchanting that even the disability movement has been captivated (much to the delight of politicians with abilities) into believing that civil rights can

provide a platform for announcing our commitment to emancipation (2001: 8).

The dangers that this critique implies are very real and need to be addressed if independent living for all is to become a reality. As noted earlier, there are inherent dangers associated with a purely legalistic approach to citizenship as, once we start to legislate, the scope of what rights people can expect to receive immediately becomes open to both legal and political (and maybe even moral/ethical) challenge. As Sayce (2003) points out, the operation of the Americans with Disabilities Act 1990 has already demonstrated the potential problems with legalistic challenges. For some groups of disabled people at least, a combination of pressure from vested interests and lack of understanding about how different aspects of the legislation should be interpreted has resulted in a progressive narrowing of the scope of the law in the courts.

> Critical Legal Studies theory would say that it is no surprise that a law has been narrowed and constrained in this way, because the drafting, interpretation and implementation of law are part of social discourse. For law to be an effective agent for social change requires it to be addressed in this context. Interventions are needed at the level of social discourse. Simply passing and enforcing a law is not enough. ... A lesson for Britain is that it is a major priority to influence public and political debate, informing people why disability rights are important and what they mean in practice. Otherwise, implementation of the law could become ever more limited by the definitions imposed on the debate by those with power to perpetuate discrimination (Sayce 2003: 632).

So, before we can even begin to consider the legal configuration of a right to independent living there is a much more fundamental challenge to transform the discourse that maintains disabled people in a state of dependency, and to develop a clear understanding of what independent living means and why it is important. For example, we need to question why, in the 21st century, it is still seen as acceptable for disabled people to be living in institutions against their wishes, to be denied access to basic support to enable them to enjoy a family or social life, and to be guaranteed no more than the bare minimum services necessary for day to day survival.

Finally, we need to win the argument that independent living is a basic universal human and civil right. Only then will it be possible for all disabled people to participate fully in the social, economic and civic life of the community.

Bibliography

Audit Commission 2002: *Special Educational Needs: A mainstream issue*. London: Audit Commission.

Beresford, P. 2000: What Have Madness and Psychiatric System Survivors Got to Do with Disability and Disability Studies? *Disability and Society*, 15 (1), 167-172.

Beresford, P., Gifford, G. and Harrison, C. 1996: What has disability got to do with psychiatric survivors? In J. Reynolds and J. Read (eds), *Speaking Our Minds: personal experiences of mental distress and its consequences*. Basingstoke: Macmillan.

Clements, L. and Read, J. 2003: *Disabled People and European Human Rights: A review of the implications of the 1998 Human Rights Act for disabled children and adults in the UK*. Bristol: The Policy Press.

Department of Health 2002: *Fair Access to Care Services: Guidance on Eligibility Criteria for Adult Social Care*. London: Department of Health.

Department of Health 2003: *Personal Social Services Statistics*. London: Department of Health.

DRC 2002: *Policy Statement on Social Care and Independent Living*. London: Disability Rights Commission.

Finkelstein, V. 1999: A Profession Allied to the Community: The disabled people's trade union. In E. Stone (ed.), *Disability and Development: Learning from action and research on disability in the majority world*. Leeds: The Disability Press.

Finkelstein, V. 2001: *A Personal Journey into Disability Politics*, Seminar presentation, Centre for Disability Studies, University of Leeds, 7th February.

Morris, J. 2002: *Fair Access to Care Practice Guidance: Discussion*. Paper for Department of Health Expert Seminar, 14th January.

Morris, J. 2004: *Barriers to Independent Living: A scoping paper*. London: Disability Rights Commission.

Oliver, M. 1996: *Understanding Disability: From Theory to Practice*. Basingstoke: Macmillan.

Oliver, M. 2001: Disabled People and the Inclusive Society? Or the times they really are changing. In S. Riddell (ed.), *Disability and Civil*

Rights in the New Millennium. Glasgow: Strathclyde Centre for Disability Research.

Prasad, R. 2002: *Independence Daze,* Guardian Society, 6 November, p. 111.

Russell, P. 2003: Access and Achievement or Social exclusion? Are the Government's Policies Working for Disabled Children and Their Families? *Children and Society,* 17, 215-225.

Sayce, L. 2003: Beyond Good Intentions: Making Anti-Discrimination Strategies Work, *Disability and Society,* 18 (5), 625-642.

SSI 2003: *Mid-Year Progress Report and Delivery Forecast for Social Services: 2002-03.* London: Social Services Inspectorate.

UPIAS 1976: *Fundamental Principles of Disability.* London: Union of the Physically Impaired Against Segregation.

Zarb, G. (ed.) 1995: *Removing Disabling Barriers.* London: Policy Studies Institute.

Zarb, G. 1999: What Price Independence? In M. Turner (ed.), *Facing Our Futures.* London: National Centre for Independent Living.

Zarb, G. 2001: Cost-effective support within a framework of independent living: measuring cost-effectiveness. In A. O'Neil and J. Lewis (eds), *Cost-effectiveness and independent living.* York: Joseph Rowntree Foundation.

INDEX (compiled by Marie Ross)